D0514931

COURT OFFICER EXAM

(INCLUDING BAILIFF, SHERIFF, MARSHALL, COURTROOM ATTENDANT, AND COURTROOM DEPUTY)

3RD EDITION

DONALD J. SCHROEDER, PH.D.

Adjunct Professor,
John Jay College of Criminal Justice
Senior Instructor, REMS Tutorial,
Exam Preparation Specialists
Former Commanding Officer,
81st Police Precinct,
New York City Police Department

FRANK A. LOMBARDO

Deputy Inspector (retired),
New York City Police Department
Adjunct Professor,
John Jay College of Criminal Justice
Former Commanding Officer,
30th Police Precinct,
New York City Police Department

BARRON'S

Dedication

Justice is the obvious legitimate goal of a fair and unbiased court system. And it is the court officer who acts to ensure that this legitimate goal is reached by our courts.

It is equally true that no society can have its courts function justly unless the society at large demands justice. This clearly begins with the supporting of justice in the primary building block of society, the family. It is to the people who first patiently explained, then demonstrated, and ultimately demanded appropriate conduct from your authors that we would like to dedicate this text. And, of all these people, we would like to specifically address the two people who held our early family lives together—namely Ann Schroeder and Anna Maria Lombardo—our mothers. We acknowledge your guidance and love. We thank you.

All inquiries should be addressed to:
Barron's Educational Series, Inc.
250 Wireless Boulevard
Hauppauge, New York 11788
www.barronseduc.com

ISBN: 978-1-4380-0105-0
ISSN: 2168-5274

PRINTED IN THE UNITED STATES OF AMERICA
9 8 7 6 5 4 3 2 1

10%
POST-CONSUMER
WASTE
Paper contains a minimum
of 10% post-consumer
waste (PCW). Paper used
in this book was derived
from certified, sustainable
forestlands.

CONTENTS

CORRECT YOUR WEAKNESSES

TEST YOURSELF

A FINAL WORD

Preface

Key in the operation of the criminal justice system of the United States are its courts. Here the actions of the police and the prosecutors are put to the test of ensuring that justice is provided both as a protection for our society against those who would commit criminal acts, as well as a prevention to possible unjust actions by the state against its citizens. In order for the courts to carry out that function properly, they must operate in an atmosphere of complete order and total safety. Such order and safety are provided for the courts by the men and women who act as their court officers, sheriffs, and bailiffs, in and around the courts. It is obvious that the pursuit of such careers is certainly a worthwhile endeavor.

The goal of becoming a court officer, sheriff, or bailiff is obtained through a selection process that includes the passing of a civil service examination. This book was written for those who are interested in learning about such careers to assist them in passing the required civil service examination. The sample test questions that appear in this book are typical of the kinds of questions a candidate would find on such civil service examinations. They are intended to develop the skills a candidate needs to deal with these examinations successfully. In addition, different strategies to use when answering these different question types have been included. This was done to assist a candidate to answer the questions not only accurately but also swiftly.

New to this edition are strategies to follow when taking a computer-based, multiple-choice examination. These strategies are designed to acquaint the candidate with such examinations, which are becoming more and more common. The new strategies give advice on how to maximize one's score during computer-based examinations. With the growing trend in the use of computer-based, multiple-choice examinations, these strategies are an appropriate and timely addition.

However, the book by itself cannot pass examinations for a candidate. The candidate must be willing to study and learn the contents of this book. Being successful on civil service examinations demands being disciplined in your study habits and dedicated to working hard. In the end, achieving the goal of becoming a court officer, bailiff, or sheriff will prove to be worthwhile. Good luck!

Don Schroeder and Frank Lombardo

Introduction

About the Court Officer Test

→ **WHAT YOU SHOULD KNOW ABOUT THE TITLE OF COURT OFFICER**
→ **WHAT YOU SHOULD KNOW ABOUT THE ENTRANCE TEST**
→ **WHAT A COURT OFFICER DOES**
→ **JOB OPPORTUNITIES**
→ **THE BENEFITS OF A CAREER AS A COURT OFFICER**
→ **GENERAL JOB REQUIREMENTS**
→ **SAMPLE TEST ANNOUNCEMENT**
→ **TYPICAL STEPS TO BECOMING A COURT OFFICER**

WHAT YOU SHOULD KNOW ABOUT THE TITLE OF COURT OFFICER

A court officer is an officer of the court who is specifically charged with the basic responsibility of keeping order in and around the many federal, state, and local courtrooms in the country. It is very important, however, to point out that the title given to such an officer of the court varies from court system to court system. The titles most commonly used are court officer, courtroom attendant, courtroom deputy, bailiff, and marshall. Therefore, for ease of understanding, whenever in this book we talk about a court officer, we mean all the positions, regardless of title, throughout the country that are charged with the basic responsibility of maintaining order in and around a courtroom.

WHAT YOU SHOULD KNOW ABOUT THE ENTRANCE TEST

The type of court officer examination that is administered throughout the country to select qualified men and women for careers as court officers has been modified greatly over the past decade. As a result of a Supreme Court decision a number of years ago, test writers are not permitted to use certain kinds of questions. For example, it is against the law to ask questions that require prior knowledge of the law or of the specific duties and responsibilities of a court officer. As a candidate, you are not required to know what exact procedure a court officer should follow under certain circumstances, such as when he or she witnesses the commission of a crime in or around a courtroom or when he or she is dealing with an unruly spectator in the courtroom. That is the kind of knowledge you acquire after you become a court officer and are trained by the specific court agency involved. Therefore, it is a waste of time to prepare for the court officer examination by learning the law or by memorizing actual court officer procedures. The proper way to prepare for a court officer examination is to learn how to deal with the types of questions contained in this book. Examiners use these types of questions to evaluate your ability to learn the skills needed to actually do the job of court officer after you become one.

The material presented in this book, including the hundreds and hundreds of practice questions, was written after a careful analysis of recent major court officer examinations and court decisions relating to entrance-level testing procedures. And, all the questions in the book are related to the job of a court officer. This is important because you will see these kinds of questions when you take the official court officer examination. Therefore, we are confident that using this book will help you achieve your goal of becoming a court officer.

The rest of this chapter is devoted to explaining the job of a court officer and outlining the steps you need to take to become one.

WHAT A COURT OFFICER DOES

Before discussing the typical duties of a court officer, we would like to point out that these duties vary somewhat from state to state. Even though that is true, it is also true that the knowledge and abilities needed to perform as a court officer are basically the same regardless of the legal and procedural differences that one encounters from court system to court system. For this reason, this book can be used by court officer candidates from all states.

The Work Day

The great majority of court officers work in uniform and are authorized to carry firearms. Court officers usually work eight-hour shifts, which are often referred to as tours. But because many courts, especially criminal courts, are in session for more than eight hours a day, some court officers work nighttime shifts. And because the volume of work of the courts fluctuates, court officers are often required to work overtime, for which they are compensated.

The Duties of Court Officers

The following duties are commonly the responsibility of court officers:

ENFORCEMENT OF CRIMINAL PROCEDURE LAWS. In many states, court officers have special authority granted to them by state law. For example, in New York State, court officers are the only category of peace officers who are authorized to conduct stop-and-frisk investigations based on reasonable suspicion. In addition, in many states, court officers have arrest authority that is greater than that of civilians. For example, in New York State, a court officer acting pursuant to his or her special duties is authorized to make arrests based on probable cause. Finally, court officers must be well versed in the area of search and seizure because they are responsible for keeping contraband out of the courtroom.

> **TYPICAL COURT OFFICER DUTIES**
> **Law enforcement**
> **Courtroom security**
> **Access control**
> **Courtroom operation**
> **Courtroom inspection**
> **Maintaining court documents and forms**

ENFORCEMENT OF CRIMINAL LAWS. As mentioned previously, court officers are usually given special arrest authority. It follows, therefore, that they are from time to time responsible for enforcing criminal laws in much the same way as police officers. In addition, all states have criminal laws meant specifically to deal with courtroom matters. Examples of such laws are those regarding tampering with evidence or witnesses and contempt of court.

MAINTAINING SECURITY IN THE COURTROOM. Court officers are responsible for creating a safe environment in the courtroom. They must be especially alert to protect such persons as the judge, members of the jury, attorneys, and witnesses.

ACCESS CONTROL. Court officers are responsible for making sure that only authorized persons are allowed in the nonpublic areas of the courthouse and that members of the general public who are authorized to enter the courthouse are not in possession of contraband, such as firearms.

COURTROOM OPERATION. The business of the court must be conducted in an orderly and systematic way. Court officers are responsible for making this happen. They do such things as announce the appearance of the judge, call cases in the proper order, verify the presence of all concerned, call defendants and witnesses to the witness stand, and make required notifications as directed by the judge.

INSPECTIONAL DUTIES. Court officers are responsible for inspecting the courtroom and surrounding area on a continuous basis, but especially prior to the start of every court session.

CLERICAL DUTIES. A very important part of a court officer's job is performing clerical duties relating to court documents and forms. Because of the legal ramifications involved if such documents and forms are incorrectly prepared, lost, or misplaced, this aspect of the court officer's job has an extremely high priority.

JOB OPPORTUNITIES

Courts cannot operate without court officers. For this obvious reason, civil service examinations for the position of court officer are held regularly in most jurisdictions in the country. In other words, job opportunities are usually plentiful. Remember that different court systems often hold their own examinations. And, don't make the mistake of overlooking the federal court system. Federal court officer tests are always held independently of those administered for state courts.

THE BENEFITS OF A CAREER AS A COURT OFFICER

The many material benefits typically associated with the position of court officer follow.

JOB SECURITY. Court officers are civil servants. Their employment is regulated by Civil Service Law. They have the same solid job security as all other civil servants.

SALARY. Even though salary rates for court officers vary from one state to another, it is safe to say that court officers all over the nation are always among the highest-paid entry-level civil servants.

INSURANCE BENEFITS. Most court officers are, as part of their compensation, covered by health, dental, prescription drug, optical, and life insurance.

LEAVE BENEFITS. Court officers have very liberal leave benefits, which usually include such things as time off at full pay for annual leave, personal leave, bereavement leave, workers' compensation leave, and sick leave.

> **CAREER BENEFITS**
> Job Security
> Salary
> Insurance Benefits
> Leave Benefits
> Retirement Benefits
> Promotional Opportunities

RETIREMENT BENEFITS. Court officers are usually part of the employee's retirement system in the state where they are employed. Normal retirement age in many state systems is 62 years old. However, in most cases, court officers are allowed to retire after 20 or 25 years of service regardless of their age. This means that early retirement is the norm for court officers.

PROMOTIONAL OPPORTUNITIES. Civil service promotion examinations are very seldom open to the general public. Promotion is usually from within the employing agency. For this reason, promotional opportunity is one of the most attractive features of the court officer's job.

OTHER BENEFITS. Court officers, depending on where they work, often receive such other benefits as credit union membership, consumer buying power, uniform allowances, education and training incentives, and disability insurance.

GENERAL JOB REQUIREMENTS

Because an overwhelming number of court officer jobs are civil service positions, the minimum requirements for such jobs are established by the Civil Service Law in the state involved. This, of course, makes it impossible to list one definitive set of job requirements. To get the specific information for the job you are seeking, you, in most cases, must contact the civil service agency that is offering the job. In some states, however, the test is developed and administered by the court system itself.

We have compiled the following set of typical job requirements to give you a general idea of the most commonly accepted standards of employment used by most court systems. If you believe you may have a problem meeting any of these standards, you should be especially alert for them and specifically inquire about any such standard when you apply for the position of court officer. Such questions should be resolved before you spend a lot of time and effort attempting to become a court officer.

These standards follow:

AGE. Very rarely are persons who are less than 18 years old eligible for appointment as a court officer, and in some states the minimum age for appointment could be as high as 22 years of age. This does not always mean that persons under 18 cannot take a court officer examination. Rather it means that such persons cannot be appointed prior to their attaining the minimum age. Candidates who are too young for appointment when they otherwise become eligible are usually put on a special list and are appointed when they reach the minimum age unless the entire list is terminated prior to that time. For this reason, we always encourage students to take the entrance examination at their earliest opportunity.

CHARACTER. To become a court officer, one is legally required to carry firearms. Therefore, proof of good character is absolutely essential for all court officer positions. However, what is considered to be "good character" varies from state to state. As a general rule, however, any of the following would typically be cause for disqualification:

- A criminal conviction for a felony. Note, however, that, under federal law, a felon who has received a Certificate of Relief from Disabilities could be eligible to carry firearms legally.
- A series of criminal convictions regardless of the seriousness of the underlying charges.
- Evidence that indicates a propensity for violence.
- A history of repeated firings from jobs or long periods of unexplained unemployment.
- Dishonorable discharge from the Armed Services.

JOB REQUIREMENTS

Age Range
Good Character
Education
U.S. Citizen
Meet Medical/Psychological Standards
Weight: In proportion with height and frame
Drug Screening
Probationary Period
Residency
Physical Fitness

The background investigation that is conducted to determine whether candidates meet the character requirements is usually quite thorough and somewhat time consuming, and it always includes the taking of the candidate's fingerprints. Candidates who are preparing to undergo a background investigation can speed up the process by having ready for the investigator originals or certified copies of such documents as birth certificates, diplomas, military discharge papers, drivers licenses, and naturalization papers, if appropriate. If a candidate has one or more arrests, then complete documentation of the details involved are essential. Candidates who are awaiting a background investigation should also prepare a chronological listing of employment from the day they finished attending school on a full-time basis to the present time.

EDUCATION. A minimum of a high school diploma or its equivalent, a General Education Development (GED) diploma is, by far, the most prevalent educational requirement. It should be noted that the diploma or its equivalent usually must be obtained prior to the date of appointment.

CITIZENSHIP. U.S. citizenship at the time of appointment is a universal standard for employment as a court officer.

MEDICAL AND PSYCHOLOGICAL STANDARDS. Prior to appointment, eligible candidates must meet the medical and psychological standards set by the hiring agency. Any candidate who has a medical or psychological problem that would impair his or her ability to carry out the duties of a court officer will be disqualified. Candidates are required to reveal their medical history to the doctors who perform the medical examination. It is strongly suggested that those candidates who have had a medical problem that resulted in hospitalization obtain, if possible, a letter from their personal physicians stating that they are now fit to do the job of a court officer. This letter should then be shown to the doctors from the employing agency along with the other pertinent information about the specific medical problem involved.

Another important consideration concerning the medical and psychological component of the entry process is the appeals process. The Civil Service Law in almost every jurisdiction allows candidates to appeal the findings of the medical and psychological board of the hiring agency. However, such appeals always must be made on a timely basis. If you must appeal, make sure that you do so in accordance with the time frames set forth in the law.

Here is one final word in this area. Most civil service hiring rules require court officer eligibles to pass an eyesight examination, including a color vision test. As a general rule, a minimum uncorrected vision of 20/70 using both eyes is acceptable if it is correctable to 20/40 vision with lenses. The point is this. If you have poor unaided vision or some other vision problem, you should investigate the eyesight requirement before you make a significant commitment of time and effort to determine if you will be able to meet the standards of the job you are seeking.

HEIGHT AND WEIGHT REQUIREMENTS. There is no minimum height requirement prescribed as a requisite for employment as a court officer. But, there is usually a weight requirement. Such a weight requirement is usually determined by a candidate's height and body frame. In other words, to be eligible for appointment, a candidate's weight must be proportionate to the candidate's height and frame. Body frame is usually categorized into small frame, medium frame, and large frame. The examining doctor from the hiring agency determines the applicable frame size of a candidate. Exceptions are generally made in those cases where excess weight is deemed by the examining doctor to be lean body mass and not fat. For those of you who think you might be overweight, we recommend that you seek a doctor's opinion and then, if necessary, initiate a weight reduction program under medical supervision prior to the official medical examination.

DRUG SCREENING TEST. Eligibles for the position of court officer are subject to drug screening tests. It is universally true that court systems are not interested in hiring those with illegal drug use habits. It is also true that those candidates who are dependent on alcohol will also be rejected.

PROBATIONARY PERIOD. Virtually every court system requires newly hired officers to complete a probationary period successfully prior to their becoming fully tenured civil service employees with all the rights and privileges that accompany such tenure. The average length of such probationary periods is about 18 months. During this time, probationary court officers are required to complete successfully a training course that has academic, physical fitness, and firearms proficiency components. Many agencies also require probationary officers to pass another full medical examination at the very end of the probationary period.

Candidates must understand that during their probationary period they can be dismissed by an agency and that such dismissals are not subject to court review. It is a term of employment. Therefore, the conduct of candidates who are serving probationary periods must be exemplary both on and off duty. Serious off-duty indiscretions are cause for dismissals. Although this is also true for tenured employees (those who are not on probation), tenured employees usually have many avenues to appeal such decisions. This is not true for those who are on probation.

RESIDENCY REQUIREMENTS. Civil Service Law typically imposes residency requirements on court officers. Usually, such requirements must be met on the date of appointment, not on test day. However, some states require candidates to be a resident of that state for a period of time, usually one year, prior to the taking of the written examination. It is strongly suggested that you make certain that you meet the residency requirements in your area before you spend a considerable amount of time and effort pursuing such employment only to find out afterward that you are ineligible for appointment.

PHYSICAL FITNESS TEST. At some point prior to becoming a tenured court officer, candidates must pass a physical fitness test. This is done in two ways. In some cases, the test is administered prior to appointment as part of the hiring process. In other cases, the physical fitness test is administered after hiring as part of the probationary process. Of all the components of the hiring and probationary processes, none is more varied from jurisdiction to jurisdiction than the physical fitness component. However, successful completion of some sort of obstacle course, during which candidates must demonstrate an ability to run, push weighted objects, jump over hurdles, and lift and carry weighted dummies, all within a certain time period, is a very common requirement. Our experience with the physical fitness test has convinced us that, with proper preparation, most candidates can successfully pass it. The key phrase is *with proper preparation*. When the test is administered as part of the probationary period, this proper preparation is built into the physical fitness component of the official training curriculum. The physical fitness component is more of a problem when it is administered as part of the hiring process. When this is the case, we always strongly advise candidates to find out the specifics of the physical fitness test and to prepare for it. In many cases, the hiring agencies offer interested candidates the opportunity to prepare for the physical fitness test at no cost. If this is the case in your jurisdiction, we strongly urge you to take advantage of the opportunity.

SAMPLE TEST ANNOUNCEMENT

As you can see, there is not just one standard set of requirements for the position of court officer. Your task is to find out the specific requirements for the position you are seeking. The first step toward obtaining this information is to obtain the examination announcement for that position. This announcement will supply you with general information about that job, the requirements for that job, and the steps to follow to obtain that job.

To assist you, we have included a sample examination announcement, also referred to as a job announcement or a notice of examination, so that you can read and become familiar with what typically appears on such announcements. You must understand, however, that the information included on our sample announcement is general information and does not relate specifically to any one court system. Therefore, when it is available, you must get the test announcement for the position you are seeking in order to learn the specific information about that test for that position.

We also remind you that the specifics listed on an examination announcement sometimes change from test to test, so it is a mistake to believe that the requirements for the last examination will definitely be the same as the requirements for an upcoming examination.

SAMPLE TEST ANNOUNCEMENT
FOR COURT OFFICER
Examination # 1007
APPLICATION INFORMATION

APPLICATION FEE: There is a nonrefundable application fee of $35, payable by money order only. Money orders must be made payable to the Office of Court Administration. The name and number of the test as well as the applicant's social security number must be included on the money order. This application fee will be waived for applicants receiving public assistance who submit proof of this status along with their application.

APPLICATION PERIOD: From May 3rd through June 30th. Completed applications may be submitted by mail or in person to the Hiring Unit of the Office of Court Administration, 300 Main Street, Metropolis, Zip Code 00000. Applications must be postmarked no later than midnight on June 30th of this year.

TESTING LOCATIONS: The examination will be conducted in the state capital and in certain other cities around the state. The specific location of the test sites will be determined after a review of the applications. All candidates will then be notified via the U.S. mail.

SALARY: The current hiring rate is $40,000, which increases over 5 years to an annual salary of $65,000. In addition, court officers receive 20 days of paid vacation during the first year of service, as well as 12 paid holidays. Participation in medical, dental, life insurance, and retirement plans is offered.

LIFE OF THE LIST: The eligible list established as a result of Court Officer Examination # 1007 shall be at least 1 year but not more than 4 years. However, the list shall be automatically terminated upon the promulgation of a subsequent list for the position of court officer.

At the time of appointment to the position, court officers must be at least 18 years of age and have a high school diploma or its legal equivalent. Because candidates are required to be legally eligible to carry firearms, a convicted felon who has not received a Certificate of Relief from Disabilities will be automatically disqualified.

CITIZENSHIP: By the date of appointment, U.S. citizenship is required.

MEDICAL STANDARDS: Eligibles will be refused employment should they have a medical condition that significantly limits their ability to perform the tasks required of a court officer. Details on medical requirements, including eyesight requirements, are posted at the Medical Unit of the Office of Court Administration and are available upon request.

PSYCHOLOGICAL STANDARDS: Candidates are required to pass a battery of standard psychological tests and may also be required to appear for personal psychological evaluation.

PHYSICAL FITNESS STANDARDS: Candidates are required to pass a job-related physical agility test at a yet undetermined date after the written test. Details of this physical fitness test are posted at the Medical Unit of the Office of Court Administration and are available upon request. Prior to the administration of this test, all eligibles will be offered an opportunity to train for the physical agility test at a site yet to be selected. Details concerning this no-cost training and the actual physical agility test will be sent to all eligibles via U.S. mail.

BACKGROUND STANDARDS: Prior to hiring, each eligible will be fingerprinted and subject to an intensive background investigation and a criminal history search, which is to be conducted by State Police. As part of the background investigation, all eligibles will be required to participate in substance abuse testing prior to appointment and thereafter at any time during the probationary period. Candidates whose overall background is not deemed suitable as determined by the appointing authority shall be rejected. Candidates who fail to cooperate fully with their assigned investigators or who fail to present required documents are also subject to rejection.

LANGUAGE STANDARDS: All candidates must be proficient in the English language so as to be able to communicate orally and in writing at a level established by the Office of Court Administration. Candidates may be required to pass a communications test at any time prior to the completion of their probationary period.

JOB INFORMATION

PROBATIONARY PERIOD: Each appointed eligible will be required to successfully complete an 18-month probationary period during which he or she shall have the title of Probationary Court Officer. Candidates must understand that the probationary period is an extension of the selection process and that they are subject to continuous evaluation during their entire period of probation. Those who do not successfully complete the probationary period shall be rejected with no right to appeal.

TRAINING REQUIREMENTS: Upon appointment and prior to assignment, each probationary court officer must successfully complete a 12-week training program. Those who do successfully complete this training will receive full peace officer status.

COURT OFFICER DUTIES AND RESPONSIBILITIES: The basic responsibilities of court officers are to maintain order in the courthouse and to provide security in and around court facilities. Court officers work under the direct supervision of security supervisors and court clerks. Tenured court officers are peace officers in the state and may be required to wear uniforms. In addition, they may be authorized to carry firearms while they are working.

WRITTEN TEST INFORMATION

TEST DATE: To be announced. All candidates will receive notification via the U.S. mail as to the date and time of the examination. Such notification will be given at least two weeks in advance of the test date.

ADMISSION CARD: Applicants will not be admitted to the test site without an admission card. Such cards will be sent to candidates via U.S. mail. Those candidates who do not receive an admission card at least five days prior to the announced test date must appear personally at the Admissions Unit of the Office of Court Administration between 9:00 A.M. and 5:00 P.M. on one of the five days preceding the test to obtain their admission card.

TEST DESCRIPTION: The written test will be of the multiple-choice type and will consist of 100 questions to be answered in a 3½-hour period. It will contain questions to test

   a. your ability to remember facts and information.
   b. your ability to comprehend and interpret written material. You will NOT be required to have any special knowledge relating to the content area covered in the written material.
   c. your ability to apply facts and information to given situations. However, all the facts and information needed to answer questions will be provided, and you do NOT need any special knowledge of court policies and procedures.
   d. your ability to understand and apply legal definitions. Here again, however, you do NOT need any special knowledge of the law.
   e. your ability to process and review forms.

PASSING SCORE: The passing score will be determined and announced after statistical analysis of the results of the test.

APPEALS: Within 60 days after the administration of the test, a tentative scoring key will be published. Candidates who petition the Department of Personnel to do so will be allowed to appeal this tentative key providing they do so within 30 days of the publication of the tentative scoring key.

NOTIFICATION OF RESULTS: All applicants who actually take the test will receive notification via the U.S. mail of their final test score and, if appropriate, their place on the eligible list within 60 days of the end of the appeals period.

TYPICAL STEPS TO BECOMING A COURT OFFICER

1. Determine the date of the next test. This can be done by watching the civil service newspaper that services the area where you are seeking employment. Or, you can contact the civil service or court agency that administers the test.
2. Obtain an examination announcement.
3. File an application.
4. Prepare for and pass the written test.
5. Prepare for and take the physical agility test, if required, prior to appointment.
6. Take the medical examination.
7. Take the psychological examination.
8. Prepare for and undergo the background investigation. (Note that steps 5–8 may occur in a different sequence.)
9. Get appointed.
10. Attend and successfully complete a training school.
11. Successfully complete your probationary period.

A NOTE FROM YOUR AUTHORS

Don't be discouraged by the apparent complexity of the required steps you must take to become a court officer. Such a job is both rewarding and satisfying. It offers financial security and promotional opportunities plus a liberal retirement benefit. Pursue the job. Make it your goal. Use this book to help you. Remember that all court officers were once in the position you are in right now. They did it, and you can too!

How to Maximize
Your Test Score

→ **GOOD STUDY HABITS—THE KEY TO SUCCESS**

→ **TEN RULES FOR STUDYING MORE EFFECTIVELY**

→ **STRATEGIES FOR TAKING COMPUTER-BASED MULTIPLE-CHOICE EXAMINATIONS**

→ **STRATEGIES FOR HANDLING MULTIPLE-CHOICE QUESTIONS**

→ **DEVELOPING AND USING A TIME MANAGEMENT PLAN**

→ **TEST MATERIAL DISTRIBUTED IN ADVANCE**

→ **DEALING WITH TESTS PRESENTED ON VIDEO**

→ **HOW TO USE THIS BOOK MOST EFFECTIVELY**

This section contains information you need to get the best return from your test preparation efforts so that you can achieve the highest possible score on your official court officer examination. Too many students approach test preparation in a slipshod manner. Consequently, they waste time and do not achieve their potential. The guidelines presented in this chapter are designed to help you avoid such wasted effort.

The first part of this section provides guidelines to help you develop good study habits. Until you are quite familiar with the rules for effective studying contained in this section, you should review them prior to each study session.

The second part of this section provides a specific strategy to deal with multiple-choice questions. This strategy has been updated to reflect the recent trend in court officer examinations to utilize computer-based testing. The era of pencil-and-paper testing is coming to a close. In multiple-choice, computer-based testing, the candidate views the test on a computer monitor and uses a mouse to click on his or her selected answer choices. Although the types of questions being asked remain the same, it is imperative that the candidate use a test-taking strategy geared for taking computer-based tests. Unfortunately, an unsophisticated test taker can do poorly on such an examination simply because of a lack of familiarity with the computer-based program. Don't let this happen to you. The whole matter is complicated by the fact that the traditional pencil-and-paper examination is still widely used. You must find out which testing method is used for the examination you are taking—pencil-and-paper or computer-based—and then use the appropriate test-taking strategy.

Also included in the second part of this section is a specific strategy to deal with material distributed in advance of the test and with tests that contain a video component. Understanding and mastering these strategies is vitally important. Make sure that you review the strategy dealing with the handling of multiple-choice questions before taking each of the full-length examinations included in this book. Finally, be sure to practice this strategy while

TIP

If you don't know how to use a computer, learn!

taking these examinations. In time, the strategy will become second nature and your organized approach to answering multiple-choice questions will serve you well.

Please note that some of the practice questions in this book are based on laws, rules, policies, and procedures that are typical of those that might be found in a typical state court. Do not assume, however, that they are the exact laws, rules, policies, and procedures that are actually in use in any specific court system.

Also note that the difficulty level of the practice questions appearing in this book is, in most cases, higher than what you may encounter on your official examination. *This is a very important point for you to understand.* If you can learn to master the questions in this book, you should have great success on your official examination. We caution you again, however, if you are taking a computer-based, multiple-choice question test, you must understand the specific strategy required to do well on such an examination. Also, remember not to get discouraged if you miss some questions when tackling the questions in this book. Instead, study the explained answers provided for every question to learn why you got them wrong, and avoid such errors in the future.

GOOD STUDY HABITS—THE KEY TO SUCCESS

Many students incorrectly believe that the amount of time spent studying is the most important factor in test preparation. Of course, all else being equal, the amount of time you devote to your studies is a critical factor. But spending time reading is not necessarily studying. If you want to learn what you read, you must develop a system. For example, a student who devotes 60 minutes a day to uninterrupted study in a quiet, private setting will generally learn more than someone who puts in twice that time by studying five or six times a day for 15–20 minutes at a time.

TIP

Make friends with
your dictionary.

TEN RULES FOR STUDYING MORE EFFECTIVELY

We list ten rules for you to follow to increase study-time efficiency. If you follow these rules, you will get the most out of this book as well as similar study efforts you might undertake.

1. **MAKE SURE THAT YOU UNDERSTAND THE MEANING OF EVERY WORD YOU READ.** Your ability to understand what you read is the most important skill needed to pass your official examination. Therefore, starting immediately, every time you see a word that you don't fully understand, write it down and make note of where you saw it. Then, when you have a chance, look up the meaning of the word in the dictionary. When you think you know what the word means, go back and apply the meaning of the word to the written material that contained the word, and make certain that you fully understand its meaning as well as the written material that contained the word.

   Keep a list of all words you didn't know the first time you saw them, and periodically review the meanings of these words. Also, try to use these words whenever you can in conversation. If you do this faithfully, you will quickly build an extensive vocabulary that will help you not only when you take your official examination but also for the rest of your life.

2. **STUDY UNINTERRUPTED FOR AT LEAST 30 MINUTES.** Unless you can study for at least an uninterrupted period of 30 minutes, you should not bother to study at all. It is essential that you learn to concentrate for extended periods of time. Remember that the official examination usually takes anywhere from three to five hours to complete.

You must be prepared to concentrate just as hard in the final hour of the test as you did in the first hour. Therefore, as the examination date approaches, study for more extended periods of time without interruption. And, when you take the full-length practice examinations in this book, do a complete examination in one sitting, just as you must do at the actual examination. Remember that not being prepared to concentrate effectively throughout the entire examination is a major reason why many candidates fail! Don't let that happen to you.

3. **SIMULATE EXAMINATION CONDITIONS WHEN STUDYING.** Insofar as possible, you should study under the same conditions as those of the examination. Eliminate as many outside interferences as you can. If you are a smoker, refrain from smoking when you study because you will not be allowed to smoke in the test room on the day of the examination.

4. **STUDY ALONE.** Studying alone is the best way to prepare for your official examination. However, if possible, form a study group of three to five serious students and meet with them for two to three hours periodically, perhaps every other week. At each such meeting, the group should be prepared to discuss one area that will probably appear on the examination. In addition, everyone in the group should keep a list of items they are confused about; these items should be discussed at the study group meetings. Items that no one is certain of should be referred to an outside source, such as a teacher or a criminal justice practitioner. Extensive debate or, worse, arguing in a study group defeats the purpose of the group and must be avoided at all costs.

5. **MAKE SURE THAT YOU UNDERSTAND THE ANSWERS TO EVERY QUESTION IN THIS BOOK.** Every multiple-choice question in this book has an explained answer. Don't overlook the tremendous value of this feature. Whenever you answer a question incorrectly, be sure to understand why you missed it so that you won't make the same mistake again. However, it is equally important to make certain that you have answered a question correctly for the right reason. Therefore, study the answer explanation to every multiple-choice question in this book as carefully as you study the question itself.

6. **ALWAYS FOLLOW OUR RECOMMENDED STRATEGY FOR ANSWERING MULTIPLE-CHOICE QUESTIONS.** Prior to the advent of computer-based testing, this was a relatively easy rule to follow. There was only one strategy to learn and follow. In the next section of this chapter we provide the time-tested, invaluable strategy for answering multiple-choice questions on a traditional pencil-and-paper examination. Because this traditional pencil-and-paper testing process is still widely used, you must learn and practice this strategy. We also include a recommended strategy to follow when taking a computer-based, multiple-choice question examination. You must learn and apply this strategy if you will be taking a computed-based test. Remember, you must not assume you will be taking the traditional pencil-and-paper examination. You must make it your business to find out which of the two types of examinations you will be taking.

7. **ALWAYS TIME YOURSELF WHEN DOING PRACTICE QUESTIONS.** Running out of time on a multiple-choice examination is a tragic error that is easily avoided. Learn, through practice, to move to the next question after you spend a reasonable period of time on any one question. This technique is explained in greater detail when we discuss strategies for answering multiple-choice questions. The bottom line is this:

TIP

Use a timer.

when you are doing practice questions, always time yourself and always try to stay within recommended time limits. In the absence of such time limits, allow yourself two minutes per question because that is the standard often used by test writers on entry-level multiple-choice examinations.

8. **CONCENTRATE YOUR STUDY TIME IN THE AREAS OF YOUR GREATEST WEAKNESS.** The diagnostic procedures we use for every practice test in this book will give you an idea of the most difficult question types for you. Even though you should spend most of your study time improving yourself in these areas, do not ignore the other question types.

9. **EXERCISE REGULARLY AND STAY IN GOOD PHYSICAL CONDITION.** Students who are in good physical condition have an advantage over those who are not. It is a well-established principle that good physical health improves the ability of the mind to function smoothly and efficiently, especially when taking examinations of extended duration, such as the court officer examination.

10. **ESTABLISH A SCHEDULE FOR STUDYING AND STICK TO IT.** Do not put off studying to those times when you have nothing else to do. Schedule your study time, and try not to let anything else interfere with that schedule. If you feel yourself weakening, review Chapter 1 and remind yourself why you would like to become a court officer.

STRATEGIES FOR TAKING COMPUTER-BASED, MULTIPLE-CHOICE EXAMINATIONS

1. **PLAN TO BE FLEXIBLE.** Because computer-based multiple-choice testing is in its infancy, there is no standard method of structuring these examinations. It is a mistake to believe that all you have to do is learn how one such test was administered. Approach each computer-based test you take with a flexible attitude. As time goes by, standardization will probably occur. For now, however, candidates must understand that an essential element of preparing for every computer-based test they take is to learn as much as they can about the computer process that will be used for that particular examination.

2. **DEVELOP BASIC COMPUTER SKILLS.** Today, most candidates for the court officer examination will probably be comfortable working with a computer. However, if you do not feel comfortable performing basic computer functions, such as using a mouse and navigating around a computer screen, you probably should avoid computer-based testing. A better alternative, however, would be to develop these basic computer skills.

3. **SAMPLE THE FIELD.** Many of the most widely used computer-based, multiple-choice examinations, like the GMAT, have tutorials to familiarize the candidate with the specific test interface used for each such examination. Without regard for the test content, court officer candidates scheduled to take a computer-based, multiple-choice examination should seek out these tutorials and learn from them. As much as possible, become familiar with the various formats employed in computer-based, multiple-choice tests. This will go a long way toward your being able to focus on seeking out the correct answers while taking a computer-based court officer test rather than having to focus on the format of the test.

4. **ASK IN ADVANCE ABOUT THE TEST FORMAT.** Contact the testing agency administering the exam you will be taking, and inquire about the test format. Find out if you can

view a tutorial for the examination you are taking prior to exam day. Another recommended step is to seek out people who have already taken the examination you will be taking. Ask them about the format of the test. Following are some of the details of the computer-based test format that you should ask about.

- Are the written directions and rules outlining the test taker's responsibilities during the test available to the candidate before the day of the test? If so, obtain them and study them.
- Is there a computer-based method to make notes during the test? If not, are candidates supplied with a notepad to take notes? If not, can the candidate bring his or her own notepad into the test room? Later on in this chapter we will present a strategy for handling multiple-choice questions. This strategy includes note taking. It is imperative that candidates taking a computer-based, multiple-choice question test understand how to make notes during the test.
- How do you navigate from one question to another?
- Does the computer screen show one question at a time?
- Does every question fit on the computer screen or will it be necessary to scroll?
- Must you answer the questions in the order they are presented or can you skip questions? Can you return to questions you have already answered?
- How do you bookmark certain questions to return quickly to them?
- How do you select your answers? Is there a separate answer sheet?
- How do you change an answer already selected?
- Is there one time frame for completing the entire examination or are there timed sections?
- Does the computer keep track of time for you?
- What is the procedure to follow in the event of a computer malfunction during the test, such as a frozen screen?

TIP

Get as much informaiton about the test format as you can.

5. **PAY STRICT ATTENTION TO THE EXAM-DAY TUTORIAL.** Virtually every computer-based, multiple-choice examination begins with a tutorial before the examination begins. Do not assume you know the instructions being discussed in the tutorial no matter how much advance preparation you have made. Keep in mind that test formats are continuously evolving. Remain flexible.

6. **CLEAR UP UNRESOLVED ISSUES BEFORE THE START OF THE TEST.** When viewing the exam tutorial, be vigilant and listen for the answers to the questions posed in strategy 4. If, after the tutorial, you are not sure of the answers to these questions, make inquiries to the test room monitor before the test begins.

7. **FOLLOW THE TEST-TAKING STRATEGIES FOR HANDLING MULTIPLE-CHOICE QUESTIONS AS THEY APPEAR IN THE NEXT SECTION OF THIS TEXT.**

STRATEGIES FOR HANDLING MULTIPLE-CHOICE QUESTIONS

A very specific test-taking strategy that is valuable for a multiple-choice examination follows. This strategy not only will serve you well on the court officer examination but also is valid for any multiple-choice exam you may take. Study the strategy and practice it; then study it again until you have mastered it.

Please note that these strategies are written to apply to both the traditional pencil-and-paper examination and the computer-based examination. Also note that at first glance some of the strategies seem overly complex. You will find, however, that if you put in the required effort to master them, you will in all likelihood find yourself at or near the top of the hiring list when the test results are published.

1. **READ THE INSTRUCTIONS.** Do not assume that you know what the instructions are without reading them. Make sure that you read and understand them. There are test instructions and question instructions. *Test instructions* are a set of general instructions that govern the entire examination and are to be read prior to the start of the exam. *Question instructions* are found throughout the test prior to each series of questions that requires specific instructions. They govern the taking of each such series of questions. On the day of your official examination, if you are unsure about the instructions, ask questions when given the opportunity.

   If you are taking a computer-based, multiple-choice question test, don't forget to pay special attention to instructions regarding the format of the examination.

2. **MAKE SURE THAT YOU HAVE THE COMPLETE EXAMINATION.** If you are taking a traditional pencil-and-paper examination, as soon as your official examination starts, check the test booklet page by page. Because these booklets have numbered pages, simply count the pages. If you do not have a complete examination, inform a test monitor immediately.

3. **UNDERSTAND HOW TO RECORD ANSWERS PROPERLY.** If you are taking a traditional pencil-and-paper examination, keep in mind that some answer sheets number the questions vertically while other answer sheets number the questions horizontally. This numbering system is used to discourage cheating. The answer sheets used in this book for the practice examination are typical of what you will see on a traditional pencil-and-paper examination. However, do not take anything for granted. Review the instructions on the answer sheet carefully and familiarize yourself with its format.

   If you are taking a computer-based, multiple-choice test, make sure you know the answers to the following questions:

   - Is there a separate answer sheet?
   - How do you select your answers?
   - How do you change an answer already selected?

4. **BE EXTREMELY CAREFUL WHEN MARKING YOUR ANSWERS.** If you are taking a traditional pencil-and-paper examination, be sure to mark your answers in accordance with the official instructions. Be absolutely certain that

   - you mark only one answer for each question, unless the instructions specifically indicate the possibility of multiple answers.
   - you do not make extraneous markings on your answer sheet.
   - you completely darken the allotted space for the answer you choose.
   - you erase completely any answer that you wish to change.

   Please note that there is a difference between making extraneous markings on your answer sheet and making notes in your test booklet, which is the booklet that contains the test questions. As you will see, good test-taking strategy demands that you make certain notations in your test booklet. The only exception would be in the very rare instance where the test instructions prohibit writing in the test booklet.

Pay attention!

If you are taking a computer-based, multiple-choice test, this is not as important an issue as it is for those taking traditional pencil-and-paper tests. Just make certain when you take a computer-based test that you understand the proper method for entering your selected answer and, if necessary, for changing an answer you have already selected.

5. **MAKE ABSOLUTELY CERTAIN THAT YOU ARE MARKING THE ANSWER TO THE RIGHT QUESTION.** Many people have failed traditional pencil-and-paper, multiple-choice tests because of carelessness in this area. All it takes is one mistake. If, for example, you mark an answer to question 10 in the space for question 11, you probably will continue the mistake for a number of questions until you realize your error. To prevent something like this from happening, we recommend that you use the following procedure when marking your answer sheet.

- Select the choice you believe is the answer, circle that choice on the test booklet, and remind yourself what question number you are working on. If, for example, you select choice C as the answer for question 11, circle choice C on the test booklet and say to yourself, "C is the answer to question 11."
- Then find the space on your answer sheet for question 11, and again say "C is the answer to question 11" as you mark the answer.

Even though this procedure may seem rather elementary and repetitive, after a while it becomes automatic. If followed properly, it guarantees that you will not fail the examination because of this type of careless mistake.

If you are taking a computer-based, multiple-choice test, this is not as important an issue as it is for those taking traditional pencil-and-paper tests. Most computer-based formats provide for automatic marking of the answer sheet upon selecting the answer for a particular question. To be on the safe side, however, make sure this is the case on the test you are taking. In fact, never assume anything about the format of the examination. Confirm everything.

6. **MAKE CERTAIN THAT YOU UNDERSTAND WHAT THE QUESTION IS ASKING.** Test takers often choose wrong answers because they fail to read the question carefully enough. Read the stem of the question (the part before the choices) very carefully to make certain that you know what the examiner is asking. If necessary, read it twice. Be certain to read every word in the question. If you do not, you could select a wrong answer to a very simple question.

7. **ALWAYS READ ALL THE CHOICES BEFORE YOU SELECT AN ANSWER.** Distracters are what test writers call incorrect choices. Every multiple-choice question usually has one best distracter, which is very close to being correct. Many times this best distracter comes before the correct choice. Therefore, don't select the first choice that looks good. Read all the choices!

8. **BE AWARE OF KEY WORDS THAT OFTEN TIP OFF THE CORRECT AND INCORRECT ANSWERS.** When you are stuck on a question and must guess at the answer, you can often select the correct choice by understanding that absolute words tend to appear more often in incorrect choices, and that limiting words tend to appear more often in correct choices. Absolute words are very broad and do not allow for any exceptions. Limiting words are not all inclusive and allow for exceptions.

TIP

Know key words.

Absolute Words

never	always	only	none
must	all	nothing	any
every	everyone	everything	sole

Limiting Words

usually	sometimes	generally	many
occasionally	possible	some	often
may	could	probably	might

9. **NEVER MAKE A CHOICE BASED ON FREQUENCY OF PREVIOUS ANSWERS.** Some students inappropriately pay attention to the pattern of answers when taking an exam. Multiple-choice exams are not designed to have an equal number of A, B, C, and D choices as the answers. Always answer the question without regard to what the letter designations of the previous choices have been.

10. **MAKE A DECISION ON EACH ANSWER CHOICE AND RECORD IT.** This strategy is designed to enable the test taker to save time and mental energy by recording his or her decisions on each choice for every question in the entire test the first time through the test. The concept is simple: Recording your thoughts on each choice as you review it facilitates speedy review of the question as the need arises.

There are three possible decisions you can make for each answer choice you review. You know *for sure* that a certain choice (1) is not the answer, (2) is the answer, or (3) may or may not be the answer. The time-saving tip for you is to record your decision for each choice you review, as described below in our three-step process.

> **THE THREE-STEP PROCESS**
> 1. Use process of elimination to arrive at the correct answer.
> 2. Reread answer choices you were not able to eliminate.
> 3. Reread the question stem.

Step One. If you are taking a traditional pencil-and-paper examination, as you consider the various answer choices to each question, put an X in the test booklet to cross out the letter designation of any choice you know for sure is not the answer. If you cross out all but one of the choices, the remaining choice should be your answer. Read that choice one more time to satisfy yourself, put a circle around its letter designation (if you still feel it is the correct answer) and transfer it to your answer sheet using strategy 5. Spend no more time on this question.

If you are taking a computer-based, multiple-choice test, use the note-taking function of the computer to record those answer choices you know for sure are *not* the answer. If you eliminate all but one answer choice, record that choice as your answer. Spend no more time on this question.

Step Two. If, however, after your initial review of the choices, you are left with more than one possible answer, you need only to reread those choices that you did not eliminate the first time by putting an X through them. Many times, the second time you read the remaining choices, the answer is clear. If that happens, cross out the wrong choice by putting an X through it, circle the correct one, and transfer the answer to the answer sheet if you are taking a traditional pencil-and-paper test. If you are taking a computer-based, multiple-choice test, use the computer to perform these tasks.

Step Three. If, after the second reading of the choices, you still not have selected an answer, reread the stem of the question and make certain that you understand the question. Then review those choices that you did not initially eliminate by putting an X through them. Keep in mind the absolute words and limiting words mentioned in strategy 8, which may give you a hint of the correct answer. If you still haven't decided which answer choice to select, skip over that question and return to it later, as discussed in strategy 12.

11. **MAKE NOTE OF QUESTIONS YOU HAVE HAD DIFFICULTY ANSWERING.** If you are taking a traditional pencil-and-paper, multiple-choice examination, when you select and record an answer to a question that you find difficult, put an asterisk or star in the margin of the test booklet next to that question. If you are taking a computer-based test, bookmark the question to provide for a speedy return to it. Then, if after answering all the questions on the test you still have time remaining, return to these difficult questions one more time to reconsider your answer choice. Very often, when the pressure of finishing the examination is over, the question will seem less difficult.

12. **SKIP OVER QUESTIONS THAT GIVE YOU TROUBLE.** The first time through the examination, do not dwell too long on any one troubling question. Spending too much time on a troubling question is a common cause of running out of time. You must avoid this error.

   - If you are taking a traditional pencil-and-paper, multiple-choice examination, simply skip these troubling questions after putting a circle around the question number in the test booklet and go on to the next question. The circle around the question number in the test booklet will help you find unanswered questions the second time through the examination, as explained in strategy 13. Keep in mind that when you skip a question you must also skip the appropriate space on the answer sheet.
   - If you are taking a computer-based test, bookmark the question to provide for speedy return to it after you have gone through the test the first time, as explained in strategy 13.

13. **RETURN TO THE QUESTIONS YOU SKIPPED AFTER YOU FINISH THE REST OF THE EXAMINATION.** After you answer all the questions you are sure of, check the time remaining. If time permits (it should if you follow our recommendations), return to each question you did not answer and reread the stem of each of these questions and any of the choices that are not crossed out. It should be easy to find the questions you have not yet answered if you have followed strategy 12. Many times the correct answer will now be easy to determine. If, however, the answer is still not clear and you are running out of time, then make an "educated guess" from among those choices that you have not already eliminated. When making an "educated guess," use the guidelines in strategy 16.

   If you still have time left after you have answered every question that you skipped, go back and review those questions that gave you difficulty when you originally answered them (see strategy 11). These questions can be found easily if you followed our recommended strategy. Reread each of these questions and reconsider your answer. Sometimes you will discover a careless mistake. If you do, you should, of course, change your answer.

14. **NEVER LEAVE QUESTIONS UNANSWERED UNLESS THE INSTRUCTIONS INDICATE A PENALTY FOR WRONG ANSWERS.** In most court officer examinations, you do not have points subtracted from your final score for wrong answers. In other words,

there is no penalty for guessing. If this is the case on your examination, guess at any question you are not sure of.

However, in rare instances, a penalty is assessed for wrong answers on multiple-choice examinations. Because this would have to be explained in the test instructions, be sure, as already recommended, to read all your instructions very carefully. If there is a penalty for wrong answers on your examination, decide how strongly you feel about each individual question before answering it. Note again that this rarely happens on entry-level examinations such as the one you are planning to take.

15. **DEVELOP A TIME MANAGEMENT PLAN.** It is extremely important for you to have a time management plan when you take your examination. Not to systematically monitor the passage of time on an examination is similar to inviting failure. The mechanics of developing a time management plan are presented later in this chapter.

16. **RULES FOR MAKING AN EDUCATED GUESS.** Your chances of selecting the correct answers to questions you are not sure of will be significantly increased if you use the following rules:

TIP

Learn how to make
an educated guess.

- Never consider answer choices you have already positively eliminated.
- Be aware of key words that give you clues as to which answer might be right or wrong.
- Always eliminate choices that are very close in meaning to each other.

EXAMPLE

Alicia's complaint about the weather was that

(A) it was too hot.
(B) it was too cold.
(C) it varied too much.
(D) it was unpredictable.

In this example, choices C and D are so close together in meaning that neither is likely to be the correct answer. Choices A and B, on the other hand, are quite opposite each other, and one of them is most likely to be the correct answer.

- If two choices are worded so that combined they encompass all the possibilities, one of them must be the correct choice.

EXAMPLE

How old is John?

(A) John is 7 years old or less.
(B) John is over 7 years of age.
(C) John is 6 years old.
(D) John is 14 years old.

In this example, it should be clear to you that the correct answer must be either A or B, because if John is not 7 years old or less (choice A), then he must be over 7 years of age (choice B).

- An answer choice that has significantly more or significantly fewer words in it is very often the correct choice.

17. **BE VERY RELUCTANT TO CHANGE ANSWERS.** Unless you have a very good reason, do not change an answer after you have chosen it. Experience has shown us that all too often people change their answer from the right one to the wrong one. This doesn't mean that you should never change an answer. If you discover an obvious mistake, for example, you should most certainly change your answer.

18. **UNDERSTAND THAT THERE ARE SPECIFIC STRATEGIES FOR DEALING WITH DIFFERENT QUESTION TYPES.** On every entry-level examination, you will encounter different question types. For example, some questions might test your ability to understand what you read, others might test your verbal or mathematical ability, and still others might test your memory or your ability to interpret graphs, charts or tables, and so forth. If you are to maximize your test score, you must understand that it is wrong to answer all question types on the test with the same strategy. Instead, you should change your approach based on the type of question you are answering at any given time. Included in this book is a discussion of each of the most common question types used on most court officer examinations throughout the country. Included in each discussion is an explanation of a strategy to follow for the question type being considered. Learn to recognize the various question types, and learn the specific strategies for answering each one of them. Then, as you take the practice examinations in later chapters, use these strategies.

TIP

Learn the different question types.

DEVELOPING AND USING A TIME MANAGEMENT PLAN

The primary goal of a time management plan is to determine the average number of minutes you should spend on each multiple-choice question on the test and then to use that information throughout the test to guard against running out of time. In order to develop a time management plan, you must know (1) the number of questions on the exam and (2) the amount of time allowed to complete the test. Many times you will not have this information until the day of the test. But, because it is a relatively simple task, you can easily develop your time management plan on test day before you begin to answer any questions.

The following step-by-step explanation details how a time management plan is developed. For the purposes of this explanation, assume that you are taking an examination that has 100 questions and a time limit of four hours.

1. Convert the time allowed to minutes and put 30 minutes aside or, as we say, in the bank. This 30 minutes is to be used when you have finished the examination to go back to the questions you have skipped and to otherwise review your exam. Using our example, convert four hours to 240 minutes and subtract 30 minutes, which leaves you with 210 minutes to answer 100 questions. Remember that this also leaves you with 30 minutes in the bank to use at the end of the test.

2. Divide the time allowed to answer the questions by the number of questions to determine the average amount of time you should spend on each question. In our example, this means that you would divide 210 minutes by 100 questions and thus determine that you should spend approximately two minutes per question.

Make sure you have a time mangement plan.

3. Use your time management plan. Knowing that you should spend approximately two minutes per question is of little value unless you then proceed to monitor your time usage from the start of the exam. On a 100-question test, we recommend that you specifically check your time every ten questions. Using our example, at the end of the first ten questions no more than twenty minutes should have passed (two minutes per question); after completing 20 questions, no more than 40 minutes should have passed, and so forth.

By developing and using a time management plan, you will find out early in the test if you are falling behind. This information is quite beneficial because you will still be able to do something about it. Contrast that situation with one where you realize much too late that you have been using too much time. Clearly the former is the preferable situation.

TEST MATERIAL DISTRIBUTED IN ADVANCE

In some jurisdictions, material about entrance examinations is distributed in advance of the test. This material typically takes the form of a test preparation and orientation booklet. Included in this advance material may be general information about the examination, a description of the types of questions that will appear on the examination, specific suggestions or hints for you to follow when taking the examination, and sample questions. In addition, you might also be given accompanying reference material containing information that you should study to prepare for the examination.

The rule to follow when dealing with advance material is both simple and obvious. You should read the material carefully and use it to prepare for the examination. Your score on the examination will, in all probability, be in direct proportion to your understanding of the advance material.

Special Considerations for Reference Materials Distributed in Advance

By reference material we mean material upon which actual test questions might be based. Concerning reference material distributed in advance, there are generally three possibilities. The way you deal with this reference material is predicated on which of the three possibilities apply to your particular examination, if indeed your examination involves the use of advance material.

The first possibility is that the advance reference material may be similar but not identical to the reference material you will be using on the day of the test. In that case, you should familiarize yourself with the format and structure of the material, but you do not need to learn it.

The second possibility is that the advance reference material may be identical to the actual reference material to be distributed on the day of the test. In that case, you should become very familiar with the advance material because the questions you will be asked will be based on that material, but it is not necessary to memorize the material because you will have it at your disposal on test day.

The third possibility is that the advance reference material will be used on the day of the test, but you will not be able to refer to it even though the questions will test your knowledge of it. In that case, you must commit the information involved to memory prior to test day. Failure to do so will result in almost certain failure.

DEALING WITH TESTS PRESENTED ON VIDEO

Another practice occasionally used in entrance-level examinations is the use of video simulations. Should a video be used on your official examination, you can expect the following. On the day of the test, you will be shown a video presentation and then asked questions about what you have heard and seen on the video tape. In some cases, the questions you are asked are designed to measure your ability to understand by observing and listening. Other questions are designed to test your ability to apply written material to the situations shown in each scenario.

In many tests that include a video component, candidates are shown a sample video tape prior to the day of the examination. If your test is structured in that way, it is absolutely essential that you view the sample video.

Strategy for Taking a Video Test

1. **MAKE CERTAIN THAT YOU UNDERSTAND WHAT THE QUESTION IS ASKING.** This general rule about the importance of reading and understanding test instructions and directions must be followed if you are to be successful on a video test. If, after reading the instructions, you are unsure about their exact meaning, ask questions when given the opportunity. Make sure that you know what to expect before the video begins because most video tests prohibit the asking of questions after the video begins.

2. **TAKE NOTES AS THE VIDEO PRESENTATION UNFOLDS, UNLESS SPECIFICALLY PROHIBITED BY THE TEST INSTRUCTIONS.** You should not try to record the scene verbatim. Make your notes as brief as possible. Use key words and phrases and not complete sentences. Use abbreviations whenever possible, keeping in mind that your notes are useless if you cannot interpret them later. Also keep in mind that candidates who get overly engrossed in taking lengthy notes often miss critical information.

3. **CONCENTRATE.** You must not let your mind wander. You must pay strict attention to what you are seeing and what you are hearing. Completely ignore the actions of those around you. Please note that you can hone your note taking skills and concentration ability through practice. Simply watch a news show on television (video tape it if possible). Make notes of what you hear and see. After the show, see how many of the important points you have captured.

4. **PAY PARTICULAR ATTENTION TO ERRORS AS YOU SEE OR HEAR THEM OCCUR.** Note what appears to be inappropriate actions on the part of the actors in the video.

5. **NOTE TIMES, DATES, AND LOCATIONS WHEN GIVEN.** Understanding the time frames and locations involved are often the subject of questions.

HOW TO USE THIS BOOK MOST EFFECTIVELY

To obtain maximum benefit from the use of this book, we recommend the following approach.

1. **LEARN THE STRATEGIES FOR HANDLING MULTIPLE-CHOICE QUESTIONS,** which appear earlier in this chapter.

2. **TAKE THE DIAGNOSTIC TEST IN CHAPTER 3.** After completing this examination and reviewing the explained answers, fill out the diagnostic chart that precedes the explained answers. This will indicate your strengths and weaknesses. You should then devote most of your study time to correcting your weaknesses.

3. **STUDY CHAPTERS 4–8.** As mentioned previously, concentrate your study efforts in your weak areas, but make certain to cover each chapter. Note that each of these chapters deals with a different type of question and that a specific test-taking strategy is offered for each question type. As mentioned previously, make a special effort to learn these different strategies and then practice them when you take the exams in chapters 10–13.

   Also, when studying chapters 4–8, be sure to follow the ten rules for studying more effectively, which appear earlier in this chapter. Also, make sure to apply the strategies for handling multiple-choice questions when doing the practice exercises at the end of chapters 4–8.

4. **TAKE PRACTICE EXAMINATION ONE IN ONE SITTING AFTER YOU HAVE COMPLETED CHAPTERS 4–8.** When you have finished this examination and have reviewed the explained answers, complete the diagnostic chart that precedes the explained answers. Then restudy the appropriate chapters in accordance with the directions on the bottom of the diagnostic chart.

5. **TAKE PRACTICE EXAMINATIONS TWO THROUGH FOUR IN THE ORDER THAT THEY APPEAR.** After you have finished each examination, follow the same procedure that you follow after finishing Practice Examination One.

6. **READ CHAPTER 14 WHEN YOUR ACTUAL EXAMINATION IS A WEEK AWAY.** Be sure to follow the recommended strategy contained in this chapter for the 7 days immediately preceding the examination.

Diagnose

YOUR PROBLEM

A Diagnostic Examination

There are 100 questions on this diagnostic examination, and you should finish the entire examination in 3½ hours. For maximum benefit, it is strongly recommended that you take this examination in one sitting as if it were the actual test.

The answers to this examination, a diagnostic chart, and their explanations are included in this chapter after the last test question. By completing the Diagnostic Chart, you can get an idea of which question types give you the most difficulty. You can then devote most of your time to these areas.

BEFORE YOU TAKE THE EXAMINATION

Before taking this examination, you should have read the Introduction. Be certain that you employ the recommended test-taking strategies previously outlined while taking the examination.

Remember to read each question and related material carefully before choosing your answers. Select the choice you believe to be the answer, and mark your answers on the Answer Sheet provided. This Answer Sheet is similar to the one used on the actual examination. The Answer Key, Diagnostic Procedure, and Answer Explanations appear at the end of this test.

ANSWER SHEET
Diagnostic Exam

Follow the instructions given in the test. Mark only your answers in the circles below.

WARNING: Be sure that the circle you fill is in the same row as the question you are answering. Use a No. 2 pencil (soft pencil).

BE SURE YOUR PENCIL MARKS ARE HEAVY AND BLACK.

ERASE COMPLETELY ANY ANSWER YOU WISH TO CHANGE.

DO NOT make stray pencil dots, dashes, or marks.

1. Ⓐ Ⓑ Ⓒ Ⓓ	26. Ⓐ Ⓑ Ⓒ Ⓓ	51. Ⓐ Ⓑ Ⓒ Ⓓ	76. Ⓐ Ⓑ Ⓒ Ⓓ
2. Ⓐ Ⓑ Ⓒ Ⓓ	27. Ⓐ Ⓑ Ⓒ Ⓓ	52. Ⓐ Ⓑ Ⓒ Ⓓ	77. Ⓐ Ⓑ Ⓒ Ⓓ
3. Ⓐ Ⓑ Ⓒ Ⓓ	28. Ⓐ Ⓑ Ⓒ Ⓓ	53. Ⓐ Ⓑ Ⓒ Ⓓ	78. Ⓐ Ⓑ Ⓒ Ⓓ
4. Ⓐ Ⓑ Ⓒ Ⓓ	29. Ⓐ Ⓑ Ⓒ Ⓓ	54. Ⓐ Ⓑ Ⓒ Ⓓ	79. Ⓐ Ⓑ Ⓒ Ⓓ
5. Ⓐ Ⓑ Ⓒ Ⓓ	30. Ⓐ Ⓑ Ⓒ Ⓓ	55. Ⓐ Ⓑ Ⓒ Ⓓ	80. Ⓐ Ⓑ Ⓒ Ⓓ
6. Ⓐ Ⓑ Ⓒ Ⓓ	31. Ⓐ Ⓑ Ⓒ Ⓓ	56. Ⓐ Ⓑ Ⓒ Ⓓ	81. Ⓐ Ⓑ Ⓒ Ⓓ
7. Ⓐ Ⓑ Ⓒ Ⓓ	32. Ⓐ Ⓑ Ⓒ Ⓓ	57. Ⓐ Ⓑ Ⓒ Ⓓ	82. Ⓐ Ⓑ Ⓒ Ⓓ
8. Ⓐ Ⓑ Ⓒ Ⓓ	33. Ⓐ Ⓑ Ⓒ Ⓓ	58. Ⓐ Ⓑ Ⓒ Ⓓ	83. Ⓐ Ⓑ Ⓒ Ⓓ
9. Ⓐ Ⓑ Ⓒ Ⓓ	34. Ⓐ Ⓑ Ⓒ Ⓓ	59. Ⓐ Ⓑ Ⓒ Ⓓ	84. Ⓐ Ⓑ Ⓒ Ⓓ
10. Ⓐ Ⓑ Ⓒ Ⓓ	35. Ⓐ Ⓑ Ⓒ Ⓓ	60. Ⓐ Ⓑ Ⓒ Ⓓ	85. Ⓐ Ⓑ Ⓒ Ⓓ
11. Ⓐ Ⓑ Ⓒ Ⓓ	36. Ⓐ Ⓑ Ⓒ Ⓓ	61. Ⓐ Ⓑ Ⓒ Ⓓ	86. Ⓐ Ⓑ Ⓒ Ⓓ
12. Ⓐ Ⓑ Ⓒ Ⓓ	37. Ⓐ Ⓑ Ⓒ Ⓓ	62. Ⓐ Ⓑ Ⓒ Ⓓ	87. Ⓐ Ⓑ Ⓒ Ⓓ
13. Ⓐ Ⓑ Ⓒ Ⓓ	38. Ⓐ Ⓑ Ⓒ Ⓓ	63. Ⓐ Ⓑ Ⓒ Ⓓ	88. Ⓐ Ⓑ Ⓒ Ⓓ
14. Ⓐ Ⓑ Ⓒ Ⓓ	39. Ⓐ Ⓑ Ⓒ Ⓓ	64. Ⓐ Ⓑ Ⓒ Ⓓ	89. Ⓐ Ⓑ Ⓒ Ⓓ
15. Ⓐ Ⓑ Ⓒ Ⓓ	40. Ⓐ Ⓑ Ⓒ Ⓓ	65. Ⓐ Ⓑ Ⓒ Ⓓ	90. Ⓐ Ⓑ Ⓒ Ⓓ
16. Ⓐ Ⓑ Ⓒ Ⓓ	41. Ⓐ Ⓑ Ⓒ Ⓓ	66. Ⓐ Ⓑ Ⓒ Ⓓ	91. Ⓐ Ⓑ Ⓒ Ⓓ
17. Ⓐ Ⓑ Ⓒ Ⓓ	42. Ⓐ Ⓑ Ⓒ Ⓓ	67. Ⓐ Ⓑ Ⓒ Ⓓ	92. Ⓐ Ⓑ Ⓒ Ⓓ
18. Ⓐ Ⓑ Ⓒ Ⓓ	43. Ⓐ Ⓑ Ⓒ Ⓓ	68. Ⓐ Ⓑ Ⓒ Ⓓ	93. Ⓐ Ⓑ Ⓒ Ⓓ
19. Ⓐ Ⓑ Ⓒ Ⓓ	44. Ⓐ Ⓑ Ⓒ Ⓓ	69. Ⓐ Ⓑ Ⓒ Ⓓ	94. Ⓐ Ⓑ Ⓒ Ⓓ
20. Ⓐ Ⓑ Ⓒ Ⓓ	45. Ⓐ Ⓑ Ⓒ Ⓓ	70. Ⓐ Ⓑ Ⓒ Ⓓ	95. Ⓐ Ⓑ Ⓒ Ⓓ
21. Ⓐ Ⓑ Ⓒ Ⓓ	46. Ⓐ Ⓑ Ⓒ Ⓓ	71. Ⓐ Ⓑ Ⓒ Ⓓ	96. Ⓐ Ⓑ Ⓒ Ⓓ
22. Ⓐ Ⓑ Ⓒ Ⓓ	47. Ⓐ Ⓑ Ⓒ Ⓓ	72. Ⓐ Ⓑ Ⓒ Ⓓ	97. Ⓐ Ⓑ Ⓒ Ⓓ
23. Ⓐ Ⓑ Ⓒ Ⓓ	48. Ⓐ Ⓑ Ⓒ Ⓓ	73. Ⓐ Ⓑ Ⓒ Ⓓ	98. Ⓐ Ⓑ Ⓒ Ⓓ
24. Ⓐ Ⓑ Ⓒ Ⓓ	49. Ⓐ Ⓑ Ⓒ Ⓓ	74. Ⓐ Ⓑ Ⓒ Ⓓ	99. Ⓐ Ⓑ Ⓒ Ⓓ
25. Ⓐ Ⓑ Ⓒ Ⓓ	50. Ⓐ Ⓑ Ⓒ Ⓓ	75. Ⓐ Ⓑ Ⓒ Ⓓ	100. Ⓐ Ⓑ Ⓒ Ⓓ

THE DIAGNOSTIC TEST

Time: 3 1/2 hours
100 questions

> **Answer questions 1–8 based on the following directions.**
>
> **Directions:** Study for 5 minutes the following illustration, which depicts items taken from two defendants immediately after they were arrested. Try to remember as many details as possible. Do not make written notes of any kind during this 5-minute period. At the end of the 5-minute period, answer questions 1–8. When answering the questions, do NOT refer back to the illustration.

ITEMS TAKEN FROM DEFENDANT CHARLES ADAMS

PEN

AUTOMOBILE REGISTRATION

1996 BUICK PLATE CA221

CHARLES ADAMS 1632 64 ROAD WHITESTONE

ADDRESS BOOK

FIVE 5¢ CENTS

DAILY APPOINTMENTS

TRAFFIC TICKET CHARLES ADAMS SPEEDING

$ TEN DOLLARS $

TWENTY FIVE 25¢ CENTS

KEY

ITEMS TAKEN FROM DEFENDANT ALICIA SMART

TISSUES

MACE

AUTOMOBILE REGISTRATION

1996 HONDA PLATE HR442

ALICIA SMART 618 24th STREET BAYSIDE

Dear Mom,
Will return home after 3pm.
I went shopping with Susan at the mall.
Love,
CATHY

ASPIRIN

KEY

KEY

SUBWAY TOKEN

DO NOT PROCEED UNTIL 5 MINUTES HAVE PASSED.

TURN TO NEXT PAGE

DIAGNOSTIC EXAM

A DIAGNOSTIC EXAMINATION   35

Answer questions 1–8 solely on the basis of the preceding illustration. Do not refer back to the illustration when answering these questions.

1. What is the total amount of money possessed by the two defendants?

   (A) $10.30
   (B) $.30
   (C) $10.25
   (D) $.05

2. Which of the defendants is more likely to have traveled on the subway?

   (A) Charles Adams
   (B) Alicia Smart
   (C) both Charles Adams and Alicia Smart
   (D) neither Charles Adams nor Alicia Smart

3. Which of the defendants carried a defensive weapon?

   (A) Charles Adams
   (B) Alicia Smart
   (C) both Charles Adams and Alicia Smart
   (D) neither Charles Adams nor Alicia Smart

4. Which of the defendants lives in Whitestone?

   (A) Charles Adams
   (B) Alicia Smart
   (C) both Charles Adams and Alicia Smart
   (D) neither Charles Adams nor Alicia Smart

5. What is Alicia Smart's address?

   (A) 1632 64th Road
   (B) 618 24th Street
   (C) 618 24th Road
   (D) 1632 24th Street

6. "Cathy" is most probably . . .

   (A) the daughter of Charles Adams.
   (B) the daughter of Alicia Smart.
   (C) the sister of Charles Adams.
   (D) the sister of Alicia Smart.

7. How many keys did Charles Adams possess?

   (A) one
   (B) two
   (C) three
   (D) four

8. License plate number CA 221 belongs to a . . .

    (A) 1996 Buick.
    (B) 1996 Honda.
    (C) 1996 Chevrolet.
    (D) 1996 Lincoln.

Answer questions 9–15 based on the following directions.

Directions: Study for 5 minutes the following narrative about the trial of defendant Mark Brown. Try to remember as many details as possible. Do not make written notes of any kind during this 5-minute period. At the end of the 5-minute period, answer questions 9–15. When answering the questions, do NOT refer back to the narrative.

MEMORY STORY

5-Minute Time Limit

On May 15th, at 9:30 A.M., the murder trial of Mark Brown commenced in Supreme Court in the Borough of Queens. The judge was the honorable Mary Jacobs, the prosecuting attorney was Dianne Adams, and the defense attorney was David Cone.

Mark Brown was born on May 31, 1968, in Seattle, Washington. He graduated from Washington University on June 25, 1990, at which time he moved to New York City. He had trouble finding work and turned to a life of crime. On June 15, 1997, a person named Claude Johnson was stabbed to death in an apparent robbery attempt in the Borough of Manhattan. Ten days later, Mark Brown was arrested for the murder of Claude Johnson. The key witness against Brown is a parking lot attendant named Walter Ford.

Thirty minutes after the trial commenced, Mark Brown became loud and boisterous, and Court Officer Henry Hightower was ordered by the judge to restrain Brown with the use of handcuffs.

At 1:00 P.M., immediately following an hour recess for lunch, the arresting officer in the case, Detective Sam Jackson, was called to the witness stand to testify. Jackson stated under oath that at about 4:30 P.M. on the day of the murder he responded to the murder scene at Vernon Boulevard and 41 Street in the Borough of Manhattan and found the victim laying in the street bleeding. His first actions were to arrange for an ambulance to respond and to have the victim removed to Elmhurst City Hospital where he was pronounced dead on arrival. Jackson further testified that during the ambulance ride to the hospital, the victim made a dying declaration naming Mark Brown as the person who stabbed him.

At 4:45 P.M., immediately after Detective Jackson concluded his testimony, the trial was recessed until 9:30 P.M. the following day.

DO NOT PROCEED UNTIL 5 MINUTES HAVE PASSED

9. What is Mark Brown's birthday?
   - (A) June 15th
   - (B) May 31st
   - (C) May 15th
   - (D) June 25th

10. When did Mark Brown move to New York City?

    - (A) upon graduation from college
    - (B) right after he was born
    - (C) around the time of the death of Claude Johnson
    - (D) never lived in New York City

11. The name of the key witness in the case against Mark Brown is . . .

    - (A) Dianne Adams.
    - (B) Mary Jacobs.
    - (C) Claude Johnson.
    - (D) Walter Ford.

12. At what time on May 15th was Mark Brown handcuffed?

    - (A) 9:30 A.M.
    - (B) 1:00 P.M.
    - (C) 10:00 A.M.
    - (D) 4:40 P.M.

13. The arresting officer in the case was a detective named . . .

    - (A) Johnson.
    - (B) Jackson.
    - (C) Brown.
    - (D) Cone.

14. What was the exact time of the death of the murder victim?

    - (A) 4:30 P.M.
    - (B) 1:00 P.M.
    - (C) 4:45 P.M.
    - (D) not given in the story

15. Mark Brown's trial took place in the Borough of . . .

    - (A) Queens.
    - (B) the Bronx.
    - (C) Brooklyn.
    - (D) Manhattan.

Directions: Answer questions 16–20 solely on the basis of the information contained in the following passage.

May North was adopted by her parents, Pat and June North. She was a month old at the time. May was recently appointed as a court officer and assigned to the Metropolis Criminal Court. Officer North, shield number 8607, has been in contact with Locate Your Parents, a volunteer group whose sole purpose is to assist men and women who have been adopted to find and contact their birth parents.

As a result of Officer North's efforts, she has been able to determine that her birth mother once served a sentence for involuntary manslaughter in Metropolis State Prison. It seems that the officer's birth mother, now identified as April Waters, was once married to Frank Waters, who was in fact Officer North's birth father. During April Waters's pregnancy, a violent quarrel took place late one night between Frank and April Waters. The quarrel centered around Frank Waters's drug habit, losses at the racetrack, and affairs with other women. The quarrel moved from verbal to physical, and the police were called. The police who responded, Officers Street, shield number 8094, and Sterns, shield number 8706, merely separated Frank and April Waters for a brief period, warned them that they both could be arrested, and then left. During the early morning hours following the night of the argument, April Waters took a kitchen knife and repeatedly stabbed Frank to death. At her trial, April Waters's defense was that she had been abused throughout her marriage and could no longer withstand the beatings she claimed she was constantly receiving.

The alleged abuse by her husband was not seen as a proper defense by the jury and April Waters was sentenced to 25 years to life. At the age of 25, she began her sentence at the Sing Prison as Inmate Number 8670. After 5 years she was transferred to the Metropolis State Prison where she stayed until the last year of her sentence, which she served at the Parks Half Way Detention House. Altogether she was confined for 25 years.

When April began serving her sentence she was in the fourth month of her pregnancy, and 5 months later she gave birth to Officer North. Widowed, incarcerated, and with no family members to turn to, April Waters gave her daughter up for adoption. The only stipulation to the adoption was that her daughter be named May after April's grandmother. The adoption authorities agreed and guaranteed that this would be done.

Officer North was able to ascertain from Detective Walker, shield number 8077, of the Rock Town Police Department, that 1 year after her mother's release from prison she died of a heart attack. Officer North was never able to meet her mother.

16. Approximately how old was Officer North at the time of her mother's death?

   (A) 26 years old
   (B) 21 years old
   (C) 30 years old
   (D) cannot be determined from the information provided

17.   What were the shield numbers of the officers who responded to a family dispute between Frank and April Waters?
(A)   8607 and 8094
(B)   8094 and 8706
(C)   8706 and 8670
(D)   8670 and 8077

18.   Where was May North born?
(A)   in the home of Pat and June North
(B)   in the Spring Hill Detention Facility for women
(C)   in Sing Prison
(D)   in the Parks Half Way Detention House

19.   The reason for the quarrel between April and Frank Waters was that Frank was . . .
(A)   using drugs.
(B)   gambling.
(C)   unfaithful.
(D)   all of the above.

20.   The weapon used to kill Frank Waters was . . .
(A)   poison.
(B)   a kitchen knife.
(C)   a revolver.
(D)   a blunt instrument.

> **Directions:** The paragraph below contains questions 21–23 in the form of three numbered blanks. Immediately following the paragraph are lists of four word choices that correspond to these numbered blanks. Select the word choice that would MOST appropriately fit the numbered blank in each question.

Court officers are often assigned to fixed posts. A fixed post is an assignment that involves a ____(Q-21)____ or extremely sensitive problem. Such assignments are often tedious, and court officers assigned to them consistently find themselves combating boredom. Fixed posts require the ____(Q-22)____ assigned to stay in a very restricted area. The area may be restricted for a variety of reasons. The____(Q-23)____ for the existence of such restrictions include everything from previous prisoner escape attempts to concern for prisoner safety. Fixed posts are created only after much intuitive thinking and deliberation on the part of the security arm of the court.

21. (A) routine
    (B) complicated
    (C) serious
    (D) fundamental

22. (A) witness
    (B) person
    (C) court officer
    (D) jury member

23. (A) rules
    (B) reasons
    (C) budget
    (D) opposition

Directions: Answer questions 24 and 25 based solely on the following information.

After a trial is ended and the jury begins its deliberations, unless so directed by a magistrate, court officers shall keep alternate jurors in a location that is separate from the jury deliberating room where the primary jurors are discussing the case. While deliberations are ongoing, a court officer must be posted directly outside the jury deliberating room in order to prevent unauthorized persons from either entering the room, from interfering in any way with the process, or from listening to the deliberations of the jury.

24. Alternate jurors . . .

    (A) are never allowed in the jury deliberating room after deliberations have started.
    (B) are allowed in the jury deliberating room only if one of the primary jurors is excused or discharged.
    (C) are sometimes allowed in the jury deliberating room while deliberations are ongoing.
    (D) have the same access to the jury deliberating room as primary jurors.

25. Unauthorized persons . . .

    (A) are subject to arrest if they interfere in any way with the deliberations of the jury.
    (B) are never allowed in the jury deliberating room while deliberations are ongoing.
    (C) are permitted in the jury deliberating room only when cleared by a magistrate.
    (D) are sometimes permitted to listen to the deliberations of the jury.

Directions: Answer questions 26–28 solely on the basis of information contained in the following passage.

Most ordinary citizens believe that juvenile defendants in criminal cases are not any different from adult defendants. They erroneously believe that the only difference is age. Nothing could be farther from the truth. Even though both groups of criminals can be held to know the difference between right and wrong, juvenile offenders often lack an appreciation for the effects of their crimes on the rest of the community.

To a lesser degree, juveniles do not see the risks of punishment to themselves as a result of their actions. They see themselves eternal and indestructible. Even though juveniles see on television how criminals are punished and are also told about prison life by ex-convicts returning to the neighborhood, they remain unaware of the punishments able to be dealt out by the state mainly because of a lack of personal experience of adult incarceration.

To try to bridge this gap of inexperience with the realities of prison life, programs such as Scared Stiff have been developed. These programs take juveniles identified by the local police as being headed in the wrong direction and have them live a day in the life of an adult inmate in an adult correctional facility. The day is complete with the feeling of being locked away in a tiny cell and even limited supervised interaction with volunteer adult inmates who pull no punches and treat the juveniles as they would any new inmate. The hope is that, by seeing what prison life is really like, some change in attitude will occur in the juvenile. Although such programs are not seen as the cure-all for rising juvenile crime nor as a replacement for the role of parents or educational institutions, some progress has been realized.

26. Based on the passage, which of the following statements is most correct?

   (A) The ordinary citizen sees great differences between an adult defendant and a juvenile one.
   (B) The only difference between an adult defendant and a juvenile defendant is age.
   (C) Juvenile criminals are not expected to know the difference between right and wrong.
   (D) Juvenile offenders often lack an understanding of the results of their criminal activity on the rest of the community.

27. Juveniles do not see the risks of punishment to themselves as a result of their actions mainly because . . .

   (A) they see themselves eternal and indestructible.
   (B) they do not see on television how criminals are punished.
   (C) ex-convicts returning to the neighborhood do not talk about their prison life.
   (D) of a juvenile's lack of personally experiencing adult incarceration.

28. Scared Stiff programs . . .

   (A) hope that a change in attitude will occur in certain juveniles.
   (B) are seen as the cure-all for rising juvenile crime.
   (C) can be a replacement for the role of parents.
   (D) are structured to take the place of educational institutions.

Directions: Answer question 29 based solely on the following information.

Although occasionally a magistrate may exercise his or her legal power to punish on the spot any person who disrupts courtroom proceedings, this is the exception rather than the rule. In practice, it is the responsibility of the court officer to handle routine violations of court decorum. When a magistrate chooses to punish any person who is disorderly in the courtroom, a fine not exceeding $250.00 and/or imprisonment not exceeding 30 days can be imposed.

29. A person who disrupts the proceedings of the court . . .

    (A) will be fined $250.00.
    (B) will be jailed for 30 days.
    (C) is usually handled by a court officer.
    (D) is usually handled by a magistrate.

Directions: Answer questions 30–37 based solely on the following data.

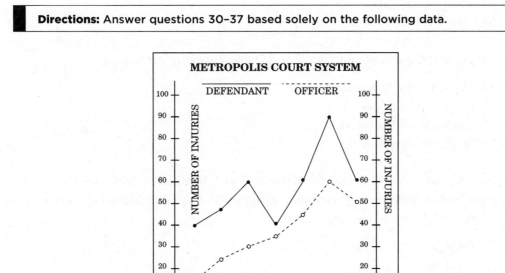

30. The day of the week during the last three years that accounted for the most injuries to defendants . . .

    (A) was Wednesday.
    (B) was Friday.
    (C) was Saturday.
    (D) cannot be determined.

31. On the average, injuries to court officers over the last 3 years . . .

    (A) were lower than injuries to defendants on every day of the week.
    (B) were higher than injuries to defendants on Thursdays.
    (C) were higher than injuries to defendants on Saturdays.
    (D) were higher than injuries to defendants on Sundays.

32. The exact number of injuries to defendants that occurred last year on Sundays . . .

    (A) is 60.
    (B) is 90.
    (C) is 50.
    (D) cannot be determined.

33. The fewest number of injuries to court officers over the last 3 years . . .

    (A) occurred on Mondays.
    (B) occurred on Wednesdays.
    (C) occurred on Fridays.
    (D) cannot be determined.

34. The greatest number of injuries to Court Officers over the last 3 years . . .

    (A) happened on Wednesdays.
    (B) happened on Fridays.
    (C) happened on Saturdays.
    (D) cannot be determined.

35. Over the last 3 years, on what day of the week was the number of injuries that happened to defendants on Wednesdays approximately equal to the number of injuries that happened to defendants?

    (A) Fridays
    (B) Saturdays
    (C) Sundays
    (D) cannot be determined

36. Over the last 3 years, the ratio of defendant injuries to officer injuries on Wednesday . . .

    (A) was about 2 to 1.
    (B) was about 3 to 1.
    (C) was about 4 to 1.
    (D) cannot be determined.

37. Over the last 3 years, on what day of the week was the number of injuries to defendants closest to the number of injuries to officers?

(A) Mondays
(B) Wednesdays
(C) Thursdays
(D) cannot be determined

Directions: Answer questions 38 and 39 based solely on the information contained in the following passage.

Court officers are professionals and as such must operate within a framework of law and procedures that carefully circumscribe their latitude of action. Because of this, it is essential that court officers respect the civil liberties of others. Civil liberties are defined as the rights derived from the U.S. Constitution, which can be asserted by the people against the government. The following are important points about the civil liberties of the people of the United States of America.

a. The first ten amendments to the U.S. Constitution are known as the Bill of Rights.

b. The First Amendment guarantees freedom of speech, freedom of the press, freedom of religion, freedom to peaceably assemble, and the freedom for citizens to seek a redress of grievances against the government.

c. The first eight amendments specify the personal and property rights of the people.

d. The Ninth Amendment stipulates the powers given to the various states to pass their own laws.

38. The civil liberties possessed by the people of the United States of America can be traced directly to . . .

(A) the Declaration of Independence.
(B) the Constitution.
(C) the First Amendment only.
(D) the first eight amendments only.

39. Freedom of Speech is guaranteed by . . .

(A) the Bill of Rights.
(B) the constitutions of each of the 50 states.
(C) the Supreme Court.
(D) the congress of the United States.

Directions: Answer questions 40 and 41 based on the following legal rule.

Court officers are legally entitled to use physical force upon another person when and to the extent they reasonably believe to be necessary to defend themselves or a third person from what they reasonably believe to be the use or imminent use of unlawful physical force by such other person. Court officers may not use deadly physical force upon another person unless they reasonably believe that such other person is using or about to use deadly physical force against them or another.

40. Which of the following represents a violation of the preceding rule?

   (A) A court officer uses physical force against a defendant who was assaulting another court officer.
   (B) A court officer uses physical force against a defendant who is assaulting him.
   (C) A court officer uses physical force against a defendant who threatens to "get him one day."
   (D) A court officer uses physical force against a defendant who is about to assault him.

41. Which of the following is NOT a violation of the preceding rule?

   (A) A court officer shoots at a defendant who is using his fists to beat another defendant.
   (B) A court officer shoots a defendant who is about to attack him with a switchblade knife.
   (C) A court officer shoots an unarmed defendant who is threatening to have another defendant shot.
   (D) A court officer shoots an unarmed defendant who is attempting to escape.

---

42. The argument that the death penalty is more financially economical than life imprisonment does not stand up under close examination. The most reasonable conclusion that can be drawn from this statement is that . . .

   (A) it is cheaper to execute prisoners than to incarcerate them for life.
   (B) the death penalty is not an effective deterrent.
   (C) the administration of the death penalty is not as financially economical as some people say it is.
   (D) the cost of administering the death penalty is equal to the cost of financing a life sentence.

43. The courts have ruled that a juvenile, someone under the age of 16, who has been accused of a crime, has the right to a lawyer. In turn, the juvenile can decide to waive the right to a lawyer providing that the parents/guardians of the juvenile concur with that decision. The lawyer may be of the juvenile's own choosing or appointed by the court for financial or other reasons. Therefore, a court officer who finds it necessary to arrest a juvenile must give notice of the juvenile's right to a lawyer. Based on the statement, the most reasonable conclusion to reach is that . . .

(A) a lawyer must be assigned to represent a juvenile.
(B) a 16 year old may waive his right to a lawyer without obtaining concurrences from a parent or guardian.
(C) a court officer who arrests a juvenile must secure a lawyer for that juvenile.
(D) the only time the court can appoint a lawyer for a juvenile is when financial considerations are involved.

44. Notification shall be made, as soon as practicable, by telegraph to the nearest relative or friend of any defendant who unsuccessfully attempts to commit suicide while in the custody of a court officer. The notification shall include an invitation to attend a private meeting with the court officer's commanding officer. The main purpose of this rule is most probably to . . .

(A) explore ways to prevent further suicide attempts.
(B) prepare loved ones for a possible tragedy.
(C) avoid civil liability.
(D) comply with the law.

45. No defendant under 19 years of age shall be held in cells with adult defendants. The main purpose of this rule is probably to prevent . . .

(A) disputes and confrontations.
(B) escape attempts.
(C) exposure of younger prisoners to the views of adult criminals.
(D) possible assaults on younger prisoners by adult prisoners.

46. A court officer shall not authorize the use of a photograph of himself in uniform in connection with any commercial enterprise. The purpose of this rule is most probably to . . .

(A) protect the identity of court officers.
(B) prevent officers from enjoying unethical personal commercial gain.
(C) maintain the image of the court officer's uniform.
(D) prevent the endorsement of substandard products.

47. To remain safe in the court environment and to accomplish the goals of the court administration most effectively, court officers must function together as a team. The most important characteristic of teamwork is . . .

    (A) individual accomplishment.
    (B) cooperation.
    (C) aggressiveness.
    (D) rigidity.

48. A court officer should be open-minded. This means that an officer should . . .

    (A) consider both sides of a story.
    (B) impose his will on others.
    (C) rigidly enforce the rules of the court system.
    (D) never exercise discretion.

49. To be effective, a court officer must be . . .

    (A) an extremely physically strong person.
    (B) a thinking person.
    (C) a very emotional person.
    (D) an inflexible person.

50. Court officers should not view their firearms as offensive weapons. This means that firearms would best be used to . . .

    (A) prevent escapes.
    (B) maintain order.
    (C) promote discipline.
    (D) defend against a threat to life.

THE LAW OF ARREST—WITHOUT AN ARREST WARRANT

a. An offense is either a felony, a misdemeanor, or a violation. A traffic infraction is not an offense. Felonies are punished most severely, followed by misdemeanors and then violations.

b. A crime is either a felony or a misdemeanor.

c. A petty offense is either a violation or a traffic infraction.

d. A court officer may arrest a person without a warrant of arrest:

- For any offense when the court officer has reasonable cause to believe that such person has committed such offense in the officer's presence; and

- For a crime when the court officer has reasonable cause to believe that such person has committed such crime, whether in the court officer's presence or otherwise.

- Close pursuit allows a court officer to arrest a person for the commission of a crime committed within the state, outside of the state, if the apprehension is made as a result of close pursuit of the perpetrator by the arresting court officer.

e. A court officer acting without a warrant, when legally arresting a person for an offense may do so at any hour of any day or night.

f. An arresting court officer must inform a person being arrested without an arrest warrant of the officer's authority and purpose and of the reason for such arrest unless the officer meets physical resistance, or flight.

g. If a person flees into his residence to avoid arrest, the arresting court officer may follow in close pursuit.

51. Which of the following is least likely to be considered an offense?

   (A) a felony
   (B) a misdemeanor
   (C) a violation
   (D) a traffic infraction

52. Petty offenses include which of the following?

   (A) all crimes
   (B) a felony
   (C) a violation
   (D) a misdemeanor

53. A court officer can legally effect the arrest of a person without an arrest warrant when the court officer has reasonable cause to believe that such person has committed which of the following in the presence of the court officer?

    (A) only a felony
    (B) only a misdemeanor
    (C) only a violation
    (D) any offense

54. Don is an experienced and knowledgeable court officer. He is approached by Pat who is a newly hired court officer. Pat asks Don to explain when an arrest can be made without a warrant. Don would be most correct if he responded, . . .

    (A) "Only on weekdays but at any hour of the day."
    (B) "On weekdays but only between the hours of 6 A.M. and 12 midnight."
    (C) "On any day of the week but only between the hours of 6 A.M. and 12 midnight."
    (D) "At any hour of any day or night."

55. In which of the following situations is it necessary according to the law of arrest to notify the person being arrested of the reason for the arrest?

    (A) an arrest for manslaughter where the defendant is found hiding under a car after a high-speed chase
    (B) an arrest for rape where the defendant has just fled the scene
    (C) an arrest for disorderly conduct where the level of the charge is only a violation
    (D) an arrest for robbery where the defendant fought with the arresting court officer

56. Ray, who is being arrested without an arrest warrant, suddenly runs into his own home to avoid arrest. In such an instance, the arresting court officer . . .

    (A) may follow in close pursuit.
    (B) must wait until Ray comes out.
    (C) must arrest all occupants of the house.
    (D) may enter only if the charge is a felony.

THE LAW OF ARREST—WITH AN ARREST WARRANT

When and How Warrants of Arrest Are Executed

a. A warrant of arrest may be executed on any day of the week and at any hour of the day or night.

b. Unless encountering physical resistance or flight, the arresting officer must inform the defendant that a warrant for his arrest for the offense designated therein has been issued.

c. If requested by the defendant, the arresting officer must show him the warrant if the officer has it in his possession. The officer need not have it in his possession, and, if he has not, the officer must show it to the defendant upon request as soon after the arrest as possible.

d. To effect the arrest of a person pursuant to the authority of an arrest warrant, the arresting officer may enter any premises if the officer reasonably believes that the defendant is present in the premises. However, if the premises is the dwelling of a third party, said officer must obtain a search warrant for said premises in addition to the currently held arrest warrant.

e. Before entering a premises to make the arrest with a warrant, the officer must make a reasonable effort to give notice of his authority and purpose to an occupant of the premises, unless the officer reasonably believes that giving such notice will

   i. result in the defendant escaping or attempting to escape, or

   ii. endanger the life or safety of the officer or another person, or

   iii. result in the destruction, damaging, or secretion of evidence.

f. If the officer is authorized by special provisions in the arrest warrant to enter the premises without giving notice of his authority and purpose, or if after giving such notice he is not admitted, he may enter such premises, and by a breaking if necessary.

57. Court Officer Frank executes a warrant of arrest on a Sunday at 5 A.M. In this instance Court Officer Frank's action was . . .

   (A) proper, mainly because a warrant of arrest may be executed on any day of the week and at any hour of the day or night.
   (B) improper, mainly because a warrant of arrest may not be executed on a weekend.
   (C) proper, as long as the Sunday is not the Sabbath of the person arrested.
   (D) improper, mainly because a warrant of arrest may not be executed before 6 A.M. regardless of the day of the week.

58. Court Officer Frank has a valid warrant of arrest for Ray. Frank reasonably believes that Ray is present in a certain premises, which happens to be the dwelling of another person named Tom. Frank rings the bell of the premises, and Tom answers the door and tells Frank that he does not want to let Frank enter his dwelling. In such an instance, it would be most appropriate for Officer Frank to . . .

(A) arrest Tom for interfering with a legal arrest.
(B) obtain a search warrant for the premises.
(C) obtain an arrest warrant for Tom.
(D) push Tom aside and forcibly enter the premises.

59. If a court officer has an arrest warrant for a person and such person is inside a premises, the officer should announce his purpose and authority to an occupant of the premises. However, in certain instances, the officer is not required to make such an announcement if the officer reasonably believes certain circumstances exist. Which of the following least accurately describes such an instance?

(A) if it might result in the defendant attempting to escape
(B) if it might result in the hiding of evidence
(C) if the person sought is wanted for a serious felony
(D) if someone's life in the premises could be endangered

60. Court Officer Drake is about to arrest Booker on the authority of a warrant of arrest as Booker is about to leave the courthouse where Court Officer Drake is assigned. However Officer Drake discovers that she does not have the warrant of arrest for Booker with her. Under these circumstances, Officer Drake would be most correct if she . . .

(A) immediately ceases any arrest action until she physically possesses the warrant of arrest.
(B) arrested Booker but realized that if Booker asks to see the warrant she must release him.
(C) detained Booker until she obtained a copy of the warrant and then arrested Booker.
(D) arrested Booker because the officer need not have the warrant in her possession.

Directions: Answer questions 61–65 based solely on the content of the legal definitions given. Do not use any other knowledge of the law that you might have. You may refer to the definitions when answering the questions.

A. Bribing a Juror—A person is guilty of bribing a juror when he offers, gives, or agrees to give a benefit to a juror with the understanding that the actions of the juror will be influenced.

B. Bribe Receiving by a Juror—A person is guilty of bribe receiving by a juror when such person asks for, receives, or agrees to receive a benefit with the understanding that such person's action as a juror will be influenced.

   Note that benefits are not limited to currency but instead include any gain or advantage to the juror or a third person pursuant to the wishes of the juror.

C. Tampering with a Juror—A person is guilty of tampering with a juror when, with intent to influence the outcome of an action or proceeding, he communicates with a juror in such an action or proceeding, except as authorized by law.

D. Misconduct by a Juror—A juror is guilty of misconduct by a juror when, in relation to a proceeding pending or about to be brought before him, he agrees to give a vote or decision for or against any party in such proceeding. The term *juror* includes someone acting as a juror in a current proceeding as well as someone who has been summoned to be a juror at a future date.

61. Rose is a juror in an ongoing criminal case. She is approached by Frank Bones who tells Rose that if she votes to acquit the defendant in the criminal case, Bob Hammers, Bones can guarantee that she will receive an easier job from her boss who is a friend of the defendant Hammers. Rose refuses the offer. In such an instance, Frank Bones has committed . . .

   (A) no crime because no money was offered to Rose.
   (B) bribery of a juror.
   (C) no crime because Rose did not accept the offer.
   (D) misconduct by a juror.

62. June has been arrested for assaulting her fiancee Tom. When June goes to trial for the assault, she finds out that her old high school friend Pat is on the jury. She calls Pat on the telephone and asks that Pat not find her guilty when the case is given to the jury by the judge. Pat listens intently and then hangs up the phone after deciding not to entertain June's request. In this instance, . . .

   (A) June is guilty of no crime because apparently Pat will not entertain her request.
   (B) June is guilty of tampering with a juror, and Pat is guilty of misconduct by a juror.
   (C) June is guilty of tampering with a juror.
   (D) neither June nor Pat are guilty of any offense because no benefit was offered to influence Pat's decision.

63. Based solely on the information provided, evaluate the following statements.

    1. A person is considered a juror only after being duly sworn as a juror by a magistrate.

    2. For something to be recognized as a benefit, it must represent a direct gain or advantage to the juror.

    Which of the following choices is most accurate concerning these statements?

    (A) Only statement 1 is correct.
    (B) Only statement 2 is correct.
    (C) Both statements 1 and 2 are correct.
    (D) Neither statements 1 nor 2 are correct.

64. Tab is a juror in an ongoing criminal trial involving a defendant named Jay who is accused of stealing money from his business partner Frank. Tab is approached by Jay's business partner Frank who asks Tab to make sure that Jay is convicted. Tab thinks nothing of the conversation and goes on about his business without considering what Frank has requested. In this instance, . . .

    (A) Frank has committed tampering with a juror.
    (B) Tab can commit misconduct by a juror only if he requests money or some other benefit to have his actions as a juror influenced.
    (C) Frank has committed no crime because his intent was to get someone convicted and not acquitted.
    (D) Tab has committed bribe receiving by a juror.

65. Bob approaches Don who is a juror in a civil court proceeding in which Bob is an involved party. Bob offers Don a new car if Don will decide in Bob's favor concerning the outcome of the proceeding. Don accepts the offer and laughs to himself because Don had already decided to act in Bob's favor prior to Bob's offer. In this instance, . . .

    (A) neither Bob nor Don has committed any crime because Don had already decided to act in Bob's favor prior to Bob's offer.
    (B) Bob has committed bribing a juror, but Don has committed no crime.
    (C) Bob has committed bribing a juror, and Don has committed bribe receiving by a juror.
    (D) Don has committed bribe receiving by a juror, but Bob has committed no crime.

Upon discovering or responding to a crime that may require safeguarding evidence and detaining witnesses for further investigation, the court officer involved shall perform the following steps in this order.

1. Request response, through the court dispatcher, of
   a. the shift supervisor and then
   b. the local police detectives.

2. Remove unauthorized persons from the area and secure the crime scene.
   a. Evidence found at the scene shall not be disturbed.

3. Detain witnesses and persons with information pertinent to the crime.

4. Make appropriate entries in memo book of
   a. observations made,
   b. identity of suspects/witnesses with addresses and telephone numbers, and
   c. any relevant statements made whether casually or as a formal statement by a witness.

5. Advise the shift supervisor and local police detectives of
   a. identity of witnesses detained and
   b. other information regarding the case.

6. Assess the crime scene.

7. Determine if the services of the local police Crime Lab Unit are required.
   NOTE: The local police Crime Lab Unit will be requested for the following incidents:
   a. any homicide,
   b. any forcible rape,
   c. a robbery or a car-jacking with injury caused by a firearm,
   d. an aggravated assault with a dangerous instrument and the victim is likely to die,
   e. any burglaries involving forced safes, or circumvented alarms, or
   f. a criminal mischief where property damage is more than $1000.

8. Request the local police Crime Lab Unit directly by telephone; if a telephone is not available, then make the request through the court dispatcher by portable radio. Include the following information in the request:
   a. exact location,
   b. time and date of occurrence,
   c. type of crime committed and type of weapons if used,
   d. number of victims involved, and
   e. name of the hospital treating persons removed from the scene.

9. Notify the court desk officer of details and request additional assistance, if required.

10. Post Crime Scene signs.

66. According to procedure, the person required to post Crime Scene signs is . . .

    (A) the shift supervisor.
    (B) a detective from the local police.
    (C) the crime lab technician who responds to the scene.
    (D) the responding court officer.

67. After responding to a crime that requires safeguarding evidence and detaining witnesses for further investigation, Court Officer Rivers properly requests the shift supervisor. The officer's next step should be to . . .

    (A) remove unauthorized persons from the area and secure the scene.
    (B) request the response of the local police detectives through the court dispatcher.
    (C) notify the court desk officer.
    (D) telephone the local police Crime Lab Unit.

68. According to procedure, which of the following has the responsibility to determine if the services of the local police Crime Lab Unit are required?

    (A) the court desk officer
    (B) the local police detectives
    (C) the shift supervisor
    (D) the responding court officer

69. In connection with a certain crime incident, the decision has properly been made to use the services of the local police Crime Lab Unit. In requesting the response of the local police Crime Lab Unit, certain information is required to be transmitted to the local police Crime Lab Unit. Which of the following is not required to be communicated to such unit?

    (A) exact location and time and date of occurrence
    (B) name of the hospital treating persons at the scene
    (C) type of crime committed and type of weapons if used
    (D) how many victims were involved

70. The first attempt to request the response of the local police Crime Lab Unit should be made . . .

    (A) through the court dispatcher.
    (B) by telephone directly.
    (C) through the court desk officer.
    (D) through the shift supervisor's portable radio.

71. According to the procedure, it would be least correct for a responding court officer to request the services of the local police Crime Lab Unit for . . .

(A) any rape taking place within the confines of the courthouse.
(B) any homicide.
(C) a car-jacking in the courthouse parking lot where someone has been shot by a firearm.
(D) any burglary within the courthouse involving a circumvented alarm.

72. Court Officer May Rudder would not be following procedure if she requested the services of the local police Crime Lab Unit for . . .

(A) a robbery in the courthouse parking lot where the victim was stabbed with a knife after being shot.
(B) a burglary of a judge's chambers where a safe had been forcibly cracked open.
(C) an aggravated assault outside a courtroom where the perpetrator had very badly beaten the victim with his fists so that the victim is likely to die.
(D) a criminal mischief in a court rest room where property damage exceeded $1200.

Directions: Answer questions 73–75 solely on the basis of the following information.

When making entries in a memo book regarding information relating to assignments and actions taken, a court officer shall make entries in ink, beginning on the first line at the top of each page and continuing thereafter accounting for each scheduled tour of duty:

a. The blank side of each page shall be used for notes, diagrams, and sketches, when necessary.

b. The memo book shall be carried in a regulation leather binder.

c. Errors shall be corrected by drawing a single line through the incorrect entry and initialing it; no erasures are permitted.

d. Begin the tour's entries on the next open line, following the previous tour of duty's closing entry. No lines or pages are to be skipped.

e. Write or print legibly; abbreviations may be used.

f. Do not remove pages for any reason or use the memo book as scrap or for note pads.

g. Store active and completed ACTIVITY LOGS in the individually assigned department locker, available for inspection at all times.

73. Court Officer Rose Carpenter is making entries in her memo book. She inadvertently makes an error. In this instance, she should . . .

(A) erase the entry and make the correct entry.
(B) circle the entry and initial the error.
(C) draw a single line through the incorrect entry and initial it.
(D) remove the entire page and rewrite the entire entry.

74. When Court Officer Frank Flores completes a memo book, the officer should . . .

(A) deliver the memo book to the court desk officer.
(B) store the memo book in his department locker.
(C) keep the memo book for 5 years before destroying it.
(D) store the completed memo book at home in a safe place.

75. According to the procedure, which of the following is least correct?

(A) A court officer shall make entries in ink.
(B) The memo book shall be carried in a regulation leather binder.
(C) Abbreviations may not be used.
(D) The blank side of each page of the memo book may be used for notes and diagrams.

Directions: Answer questions 76–83 solely on the basis of the following information.

To protect court officers from injury while conducting investigations involving stop-and-question situations, the following procedure will be followed by court officers.

  a. To stop means to detain a person temporarily for questioning.

  b. To frisk means to run the hands over the clothing, feeling for a weapon.

  c. To search means to place hands inside a pocket or other interior parts of clothing to determine if an object felt during a frisk is a weapon.

When a court officer reasonably suspects that a person has committed, is committing, or is about to commit a felony or misdemeanor as defined in the State Penal Code, the officer shall

  1. Stop the person and request identification and an explanation of the person's conduct.

    a. If not in uniform, the officer shall identify himself as a court officer.

  2. If the officer reasonably suspects he or she is in danger of physical injury, the officer may frisk the suspect.

  3. If the frisk reveals an object that may be a weapon, the officer may search the suspect.

    NOTE: Only that portion of the suspect's clothing where an object is felt may be searched.

4. Detain the suspect while conducting the investigation to determine whether there is probable cause to believe an offense has been committed by the suspect.

   a. A suspect may be detained for a period of time reasonably related to the facts that initially justified the stop or are discovered during the stop.

   b. Complete the investigation as expeditiously as possible.

5. Release the suspect immediately after completing the investigation if probable cause to arrest does not exist.

6. Prepare a STOP AND FRISK CARD for each person stopped, if

   a. Person is stopped by use of force.

   b. Person stopped is frisked or frisked and searched.

   c. Person stopped is arrested.

   d. Person stopped refused to identify himself.

   NOTE: If person stopped refuses to identify himself (and there is no reason to take further action), enter *REFUSED* in the appropriate space on the STOP AND FRISK CARD and allow the suspect to depart only after completing the investigation and only if the investigation does not establish probable cause to believe that the suspect has committed an offense. Request the shift supervisor to respond and confirm the refusal and to review STOP AND FRISK CARD and action taken.

   Do not detain the suspect while awaiting the arrival of the shift supervisor if the investigation is completed and no probable cause to arrest the suspect exists.

7. Enter the details in the court officer memo book.

8. Inform the court desk officer of the facts.

9. Submit STOP AND FRISK CARD(S), if prepared, to the court desk officer who shall review the STOP AND FRISK CARD(S).

A suspect should not be moved or transported from the location where he is stopped for questioning unless he voluntarily consents, there is an exigency (e.g., hostile crowd gathers) and the officer must move suspect from area for safety purposes, or victim/witness is injured and cannot be brought to the location where the suspect is being detained, and so officer transports the suspect to injured party.

Some factors that would create a reasonable suspicion include:

   a. The demeanor of the suspect.

   b. The gait and manner of the suspect.

   c. Any knowledge the officer may have of the suspect's background and character.

   d. Whether the suspect is carrying anything and what he is carrying.

   e. Manner of dress of suspect including bulges in clothing.

   f. Time of day or night.

   g. Any overheard conversations of the suspect.

   h. The particular location and areas involved.

   i. Any information received from third parties.

   j. Proximity to scene of a crime.

76. Concerning stop-and-question situations, which of the following is the most correct statement?

    (A) A frisk has the exact same meaning as a search.
    (B) A search usually precedes a frisk.
    (C) A frisk involves going inside a suspect's pockets.
    (D) A search is often preceded by a frisk.

77. The minimum level of proof required for a court officer to stop a person legally and request identification and an explanation of such person's conduct is . . .

    (A) reasonable suspicion.
    (B) a hunch.
    (C) absolute certainty that something has occurred.
    (D) an educated guess.

78. Court Officer April Horizons is conducting a frisk of a suspect she has stopped when she feels something hard in the suspect's coat pocket. The officer then searches the suspect's coat pocket and then pants pocket. In the suspect's pants pocket the officer finds a knife. In this instance, the officer acted . . .

    (A) properly, mainly because she was able to find a weapon that could be used to injure someone.
    (B) improperly, mainly because she was legally allowed to search only the suspect's coat pocket.
    (C) properly, mainly because she was following up on what her frisk revealed.
    (D) improperly, mainly because a search of inside pockets should be conducted only after an arrest is made.

79. The amount of time an officer may legally detain a person who has been stopped for questioning is . . .

    (A) 5 minutes.
    (B) 15 minutes.
    (C) 1 hour.
    (D) not a fixed period.

80. If, as a result of a stop-and-question incident, the officer concerned finds no probable cause to arrest the suspect, the officer should . . .

    (A) bring the suspect to the court desk officer.
    (B) release the suspect immediately after completing the investigation.
    (C) give the suspect a summons.
    (D) take a photo of the suspect.

81. In which of the following situations would it be least appropriate for a STOP AND FRISK CARD to be prepared by a court officer?

    (A) whenever a person is stopped
    (B) whenever a person is frisked
    (C) whenever a person who was frisked is arrested
    (D) whenever a person who is stopped refuses to identify himself

82. According to the procedure, when STOP AND FRISK CARDS are prepared, they are reviewed by . . .

    (A) only the shift supervisor.
    (B) only the court desk officer.
    (C) by neither the shift supervisor nor the court desk officer.
    (D) by both the shift supervisor and the court desk officer.

83. Court Officer Rays observes a person on a hot, dry August afternoon, standing in front of the courthouse wearing a long heavy raincoat under which the officer observes what looks like a rifle bulging out. The officer decides to stop the person and request identification and an explanation of the person's conduct. In this instance the Court Officer Rays acted . . .

    (A) properly, mainly because at this point enough proof exists to immediately arrest the person.
    (B) improperly, mainly because the officer has no further information about the person.
    (C) properly, mainly because at this point the officer has enough proof to create a reasonable suspicion.
    (D) improperly, mainly because a person can at any time wear whatever that person wants.

Directions: Answer questions 84 and 85 solely on the basis of the following information.

When counterfeit money is detected by a court officer and it is determined that the passer is an innocent victim or there is no indication who passed it:

   a. The court officer shall have the person last in possession write his name and date across the face of the bill or scratch his initials on a coin.

   b. The court officer shall sign his or her rank, name, badge number, and date on the bill or scratch his or her initials on the coin.

   c. The court officer shall prepare four copies of a report describing in detail how the money came into the possession of the officer, including the amount and serial numbers of all bills. The court officer shall deliver the counterfeit items to the court desk officer.

   d. The court desk officer shall assign a messenger to deliver the report and the money to the Special Agent-In-Charge of the local office of the U.S. Secret Service.

84. Court Officer Barns is called to the employees' cafeteria located in the courthouse. A cashier states that while counting the money in the cash register, the cashier noticed what has turned out to be a counterfeit $10 bill. The cashier does not recall the user of the bill. In this instance, the officer should . . .

    (A) initial the bill.

    (B) have the attendant initial the bill.

    (C) have only the attendant sign the bill.

    (D) sign the bill along with the attendant.

85. In connection with question 84, after coming into possession of the counterfeit bill, Court Officer Barns takes possession of the bill and immediately delivers it to a local office of the Secret Service. In this instance, the officer acted . . .

    (A) properly, mainly because the Secret Service stores counterfeit bills.

    (B) improperly, mainly because the Secret Service should respond to the cafeteria to take possession of the counterfeit bill.

    (C) properly, mainly because the quicker an investigation can be commenced by the Secret Service, the quicker arrests can be made.

    (D) improperly, mainly because the court desk officer will have the money delivered to the Secret Service.

Directions: Answer questions 86–90 solely on the basis of the following information.

Court officers should recognize that the firearm is mainly intended to provide protection for the court and the officer. As such, court officers should be constantly aware that their firearms, if improperly used, or if they fall into the hands of criminals, can obviously cause serious and even fatal injury. Therefore, court officers should adhere to the following guidelines:

  a. The firearm is to be kept under physical control at all times. For example, it should never be left in an unattended vehicle.

  b. A court officer shall never leave his or her firearm in an unlocked desk or cabinet in the courthouse.

  c. Detention areas shall not be entered by any court officer while wearing a firearm.

  d. While armed, caution shall be exercised when entering public elevators in the courthouse.

  e. A court officer shall not remove his or her weapon from the holster unnecessarily nor display it to another in a public area of the courthouse.

  f. The practice of dry firing in any location within the courthouse or its contiguous grounds or parking lot(s) is strictly prohibited. N.B. Dry firing is the practice of unloading one's firearm and then practicing the pulling of the trigger while target site alignment is maintained.

  g. The cleaning of firearms on court property is strictly prohibited unless permission is obtained from the court desk officer.

  h. A court officer shall be particularly vigilant while in the court officers locker room. A significant number of accidental discharges of firearms have occurred during such times. Firearms shall not be left unattended on the tops of lockers or on chairs.

86. Evaluate the following statements.

    1. The main reason for firearms regulations is to apprehend criminals in and around the courthouse.

    2. Court officers should always take unoccupied elevators while in the courthouse.

    Which of the following choices is most accurate concerning these statements?

    (A) Only statement 1 is correct.
    (B) Only statement 2 is correct.
    (C) Both statements 1 and 2 are correct.
    (D) Neither statement 1 nor 2 is correct.

87. Court Officer Ben Drake decides to visit a health spa after work. Not wishing to take his firearm into the spa, he unloads it and places the firearm in the trunk of his private vehicle and securely locks the trunk. After putting the bullets in his pants pocket, the officer enters the spa. In this instance, the actions of Court Officer Drake were . . .

    (A) proper, mainly because the firearm was unloaded and the bullets were with him.
    (B) improper, mainly because the firearm should not have been left in the vehicle under any circumstances.
    (C) proper, mainly because the trunk of the vehicle was securely locked.
    (D) improper, mainly because the bullets could be stolen while Officer Drake is visiting the spa.

88. Court Officer Mallard is armed and on duty assigned to what is known as the feeder pens, detention areas where prisoners who are about to be arraigned by the judge are held pending their appearances in the courtroom. Suddenly, Tom Mixes, a prisoner, being detained along with other prisoners in the feeder pens, collapses, apparently bleeding from some type of stab wound. Officer Mallard opens the feeder pens and rushes in to deal with the situation. In such an instance, the actions of the officer were . . .

    (A) proper, mainly because when dealing with a stab wound, time is of the essence.
    (B) improper, mainly because the officer should have called for another armed officer to enter the feeder pens with him to watch his back.
    (C) proper, mainly because there is someone in the feeder pens who is apparently armed and such a threat should be met equally with armed force.
    (D) improper, mainly because such areas are not to be entered by a court officer who is armed.

89. Court Officer Brown is properly on his lunch break. Wishing to maximize the use of his time, he quickly finishes his lunch and goes to the court officers locker room, which is located in another part of the courthouse and is presently completely empty. While there alone, Officer Brown unloads his firearm and begins cleaning it. In such an instance, the actions of the officer were . . .

(A) proper, mainly because no one else was present in the locker room.
(B) improper, mainly because the cleaning of firearms on court property is strictly prohibited by regulation.
(C) proper, mainly because the gun was unloaded while the officer cleaned it.
(D) improper, mainly because the permission of the court desk officer was not obtained.

90. Evaluate the following statements.

1. Dry firing in the court officers locker room is permitted if the permission of the court desk officer is obtained.

2. A court officer shall be particularly careful concerning firearm safety while in the court officers locker room.

Which of the following choices is most accurate concerning these statements?

(A) Only statement 1 is correct.
(B) Only statement 2 is correct.
(C) Both statements 1 and 2 are correct.
(D) Neither statement 1 nor 2 is correct.

Directions: Use the information in the following reference table to answer questions 91–100. Each number in the table is to be associated with the letter appearing above it. For example, 3 is associated with B, and 4 is associated with N.

REFERENCE TABLE

B	I	N	G	O
3	25	24	10	19
16	1	4	9	7
17	2	14	23	18
11	12	6	21	5
8	20	22	13	15

Directions for questions 91–95: Compare the letters in Column 1 in each question with the numbers in Column 2, and then select as the answer the choice that contains the sets of letters and numbers that are correctly associated with each other according to the reference table. For each question there are four possible answers. Select the lettered choice A, B, or C if one of those choices contains a set of letters that have been accurately associated with the corresponding numbers. However, you should select choice D if all or none of the sets has been accurately associated according to the reference table.

	Column 1	Column 2
91.	(A) GNO	15 - 4 - 10
	(B) IOG	1 - 19 - 23
	(C) IGN	8 - 10 - 22
	(D) all or none of the sets	

	Column 1	Column 2
92.	(A) BNG	2 - 14 - 9
	(B) BGO	6 - 10 - 5
	(C) BGN	17 - 6 - 4
	(D) all or none of the sets	

	Column 1	Column 2
93.	(A) NGO	14 - 9 - 7
	(B) INO	11 - 4 - 15
	(C) IGO	11 - 23 - 19
	(D) all or none of the sets	

	Column 1	Column 2
94.	(A) OBN	19 - 3 - 5
	(B) BOB	3 - 18 - 1
	(C) NNN	6 - 24 - 14
	(D) all or none of the sets	

	Column 1	Column 2
95.	(A) INB	12 - 4 - 16
	(B) BIN	17 - 2 - 22
	(C) NIG	6 - 1 - 9
	(D) all or none of the sets	

> **Directions for questions 96–100:** Select the choice containing the numbers, which when associated with their corresponding letters according to the reference table, represents the letters in best alphabetical order.

96. (A) 3,   18,   4
    (B) 3,   1,   9
    (C) 1,   4,   7
    (D) 10,   3,   19

97. (A) 2,   7,   6
    (B) 21,   24,   1
    (C) 11,   12,   5
    (D) 21,   5,   6

98. (A) 17,   14,   2
    (B) 17,   14,   23
    (C) 17,   18,   14
    (D) 17,   23,   2

99. (A) 10,   25,   19
    (B) 23,   19,   14
    (C) 21,   2,   16
    (D) 17,   20,   23

100. (A) 19,   25,   24
    (B) 18,   17,   13
    (C) 5,   9,   4
    (D) 11,   6,   7

ANSWER KEY
Diagnostic Exam

1.	A	26.	D	51.	D	76.	D
2.	B	27.	D	52.	C	77.	A
3.	B	28.	A	53.	D	78.	B
4.	A	29.	C	54.	D	79.	D
5.	B	30.	C	55.	C	80.	B
6.	B	31.	A	56.	A	81.	A
7.	A	32.	D	57.	A	82.	D
8.	A	33.	A	58.	B	83.	C
9.	B	34.	C	59.	C	84.	D
10.	A	35.	A	60.	D	85.	D
11.	D	36.	A	61.	B	86.	D
12.	C	37.	C	62.	C	87.	B
13.	B	38.	B	63.	D	88.	D
14.	D	39.	A	64.	A	89.	D
15.	A	40.	C	65.	C	90.	B
16.	A	41.	B	66.	D	91.	B
17.	B	42.	C	67.	B	92.	D
18.	C	43.	B	68.	D	93.	A
19.	D	44.	A	69.	B	94.	C
20.	B	45.	C	70.	B	95.	D
21.	C	46.	B	71.	A	96.	C
22.	C	47.	B	72.	C	97.	C
23.	B	48.	A	73.	C	98.	D
24.	C	49.	B	74.	B	99.	A
25.	B	50.	D	75.	C	100.	D

DIAGNOSTIC CHART

Directions: After you score your test, complete the following chart by inserting in the column entitled "Your Number Correct" the number of correct questions you answered in each of the eight sections of the test. Then compare your score in each section with the ratings in the column entitled "Scale." Finally, to correct your weaknesses, follow the instructions found at the end of the chart.

Section	Question Numbers	Area	Your Number Correct	Scale
1	1–15	Memory (15 questions)		15 Right—Excellent 13-14 Right—Good 11-12 Right—Fair Under 11 Right—Poor
2	16–50	Reading Comprehension (35 questions)		33-35 Right—Excellent 30-32 Right—Good 27-29 Right—Fair Under 27 Right—Poor
3	51–65	Legal Definitions (15 questions)		15 Right—Excellent 13-14 Right—Good 11-12 Right—Fair Under 11 Right—Poor
4	66–90	Applying Court Officer Procedures (25 questions)		25 Right—Excellent 22-24 Right—Good 18-21 Right—Fair Under 18 Right—Poor
5	91–100	Clerical Ability (10 questions)		10 Right—Excellent 8-9 Right—Good 7 Right—Fair Under 7 Right—Poor

How to correct weaknesses:

1. If you are weak in Section 1, concentrate on Chapter 2.
2. If you are weak in Section 2, concentrate on Chapter 1.
3. If you are weak in Section 3, concentrate on Chapter 4.
4. If you are weak in Section 4, concentrate on Chapter 3.
5. If you are weak in Section 5, concentrate on Chapter 5.

Note: Consider yourself weak in a section if you receive a score other than excellent in that section.

ANSWERS EXPLAINED

1. **(A)** Charles Adams had a $10 bill, a quarter, and a nickel. Alicia Smart did not have any money. Always count money in these type of questions.

2. **(B)** Remember that it is OK to make assumptions as long as the assumptions are based on fact. The fact here is that Alicia Smart had a subway token. There is nothing to support an assumption that Charles Adams traveled on the subway.

3. **(B)** Alicia Smart possessed mace, which, of course, is a weapon commonly carried to ward off physical attacks.

4. **(A)** According to his automobile registration, Charles Adams lives in Whitestone.

5. **(B)** If you noticed that Alicia Smart's address was in multiples of 6 (e.g., 6-18-24), you would have had an easy time with this question.

6. **(B)** Among Alicia Smart's possessions was a letter addressed to "Dear Mom" and signed "Cathy." Although it is true that Cathy might not be Alicia Smart's daughter, of all the choices, the one that is probably correct (the wording used in the stem of the question) is Choice B. The point is that when the question asks for something that is most probable, the answer does not need to be proven to a certainty; probability is all that is required.

7. **(A)** By now you should certainly understand the need to count similar items.

8. **(A)** According to the automobile registration of Charles Adams, plate number CA 221 belongs to a 1996 Buick.

9. **(B)** Notice that all four dates mentioned in the question appear in the passage, and note their similarity. Dates are prime targets of examiners. Make associations to deal with dates in a memory story.

10. **(A)** Upon his graduation from Washington University, Mark Brown moved to New York City.

11. **(D)** Walter Ford, who is a parking lot attendant, is the key witness. After you read the memory chapter in this book, questions such as this one with an obvious association between Walter Ford and his job as a parking lot attendant will be easy for you to answer correctly.

12. **(C)** This type of time question is very common. The answer, 10:00 A.M., Choice C, is not stated directly in the story. Instead, it is keyed off a point of reference. In other words, the trial commenced at 9:30 A.M., the point of reference, and the handcuffing occurred 30 minutes later.

13. **(B)** Note the similarity between the name of the victim, Johnson, and the name of the detective, Jackson. When names in a memory story are similar, it is highly likely that a question will be asked about those similar names.

14. **(D)** The victim was pronounced dead on arrival at the hospital, but the exact time of that arrival is not given. When one of the choices suggests that the answer is not given in the passage, always give that choice special attention, for it is often the correct answer.

15. **(A)** The murder was committed in the Borough of Manhattan, but the trial was held in the Borough of Queens.

16. **(A)** This is one of those reading comprehension questions that requires you to consult more than one portion of the reading passage. April Waters gave birth to her daughter, May North, in the first year of April's incarceration. Twenty-five years later, April was released from prison, and 1 year after her release she died. This would make May approximately 26 years old at the time of her mother's death.

17. **(B)** Examiners often ask questions like this one that require attention to detail.

18. **(C)** April Waters began her sentence in Sing Prison. At that time, she was in the fourth month of her pregnancy, and 5 months later she gave birth to Officer North.

19. **(D)** The quarrel centered around Frank Waters's drug use, losses at the racetrack, and affairs with other women. This is a question that emphasizes the importance of reading all the choices before selecting an answer.

20. **(B)** April Waters took a kitchen knife and repeatedly stabbed Frank Waters to death.

21. **(C)** According to the paragraph, a fixed post is required for an extremely sensitive security problem. Hence, the security problem obviously requires heightened concern. Choices A, B, and D do not necessarily bring about heightened security concerns. A *serious* problem, Choice C, would bring about such concerns.

22. **(C)** Choices A, B, and D are not appropriate in that the paragraph consistently indicates that it is a *court officer* who is assigned to a fixed post.

23. **(B)** The paragraph clearly indicates that fixed posts are a result of deliberation and intuitive thinking. Such an effort would certainly have to be based on sound *reasons*. Hence, Choice B is the most appropriate response.

24. **(C)** At the direction of a magistrate, an alternate juror may be allowed into the jury deliberating room.

25. **(B)** It is unequivocally stated that unauthorized persons are to be prevented from entering the jury deliberating room during deliberations. You must learn to distinguish between qualified statements such as the one that was the basis for the answer to question 24 and unqualified statements, which is the basis for the answer to this question.

26. **(D)** Most ordinary citizens believe that juvenile defendants are not any different from adult defendants and that the only difference is age. Nothing could be farther from the truth. Even though both groups of criminals can be held to know the difference between right and wrong, juvenile offenders often lack an appreciation (understanding) of the effects (results) of their crimes on the rest of the community. At times, an examiner may change the words in an answer choice slightly, but the choice still reflects the meaning or intent of the passage.

27. **(D)** Choices B and C are incorrect statements in that juveniles do see how criminals are treated in prison on television and are told some things about prison life by neighborhood ex-convicts. Choice A is correct, but the main reason that juveniles do not see the risks of punishment to themselves is as stated in Choice D.

28. **(A)** The hope of such programs is that, by seeing what prison life is really like, some change in attitude will occur in the juvenile. Although such programs are not seen as the cure-all for rising juvenile crime nor as a replacement for the role of parents or educational institutions, progress is being made.

29. **(C)** The rule is for court officers to handle routine breaches of courtroom decorum and the exception is for magistrates to handle them. As for Choices A and D, the use of the word *will* makes them wrong.

30. **(C)** In the last 3 years, about 90 injuries occurred to defendants on Saturday.

31. **(A)** There was no day of the week that had a higher average number of injuries to officers than to defendants. Please note that reading comprehension questions, as explained in a later chapter, can involve the reading of pictorial material, such as the graph in this series of questions.

32. **(D)** There is no way of knowing from this graph the exact number of injuries that occurred on any given day.

33. **(A)** For the whole 3-year period, only about 15 officers were injured on Mondays.

34. **(C)** Approximately 60 injuries happened to officers on Saturdays over the entire 3-year period.

35. **(A)** There were approximately 60 injuries to defendants on both Wednesdays and Fridays for the period covered by the graph, which was the last 3 years.

36. **(A)** There were about 60 defendant injuries on Wednesdays and about 30 officer injuries, which is a ratio of 60 to 30, or 2 to 1.

37. **(C)** There were about 40 defendant injuries on Thursdays, and about 35 officer injuries on Thursdays.

38. **(B)** Civil liberties are defined as the rights derived from the U.S. Constitution, which can be asserted by the people against the government.

39. **(A)** Students of constitutional law know that Choice B is a correct answer for this question in the real world. But, the instructions clearly state that the questions must be answered solely on the information contained in the passage. The passage states that the first ten amendments are known as the Bill of Rights, and that the First Amendment guarantees freedom of speech.

40. **(C)** The rule allows court officers to defend themselves against the use or imminent use of force. It does not allow the use of force to defend against future threats such as, "I will get you one day."

41. **(B)** According to the rule, court officers may not use deadly physical force upon another person unless they reasonably believe that such other person is using or about to use deadly physical force against them or another. Choice B is the only example that satisfies this rule.

42. **(C)** According to the statement in the stem of the question, there are those who argue that the death penalty is more financially economical than life imprisonment, but that argument does not stand up.

43. **(B)** The passage defines a juvenile as being under 16 years of age. Choice B speaks of a person who is already 16 years of age and is not, therefore, subject to the rules governing the arrests of juveniles.

44. **(A)** The thinking behind such a rule is that those most close to a person can shed insight into preventive measures that may be taken to avoid repeat suicide attempts.

45. **(C)** The thinking behind this rule is that younger prisoners have a better chance of rehabilitation if they do not associate with hardened adult criminals.

46. **(B)** It is unethical for an officer to use his uniform or any symbol of his public office for personal gain or profit.

47. **(B)** In the court system, cooperation among court officers (teamwork) is essential. Aggressiveness and rigidity are not characteristics of teamwork.

48. **(A)** A person with an open mind is flexible and not rigid. Such a person considers all the facts, including both sides of a story.

49. **(B)** Even though a court officer must be sound in mind and body, the word *extremely* makes Choice A incorrect. The ability to think on one's feet is, however, an essential attribute of a court officer.

50. **(D)** The firearm is not an offensive weapon. It is to be used for defensive purposes. And, remember that, even when used to protect lives, firearms should be used only as a last resort.

51. **(D)** The term *offense* includes felonies, misdemeanors, and violations.

52. **(C)** Petty offenses include violations and traffic infractions.

53. **(D)** A court officer who has reasonable cause to believe that a person has committed an offense in the officer's presence can arrest such person. Because an offense is either a felony, a misdemeanor, or a violation, Choice D is correct.

54. **(D)** There are no time restrictions on arrests made without arrest warrants.

55. **(C)** An arresting court officer must inform a person being arrested of the reason for such arrest unless the officer meets physical resistance or flight. All choices except Choice C, the correct choice, indicate either physical resistance or flight.

56. **(A)** An arresting officer may follow in close pursuit if a person flees into his own residence to avoid arrest.

57. **(A)** According to the information provided, a warrant of arrest may be executed anytime on any day of the week. Remember to read and follow the instructions when answering legal definition questions, which in this case told you to base your answers *solely* on the information provided.

58. **(B)** Because the premises is the dwelling of a third party, namely Tom, Frank must obtain a search warrant for the premises in addition to the currently held arrest warrant for Ray.

59. **(C)** Choices A, B, and D are all valid reasons for an officer not announcing his purpose and authority to an occupant of the premises. Choice C is not.

60. **(D)** Although the officer need not have a warrant of arrest in her possession, the officer must show it to the defendant upon request as soon after the arrest as possible.

61. **(B)** A person is guilty of bribing a juror, when he merely offers to give a benefit to a juror with the understanding that the actions of the juror will be influenced. It is not necessary for the benefit to be actually given nor is it necessary that the juror actually agree to be influenced. Note that the benefit can be any gain or advantage such as indicated here (e.g., an easier job).

62. **(C)** If a person communicates with a juror with the intent to influence the outcome of a proceeding, it is tampering with a juror. According to the definitions provided, when such defendant offers a benefit to the juror to achieve such a purpose, the crime becomes bribing a juror.

63. **(D)** Benefits also include any gain or advantage to a third person pursuant to the wishes of the juror. A juror includes someone who has been summoned to be a juror at a future date. Therefore someone who has not yet been officially sworn in as a juror is still considered a juror. Both statements are incorrect; the answer is Choice D.

64. **(A)** Frank's intent was to influence the outcome of an action or proceeding when he communicated with a juror in such an action or proceeding. It is irrelevant whether he wanted to have the defendant Jay convicted or acquitted. The wrongful act lies in the intent to influence the action of a juror in a proceeding and the offering of a benefit is not required to commit the crime of tampering with a juror.

65. **(C)** Bribing a juror is committed when a person offers, gives, or agrees to give a benefit to a juror with the understanding that the actions of the juror will be influenced. A person is guilty of bribe receiving by a juror when such person asks for, receives, or agrees to receive a benefit upon the understanding that such juror's action as a juror will be influenced. Whether or not the benefit actually influences the juror's decisions or actions is not important. It is the giving or merely offering of a benefit based on the *understanding* that the juror's actions will be influenced that is significant.

66. **(D)** The actions described in the procedure are to be performed by the responding court officer.

67. **(B)** Whenever the words *in this order*, or similar such words are used in a procedure to indicate that the steps in the procedure are sequential, you can expect a question about the sequence of the steps to be taken. In this instance, after the shift supervisor is requested by the court officer, the court officer shall then request the response of the local police detectives.

68. **(D)** It is the duty of the responding court officer to determine whether the services of the local police Crime Lab Unit are required after assessing the crime scene.

69. **(B)** The name of the hospital treating persons removed from the scene, not at the scene is required. Read carefully. The information contained in the remaining choices is required to be communicated to the Crime Lab Unit.

70. **(B)** The first attempt to request the response of the local police Crime Lab Unit should be made directly by telephone. If a telephone is not available, the request is then made through the court dispatcher by portable radio.

71. **(A)** The services of the local police Crime Lab Unit are to be requested for any forcible rape, not any rape. An act that, because of the age of the victim, amounts to rape could occur without force being used. The situations described in the remaining choices are examples of when the services of the local police Crime Lab Unit are to be requested.

72. **(C)** For the services of the local police Crime Lab Unit to be requested, the assault should be an aggravated assault involving a *dangerous instrument* with the victim likely to die.

73. **(C)** Choice D is incorrect because pages are not to be removed. Choice A is incorrect because no erasures are permitted. The correct procedure is to draw a single line through the incorrect entry and initial it.

74. **(B)** According to the procedure, a court officer shall store both active and completed memo books in the officer's department locker, available for inspection at all times. Note that the procedure makes no mention of time limits. This obviously seems unreasonable. However, remember that according to the directions, your answers are to be based solely on the information provided.

75. **(C)** Statements A, B, and D are all found in the procedure and are therefore correct statements. However, Choice C is incorrect because abbreviations may be used.

76. **(D)** A search means to place hands inside a pocket or other interior parts of clothing to determine if an object felt during a frisk is a weapon. Thus it is clear that a search is often preceded by a frisk.

77. **(A)** If a court officer reasonably suspects a person has committed, is committing, or is about to commit a felony or misdemeanor as defined in the State Penal Code, the court officer may stop the person and request identification and an explanation of such person's conduct. Mere hunches and guesses are not enough to stop someone, and absolute certainty is much more than is required.

78. **(B)** Only that portion of the suspect's clothing where an object is felt as a result of a frisk may be searched. Because the officer felt an object in the suspect's coat pocket, that would be the area that could be legally searched by the officer, not the suspect's pants pocket.

79. **(D)** The amount of time is not a fixed period but is instead reasonably related to the facts that initially justified the stop or are discovered during the stop.

80. **(B)** The procedure clearly states that the suspect under such circumstances must be immediately released.

81. **(A)** Choices B, C, and D are instances when a STOP AND FRISK CARD is to be prepared by a court officer. A court officer should prepare a STOP AND FRISK CARD when a person is stopped but only if the use of force was required.

82. **(D)** Both the shift supervisor and the court desk officer are required to review STOP AND FRISK CARDS.

83. **(C)** The manner of dress of a suspect, including bulges in clothing, is enough to yield reasonable suspicion but not enough for an immediate arrest.

84. **(D)** Choices A and B are incorrect because counterfeit coins and not bills are to be initialed. Choice C is incorrect because, as stated in Choice D, both the officer and the attendant should sign the bill.

85. **(D)** The court desk officer shall assign a messenger to deliver a report and the money to the Special Agent-In-Charge of the local office of the U.S. Secret Service.

86. **(D)** The firearms of court officers are mainly intended to provide protection for the court and the officer. Also, the procedure merely requires that court officers exercise caution when entering public elevators in the courthouse. Neither statement 1 nor 2 is correct.

87. **(B)** A court officer's firearm should never be left in an unattended vehicle. When you see a statement that leaves no room for exception, make note of it. Examiners often use such statements as the basis for questions. We call such statements *absolutes*.

88. **(D)** The procedure clearly states that detention areas, which are what feeder pens are, shall not be entered by any court officer while wearing a firearm.

89. **(D)** The cleaning of firearms on court property is strictly prohibited unless permission is obtained from the court desk officer.

90. **(B)** Statement 1 is incorrect because the practice of dry firing in any location within the courthouse or its contiguous grounds or parking lot(s) is strictly prohibited. Statement 2 is correct because a significant number of accidental discharges of firearms have occurred in court officer locker rooms.

91. **(B)** Choice A should be eliminated because the letter G is incorrectly associated with the number 15. Eliminate Choice C because the letter I is incorrectly associated with the number 8. A close comparison of letters with the numbers suggested by Choice B indicates that B is the answer. A helpful hint in actually comparing the letters and their corresponding numbers is to use the index finger of your left hand to point to the letter in the choice you are examining. Then with your eye find the numbers in the reference table that are associated with the letter you are pointing at. If the number in the choice you are examining is not associated with that letter in the reference table, eliminate that choice. Also circle the letter along with the number in the choice that has been identified via the reference table as not being correctly associated with the letter in the answer choice you are examining. As soon as you have identified one incorrectly associated letter and number move on to the next choice. The reason for circling the incorrectly associated letters and numbers is so that when you check your work, you will be quickly reminded why you have eliminated a choice.

92. **(D)** None of the sets is accurately associated. In Choices A and B, the letter B is incorrectly associated. In Choice C, the letter G is incorrectly associated. Thus, Choice D is the answer.

93. **(A)** Choices B and C can both be quickly eliminated because the letter I in both choices is incorrectly associated with the number 11, which is inaccurate according to the reference table.

94. **(C)** Choice A is incorrect because the letter N is incorrectly associated with the number 5, and Choice B is incorrect because the second letter B is incorrectly associated with the number 1. Choice C is accurately associated.

95. **(D)** They are all appropriately associated.

96. **(C)** The numbers in the choices represent the following:
(A) BON (B) BIG (C) INO (D) GBO. Choice C represents the best alphabetical order because the letter I comes before the letter N and the letter N comes before the letter O. In doing this type of coding question, we recommended that you first replace the numbers in each choice with the associated letters from the reference table. Then determine which of the individual choices is in best alphabetical order. Unfortunately each choice must be examined. That is why this type of coding question can be time-consuming.

97. **(C)** The numbers in the choices represent the following:
(A) ION (B) GNI (C) BIO (D) GON. Choice C represents the best alphabetical order.

98. **(D)** The numbers in the choices represent the following:
(A) BNI (B) BNG (C) BON (D) BGI. Choice D represents the best alphabetical order.

99. **(A)** The numbers in the choices represent the following:
(A) GIO (B) GON (C) GIB (D) BIG. Choice A represents the best alphabetical order.

100. **(D)** The numbers in the choices represent the following:
(A) OIN (B) OBG (C) OGN (D) BNO. Choice D represents the best alphabetical order.

Correct
YOUR WEAKNESSES

Reading Comprehension Questions

1

→ **THE IMPORTANCE OF CONCENTRATION**

→ **INCREASE YOUR VOCABULARY**

→ **STRATEGY FOR HANDLING READING COMPREHENSION QUESTIONS**

→ **UNDERSTANDING GRAPHIC WRITTEN MATERIAL**

→ **READING COMPREHENSION QUESTIONS INVOLVING WORD SELECTION**

Reading comprehension questions are designed, as the name implies, to measure the candidate's ability to comprehend or understand written material. In effect, reading comprehension questions on a court officer examination measure a candidate's ability to read and understand the type of written material that is used by court officers in the performance of their everyday duties. For example, the written material could be a narrative or story about a courthouse incident, or it could be in the form of a rule or procedure that a court officer is supposed to follow.

Reading comprehension questions appear on virtually all court officer examinations, and they represent the question type that accounts for the greatest number of questions. In addition, most of the other question types used also require good reading comprehension ability. Therefore, you should improve your reading comprehension skills through diligent practice and make certain that you master the strategy presented in this chapter for handling reading comprehension questions.

THE IMPORTANCE OF CONCENTRATION

How often do you "read" something by looking at the words without concentrating on what they mean. This is the biggest roadblock to overcome if you want to become a good reader. Actually, letting your mind wander is not bad for light reading. However, for the kind of reading that is essential to master almost any examination, *you must learn how to concentrate on the material totally.* One way to accomplish this is to continuously ask yourself questions about what you are reading. Another way is to use your imagination and create mental impressions about what you are reading. Above all, don't let your mind wander! You must learn to concentrate exclusively on what you are reading.

A simple way to practice concentration is to read an article from the newspaper. As you read, have a pencil in your hand and underline or circle key points. After reading the article, write down the key points you remember. Then return to the passage and see how well you did. You will become better with practice. Remember that the key is *concentration.*

INCREASE YOUR VOCABULARY

Concentration alone will not help if a reading passage contains a significant number of words that you don't understand. Therefore, follow these suggestions to increase your vocabulary.

TIP

Use your new vocabulary.

1. When you read a word you don't fully understand, make a note of it along with a reminder of where you read it. Keep a special notebook for this purpose. It is especially important for you to do this with any word in this book you do not understand because the words in this book are typical of the ones you will see on your official examination.

2. Look up the meaning of the word in the dictionary as soon as possible.

3. Return to the material where you read the word and make sure that you now understand its meaning and how it fits into the material.

4. Try to use these words in your everyday conversation.

5. Review these words periodically until you are certain you have mastered them.

6. Ask a friend or another student to test you on the meanings of these words.

STRATEGY FOR HANDLING READING COMPREHENSION QUESTIONS

Please note that some students do not completely understand our recommended test-taking strategies until they practice using them. It is vital, therefore, that you study each such strategy and then practice using it. Throughout this book, we give you practice questions with explained answers. These explanations, when appropriate, include a review of the strategy you should have used. Our experience is that, with practice, our strategies produce candidates who achieve a high degree of accuracy in a minimum amount of time. But, you must practice using the strategies to benefit from them. The strategy for reading comprehension questions follows.

QUESTION STRATEGIES

Read the directions.
Use information from the passage only.
Read the question stem.
Read the passage.
Answer the questions.

1. **READ THE DIRECTIONS.** As mentioned previously, court officer examinations contain general instructions at the beginning of the examination along with specific instructions preceding certain question types. Be sure to read all instructions carefully before proceeding to the questions. When the instructions tell you to answer one or more questions based *solely* (or only) on the information contained in a reading passage, you should recognize the fact that you are dealing with a reading comprehension question.

2. **USE ONLY INFORMATION CONTAINED IN THE PASSAGE TO ANSWER THE QUESTIONS.** You must understand that the answers to reading comprehension questions are contained in the written passage that comes before the questions. Do not introduce personal knowledge into a reading comprehension question. As the instructions state, the question is to be answered solely (or only) on the basis of the information contained in the written material that appears before the question(s).

3. **READ THE STEM OF EACH QUESTION PERTAINING TO THE PASSAGE.** It is a mistake to read the passage first and then look at the choices. It's too time-consuming. Instead, read the stem of each question before reading the passage. Also take a quick look at the choices. The stem of the question is the part of the question that comes before

the choices. It tells you what information is needed to answer the question. When you use this strategy you know what information you need to answer the question before you read the passage. This enables you to disregard unimportant information when you read the passage and saves you time.

4. **READ THE PASSAGE CAREFULLY.** Because you already have read the question stems, you know what information you need to answer the questions. The next step is to read the passage very carefully. As you come across the information needed to answer a question, circle that information. If necessary, stop reading periodically and refresh your memory concerning the information you are looking for by rereading the question stems. After you have located the information you need to answer all the questions involved, you can quickly answer the questions.

5. **ANSWER THE QUESTIONS.** As mentioned previously, after you locate all the information you need to answer the questions, you can answer the questions. Simply use the information you located and circled in the passage and select the answer choice that contains that information.

Using Judgment When Answering Reading Comprehension Questions

Sometimes you must infer the answer to reading comprehension questions based on information included in the passage. Some testing experts take the position that these questions are most properly classified as judgment questions. We do not agree entirely with that position because the information upon which the answer should be based MUST be included in the written material that accompanies the question. To clear this up in your mind, consider the following question.

EXAMPLE

Answer question Q1 based solely on the following rule.

A court officer must notify the clerk of the court whenever an emergency situation is occurring in the courtroom.

Q1.   According to this rule, for which of the following situations should a court officer notify the court clerk?

(A) A defendant in a case is not present in the courtroom.
(B) There is a distinct odor of gas in the courtroom.
(C) An attorney in the courtroom is engaged in a loud conversation with her client.
(D) A defendant in a case offers a bribe to the court officer who is guarding that defendant.

The answer to this question is Choice B because it is the choice that best describes an emergency. In essence, the test taker's task in this type of question is to apply the information contained in the question. In our example, the rule is that court officers must notify the court clerk when an emergency occurs. Even though some other rules might require the court clerk to be notified when the situations described in the other choices occur, that is NOT what is being asked. Take Choice D as an example. Surely, under the circumstances described in that choice, good judgment dictates that the court officer should probably notify the court clerk. But, the question demands that the answer spell out an emergency situation. And, of the four choices, Choice B is best classified as an emergency.

Strategy for Taking Judgment/Reasoning Questions

Take time to understand the rule.

1. If a rule is given, as is the case most of the time, you MUST spend a little time making sure that you understand the rule before you look at the question.

2. Before reading the choices, you must determine whether you are looking for an example of the rule or an example of an exception to the rule. In other words, sometimes there are three good statements which support the rule and one bad one, and you must find the bad one. This kind of question might have a stem that reads something like this:

   Q. All the following actions are in accordance with the given rule except . . .

   In this case, the choices would contain three good actions and one bad one. Your job is to select the bad one.

   Other times there are three bad statements and one good one. This kind of question might have a stem that reads something like this:

   Q. Which one of the following actions is in accordance with the given rule?

   In this case, the choices would contain three bad actions and one good one. This time your job is to select the good one.

3. Evaluate each choice as being "good" or "bad." Do this by writing *good* or *bad* in the test booklet next to each choice. If you are not sure, put a question mark next to that choice. After you have evaluated each choice, if you have three *goods* and one *bad*, or three *bads* and one *good*, the answer is obvious. If, however, you have three *goods* and a question mark, the question mark is probably the "bad" choice and the choice to select as the answer.

UNDERSTANDING GRAPHIC WRITTEN MATERIAL

Sometimes court officer examinations contain reading comprehension questions that use graphs, sketches, or drawings. In other words, the written material upon which the questions are based uses a combination of words and graphic illustrations, usually sketches, drawings, pictures, or graphs. Nonetheless, the strategy is the same. Before you look at the graphic illustrations, you should first look at the stem of the questions to get an idea of what you will be asked about.

READING COMPREHENSION QUESTIONS INVOLVING WORD SELECTION

This type of reading comprehension question is yet another way to test if you understand what you are reading. It consists of a paragraph from which words have been left out, as indicated by numbered blank spaces representing question numbers. Your task is to read the paragraph and then select from a group of words, usually four, which word most appropriately fits in the numbered blank.

Strategies for Taking Word Selection Questions

1. Scan the entire paragraph to get a sense of the overall meaning or purpose of the paragraph.

2. When initially scanning the paragraph, do not try to think of words that might fit in the numbered blank spaces. It is a waste of time, since your task will be to select the word that most appropriately fits in the numbered blank from among the choices the examiner has provided.

3. When appropriate, pay particular attention to whether the paragraph is referring to only one specific person or to many people in general. Is the paragraph describing a general procedure to follow or is it referring to a specific incident? Effort here will help to decide whether a general or specific type of word should be used. For example, if you see "_____ defendant," selecting the word *this* when the paragraph is referring to any defendant in general would not be appropriate. Rather, a better selection might be *a* defendant.

4. If a person's role is established and such person is identified by name early on in the paragraph, then it would be appropriate to select that person's name when it appears later in the paragraph. But it would NOT be appropriate to suddenly select a person's name in a paragraph without the paragraph having first identified that person and what relation or role that person has to the paragraph.

5. Make sure to keep genders straight in your mind. If the paragraph is referring to a female, the use of female gender words such as *she* or *her* and not *he* or *him* would be appropriate.

After you study the above strategies, see if you can successfully apply them to the following three Word Selection questions. Following each question is the answer as well as an answer explanation.

EXAMPLE OF WORD SELECTION QUESTIONS

Answer questions 1–3 based on the following directions.

> **Directions:** The paragraph below contains questions 1–3 in the form of three numbered blanks. Immediately following the paragraph are lists of four word choices that correspond to these numbered blanks. Select the word choice that would MOST appropriately fit the numbered blank in each question.

The purpose of an arraignment in court includes formally charging a defendant with an offense and deciding the terms of bail. Bail usually is a sum of money that ___(Q-1)___ defendant deposits with the court and can lose if that defendant does not appear the next time he or she is scheduled to appear in court. Bail is therefore intended to ensure that a ___(Q-2)___ will appear at the next scheduled court date. If the defendant does not appear at the next scheduled court date, ___(Q-3)___ bail will be forfeited.

1. (A) a
   (B) that
   (C) his
   (D) our

The answer to Question 1 is Choice A, which is the most appropriate response since the paragraph is referring to any defendant in general. Because there is no specific reference in the paragraph to any specific person or gender, Choices B, C, and D are incorrect.

2. (A) lawyer
   (B) judge
   (C) defendant
   (D) police official

The answer to Question 2 is Choice C. The paragraph clearly indicates that it is the defendant who will lose the amount of the bail if the defendant does not appear the next time he or she is scheduled to appear in court.

3. (A) her
   (B) his
   (C) their
   (D) the

The answer to Questions 3 is Choice D. There is no reference to one specific gender in the paragraph. Thus, Choices A and B are incorrect. Choice C is incorrect because the paragraph is referring to a single defendant. Therefore, the selection of "their"—which would be describing more than one defendant—would not be appropriate.

PRACTICE EXERCISE

It is now time for you to take some practice reading comprehension questions. Remember to use the recommended strategies when answering these questions. Also remember that the practice questions we use throughout this book have a high level of difficulty.

Allow yourself 20 minutes to do the 10 questions in this practice exercise.

> **Directions:** Answer questions 1–4 based solely on the following information.

Most court officers are required to interact with the public on a daily basis. During these interactions, all officers must try to exercise common sense and to be fully objective. Acting with impartiality, courtesy, and objectivity is the ideal. However, from time to time, situations that require firmness of action and even the use of physical force will occur. When these exceptional situations occur, court officers must be ready for them and take the required action. When maintaining the decorum of the courtroom, the following guidelines must be followed:

a. According to law, the judge has the responsibility to maintain the decorum of the courtroom.

b. A judge is authorized to punish any person in the courtroom who acts in a disorderly manner. This punishment can amount to a fine not exceeding $500.00 or imprisonment not exceeding 15 days, or both.

c. It is the job of a court officer to assist the judge in maintaining the decorum of the courtroom. When so doing, the court officer's conduct must be in conformity to the directions of the judge.

d. Even though a judge may on occasion punish a person in the courtroom for contempt, it is the responsibility of the court officer to handle routine breaches of courtroom decorum. While doing so, court officers are expected to act tactfully and to exercise common sense.

e. Court officers must remember that most minor breaches of courtroom decorum stem from ignorance of protocol and are not violations of law. Such breaches of decorum should be handled discreetly and, insofar as possible, should be corrected on an individual basis without involvement of the judge.

1. While attempting to maintain courtroom decorum, court officers . . .

    (A) must never resort to the use of physical force.
    (B) are encouraged to use physical force.
    (C) must sometimes use physical force.
    (D) may use physical force only when directed to do so by a judge. Ⓐ Ⓑ Ⓒ Ⓓ

2. Who has the legal responsibility to maintain the decorum of the courtroom?

    (A) court officers
    (B) court clerks
    (C) judges
    (D) court officers, court clerks, and judges Ⓐ Ⓑ Ⓒ Ⓓ

3. The punishment for a person who acts in a disorderly manner in the courtroom . . .

    (A) can be imposed by a court officer.
    (B) is limited to a fine only.
    (C) is limited to a term of imprisonment only.
    (D) could amount to a fine of $400.00. Ⓐ Ⓑ Ⓒ Ⓓ

4. The majority of breaches of courtroom decorum . . .

    (A) are violations of law.
    (B) must be settled by a judge.
    (C) happen because people are not aware of the rules of the court.
    (D) must be dealt with immediately. Ⓐ Ⓑ Ⓒ Ⓓ

Court officers are sometimes called upon to control demonstrations in the courthouse area. Generally speaking, however, areas inside courthouses are not permissible places for organized demonstrations because the potential for danger is much greater than outdoors. In courthouses, court officers most often deal with crowds that tend to be orderly and are amenable to control. From time to time, however, organized groups come into the courthouse with the specific intent to create a disruption. If such acts of disruption occur in a courtroom, the judge presiding is ultimately responsible for maintaining order and decorum. In these cases, the actions of court officers should usually be based on orders from the judge. If disruptive acts occur anywhere else in the courthouse, the course of action for court officers to follow is to be established by the highest ranking superior officer present, after consultation with the appropriate officers of the court.

5. Court officers working inside courthouses usually are responsible for handling crowds that . . .

   (A) are responsive to control.
   (B) tend to be disorderly.
   (C) have great potential to riot.
   (D) intend to be disruptive. Ⓐ Ⓑ Ⓒ Ⓓ

6. When acts of disruption occur inside a courthouse, court officers should be guided by instructions from judges or from superior officers depending on . . .

   (A) the time the disruptive acts occur.
   (B) where in the courthouse the disruptive acts occur.
   (C) the seriousness of the disruptive acts.
   (D) the nature of the disruptive acts. Ⓐ Ⓑ Ⓒ Ⓓ

A court officer should not sleep while on duty. He or she shall not engage in games of chance of any kind while on duty. Except in the line of duty, he or she shall not bring cards or dice into a court facility.

7. While working, a court officer is sometimes permitted to . . .

   (A) sleep.
   (B) play cards.
   (C) play dice.
   (D) bring a deck of cards into a court facility. Ⓐ Ⓑ Ⓒ Ⓓ

Personal telephone calls by on-duty court officers that are made without prior authorization are prohibited.

8. According to the rule, court officers . . .

    (A) can never make personal telephone calls while on duty.
    (B) can always make personal telephone calls while on duty.
    (C) can make personal telephone calls while on duty if they obtain permission immediately after the call.
    (D) can make personal telephone calls while on duty if they obtain permission before making the call.   Ⓐ Ⓑ Ⓒ Ⓓ

Court officers, while in uniform, are not allowed to smoke while performing any duties that require them to be in contact with the public. The term *public* does not include the defendants in criminal court. In addition, court officers are prohibited from smoking in those areas of a court facility that are designated as No Smoking areas.

9. Court officers who are in uniform . . .

    (A) are never allowed to smoke.
    (B) can sometimes smoke when in contact with defendants in criminal court.
    (C) can smoke when dealing in person with the public.
    (D) can smoke at all times.   Ⓐ Ⓑ Ⓒ Ⓓ

Off-duty court officers have the option to carry their firearms or to leave their firearms in a safe and secure location at their residence or at the courthouse where they are assigned. It is strongly suggested that off-duty court officers who are planning to consume alcoholic beverages do so while unarmed. When unarmed, court officers should not attempt to enforce the law.

10. Off-duty court officers . . .

    (A) must be armed at all times.
    (B) must leave their guns at work when they go off duty.
    (C) must be unarmed when consuming alcohol.
    (D) must be armed when enforcing the law.   Ⓐ Ⓑ Ⓒ Ⓓ

ANSWER KEY

1. **C**	6. **B**
2. **C**	7. **D**
3. **D**	8. **D**
4. **C**	9. **B**
5. **A**	10. **D**

ANSWERS EXPLAINED

QUESTIONS 1–4

Note that before reading the passage, according to our strategy you should have first looked at the stems of questions 1–4. You would have then realized that, while reading the passage, you were looking for the answers to the following questions:

a. When should a court officer resort to the use of physical force while maintaining courtroom decorum?

b. Who has the legal responsibility to maintain the decorum of the courtroom?

c. What punishment can be imposed on a person who acts in a disorderly manner in the courtroom?

d. What is the cause of the majority of minor breaches of courtroom decorum.

Remember that, after you have identified the questions you are seeking to answer, you can engage in sensitized reading of the passage. In other words, you know what you are looking for as you are reading. This will increase both your accuracy and your speed when doing reading comprehension questions.

1. **(C)** The passage clearly states that from time to time situations that require the use of physical force will occur.

2. **(C)** This question clearly establishes the need to answer reading comprehension questions solely on the basis of the written passage. Intuitively, one would think that court officers have a legal responsibility to maintain the decorum of the courtroom, and they probably do. But, no mention of legal responsibility is made anywhere in the passage. It does, however, clearly state that, according to law, the judge has the legal responsibility to maintain the decorum of the courtroom.

3. **(D)** The authorized punishment cannot exceed a fine of $500.00. Therefore, Choice D represents an authorized punishment.

4. **(C)** The passage very clearly states that most (the majority) of minor breaches of courtroom decorum (conduct) stem from ignorance (lack of awareness) of protocol (rules).

QUESTIONS 5 AND 6

Note that if you read the stems of the questions before you read the passage, you should have determined that you were looking for the answers to these two questions:

   a.   What kind of crowds do court officers deal with inside courthouses?
   b.   Concerning the controlling of disruption, when do court officers receive instructions from judges and when do these instructions come from superior officers?

Then when you read the passage, you could look for these two pieces of information.

5. **(A)** This question emphasizes the necessity for you to have a good vocabulary to do well on the court officer's test. The passage says that in courthouses, court officers most often deal with crowds that tend to be orderly and are amenable to control. Choice A, the answer, says that such crowds are responsive to control. Because *responsive* is a synonym for *amenable*, A is clearly the correct choice.

6. **(B)** If the disruption occurs in a courtroom, the judge takes charge. Anywhere else in the courtroom, it is the superior officer's responsibility.

QUESTIONS 7–10

7. **(D)** An officer can bring a deck of cards into a court facility if it is in the line of duty. In other words, it is permissible if he is told to do so as part of his job.

8. **(D)** Prior authorization means that permission must be obtained before the call is made.

9. **(B)** Defendants are excluded from the definition of the public. Therefore, court officers in uniform can sometimes smoke when in contact with defendants.

10. **(D)** When unarmed, court officers should not attempt to enforce the law. Therefore, they must be armed when enforcing the law.

Memory Questions

2

Earlier in this text, strategies were provided for reading comprehension questions, which, as you now know, are questions that measure whether you understand written material that may be referred to when actually answering such questions.

In this chapter we will go one step farther. Now you will learn to answer questions that measure whether you can understand and remember written or pictorial information that is given to you for a period of time to study and is then taken away while you answer questions about it. This is why we call these questions "memory" questions. To correctly answer memory questions, you must be able to commit information to memory and then retain that information long enough to answer the questions.

THE IMPORTANCE OF MEMORY QUESTIONS

In our opinion, memory questions are of special importance. We feel this way for two reasons. First, memory questions are typically the question type that causes the greatest difficulty for test takers. In fact, statistics that we have gathered over the years indicate that the average untrained test taker misses about 50% of these questions. This means that test takers who do well on memory questions have a distinct advantage over most of the other candidates taking the test.

The second factor contributing to the importance of memory questions is that such questions almost always appear at the beginning of the test. When test takers experience difficulty answering these questions, it almost always has a negative impact on their performance for the rest of the examination. Conversely, those test takers who have no trouble answering memory questions tend to develop a high level of confidence, which carries over to the remainder of the test.

The bottom line is this. If you master the technique for answering memory questions and do well with them on the official test, you will be taking a giant step toward reaching your goal of becoming a court officer.

TWO WIDELY USED TYPES OF MEMORY QUESTIONS

There are two widely used memory question formats in general use on court officer examinations. We call the first type pictorial memory questions, and the second type we refer to as narrative memory questions.

Pictorial Memory Questions

In pictorial memory questions, you are given a drawing, sketch, or some other form of illustrated material, and you are permitted to study it for a specified time period, usually between 5 and 10 minutes. In the great majority of cases, the illustration you are given to study has some relationship to the job of a court officer. You are then asked a series of questions based on information that is contained in the illustration you were given to study. In most cases, the test instructions make it clear that you are not permitted to make notes while studying the pictorial material and that you cannot refer back to it when answering the questions. In fact, the pictorial material is usually collected before the questions are started.

Narrative Memory Questions

In narrative memory questions, which are really quite similar to the pictorial memory questions, you are given written material and are permitted to study it for a specified time period, usually about 10 minutes. As is the case with the pictorial memory questions, the written material you are given to study should have some relationship to the job of a court officer. You are then asked a series of questions based on information that is contained in the narrative material you were given to study. In most cases, the question instructions make it clear that you are not permitted to make notes while studying the material, and you cannot refer to it when answering the questions. In fact, as is the case with pictorial material, the narrative material is usually collected before the questions are started.

Please note that in some cases the written material you must commit to memory is distributed well in advance of the day of the test to all candidates who have registered or filed to take the test. Then, on the day of the test, a series of questions about this material is asked. As is the case with all memory questions, candidates are not allowed to refer to the material when answering the questions. As you might expect, when the narrative material that is used as the basis for memory questions is distributed in advance of test day, it is always more lengthy and somewhat more complicated than narrative material distributed on the day of the test.

USING ASSOCIATIONS—THE KEY TO SUCCESS

Unless you are one of those very rare individuals who have a photographic memory, it is a big mistake for you to rely strictly on brute memory to remember the material, whether it is written in narrative form or presented in pictorial form. Instead, we strongly recommend that you use a memory technique that we refer to as association. Interestingly, if you learn and master the association technique, it will not only help you to be quite successful when taking memory questions on any examination, it will also help you in the future to remember important matters in your everyday life.

Proving Our Point

In the many classroom sessions we have conducted to assist students who are preparing to take memory questions, we have learned that it is important to convince those students of the value of using associations as a memory aide. That is what we intend to do with you right now by asking you to take two practice exercises. It is important that you take these two exercises before reading the rest of this chapter.

PRACTICE EXERCISE ONE

Twenty common words are listed here. Right now, take 5 minutes to study and commit these words to memory. At the end of 5 minutes, stop studying these words, let 10 minutes pass, and then see how many of these words you can remember by writing down as many of them as you can. Do not take notes during your 5-minute study period, and do not refer back to the list when you are attempting to write them all down. Then, when you cannot remember any more of the 20 words, check the actual list and record the number of words you were able to remember. Then resume reading this chapter starting with the next paragraph, which is entitled "Practice Exercise Two."

1.	peach	11.	automobile
2.	ring	12.	camp
3.	razor	13.	missile
4.	champion	14.	lamp
5.	lettuce	15.	children
6.	universe	16.	balance
7.	final	17.	listen
8.	teacher	18.	jump
9.	justice	19.	speak
10.	prisoner	20.	tank

PRACTICE EXERCISE TWO

In all probability you were able to remember about 10 to 12 of the words from Practice Exercise One after studying them for 5 minutes. We now want you to take a similar exercise with one big difference. This time we are going to give you associations to use to help you remember the 20 words that appear in Practice Exercise Two, as follows:

a. When you study the following 20 words, be aware that there is one word in the list that begins with the letter a, one word that begins with the letter b, and so forth. For example, the a word is apple, the b word is bread, and so forth. As you study each word in the list, make sure that you note the first letter of each word and associate it with the alphabet. Then, later on when you are trying to remember the words, you will easily remember the first letter of each word you cannot readily recall. You will find that this will help you remember the actual words you are unable to recall.

b. An *elephant* (word 7, the e word) is *gigantic* (word 17, the g word), usually travels in a *herd* (word 6 the h word), and has an occasional fight with a *lion* (word 12, the l word), who is the *king* (word 10, the k word) of the jungle and has a *queen* (word 9, the q word).

c. *Twenty* (word 2, the t word) rhymes with *plenty* (word 14, the p word), and is a number that is used in *mathematics* (word 8, the m word).

d. *Apple* (word 1, the a word) *jelly* (word 19, the j word) is *sweet* (word 15, the s word), and can be spread on *bread* (word 4, the b word).

Now take the same amount of time, 5 minutes, that you used in Practice Exercise One and study the following list of 20 words remembering to use the associations suggested previously. Then, as you did for Practice Exercise One, let 10 minutes pass and see how many of the words from Practice Exercise Two you can remember. Remember, do not make notes when studying the words, and do not refer back to the list when you are trying to remember its contents. Instead, use the suggested associations to help you remember.

1.	apple	11.	dark
2.	twenty	12.	lion
3.	sun	13.	office
4.	bread	14.	plenty
5.	candle	15.	sweet
6.	herd	16.	nonsense
7.	elephant	17.	gigantic
8.	mathematics	18.	idle
9.	queen	19.	jelly
10.	king	20.	finish

Learn to Develop and Make Your Own Associations

In all probability, you were much more successful in Practice Exercise Two, and you should now be convinced of the benefit of using associations as a memory aide. You probably also understand that when we say "making associations" we mean associating (or connecting) the information you want to remember with some other information so that it is easier to recall the information you want to commit to memory. Association is a necessary process because trying to remember things by brute memory alone is very difficult.

The type of associations made by different people varies tremendously from individual to individual, depending upon background, interests, and imagination. This is where practice will help you the most. The technique involves associating or relating what you are trying to remember with something you already know or with something else you are trying to remember. As a further example of how this works, listed below are some facts that you might want to remember about a story and some suggested associations to help you remember them. You must remember, however, that these are only suggestions offered to give you an idea of how the technique of association works.

Facts	Possible Associations
• The defendant is 25 years old.	• You or someone you know well is 25 years old.
• Altogether 10 court officers reported sick.	• They could have had a full court basketball game (10 players).
• One officer was 42 and the other was 24.	• The reverse of one age equals the other age.
• The escaped prisoner, Michael Murphy, is wanted for murder.	• Mike Murphy is missing and wanted for murder. This is an alphabetical association — note all the m words.

These examples should help you understand how to use associations to aid memory. Bear in mind, however, that your degree of success with this technique depends upon practice. Incidentally, you do not need special court-related material to practice. Your daily newspaper will do just fine. Study a news story for about 5–10 minutes while developing associations to remember the details of the story, then put the paper down, and see how many details you can remember.

GROUPING AND CONTRASTING ITEMS

Many times, especially when the material to be remembered is in the form of a list, it is helpful to group similar items together. If, for exmple, you are looking at a number of legal definitions that classify crimes as misdemeanors or felonies, group the misdemeanors with other misdemeanors and the felonies with other felonies. Conversely, if a piece of information is in contrast to other information, you should use that contrast to assist you in remembering that information. For example, if three wanted persons are non-violent, you should make note of the wanted person who is violent. Or, if every person in a group picture is wearing glasses, you should remember the person who is not wearing glasses.

FOCUSING ON THE KEY FACTS

Every court officer is taught during his or her entry-level training how to capture the key facts in a story in order to write an accurate report. More often than not, they are taught to use the code word "NEOTWY." This code word is derived by taking the last letter from each of the six key facts that must be contained in any thorough narrative report of an occurrence.

> ### THE KEY FACTS
>
> wheN
>
> wherE
>
> whO
>
> whaT
>
> hoW
>
> whY

If you answer these questions when you are investigating an occurrence (e.g., When did it happen?, Where did it happen?, Who was involved?, What happened?, How did it happen?, and Why did it happen?), you have captured all the key information. Therefore, when you are taking memory questions, either pictorial or narrative, concentrate on remembering information that answers these questions. To help you, we will now list the most common kinds of information to be found in each of the six categories.

1. **WHEN.** Times and dates are favorite targets of test writers. If, for example, when looking at a pictorial representation of a holding cell, there is a clock showing the time, a calendar showing the day or date, or both a clock and a calendar, you can be sure that you will be asked a when question. When the memory questions are based on a narrative, the most common dates and times used involve the time of occurrence of an incident, the time it was reported, the time escapes were made, and the time arrests were made.

2. **WHERE.** A critical element in any court-related incident is where the incident took place. If more than one incident took place, make sure you can relate each incident to its location. When you are taking a pictorial memory question, a favorite where question involves the placement of items in relation to one another. Incidentally, if a narrative or a pictorial representation mentions or shows any kind of weapon, you can be certain that you will be asked a question about that weapon. And, the answer may well be given in relation to some other object. For example, you could be given a sketch of a courtroom scene and asked where the man with the gun is located; the answer could be "next to the woman wearing glasses."

3. **WHO.** There are a number of who's in every court-related story, including who is the judge, who is the defendant, who is the officer, and who is the victim. Remember also that physical description of the various who's in the story or illustration are fair game for questions. Things such as beards, glasses, scars, and clothing are often the subject of questions. Or, if there is a vehicle of some sort involved, then it is a sure bet that you will see a question or two about the vehicle, especially its license plate number.

4. **WHAT.** The most common what question is What is happening? For example, Has someone been injured? or What kind of emergency is taking place?

5. **HOW.** How many? is a question that is almost always asked. For example, How many weapons? or How many defendants are in the picture? How things happened is also a favorite question area.

6. **WHY.** Motive is the primary why question. Why people do things is always of concern to the judge and other court personnel. Always look for indications of motive when reading a story or looking at a picture. Another why in pictorial formats involves things that are unusual. When something unusual is shown, you will be asked about it, and/or the reason why the unusual condition exists.

STRATEGIES FOR RECALLING PICTORIAL DETAILS

The illustration you are given to study is never very complicated. Therefore, all you need to become proficient at answering these questions based on the picture is a strategy, concentration, and practice. The concentration must be developed through practice. You can practice every time you look at a picture or read a story. The strategy follows.

1. **DEVELOP A STANDARDIZED METHOD OF STUDYING THE MATERIAL.** If you want to remember all the details in a pictorial representation, you must look at the picture in an organized fashion. You cannot stare at it with the mistaken belief that your mind is recording all the details. You must look at the picture methodically. You must start looking in one certain place, proceed through the picture carefully, work yourself back to the starting place, begin again, and repeat the process. You continue in this manner until your entire amount of allotted time has been used.

> **PICTORIAL QUESTION STRATEGIES**
> Standardize your study method.
> Focus on the key facts.
> Look at all readable matter.
> Look for oddities.
> Use associations.
> Count objects.
> Concentrate.

2. **FOCUS ON THE KEY FACTS.** As you observe the details shown in the illustration, you should focus on the key facts as they were described previously.

3. **OBSERVE ALL READABLE MATTER.** If there is information in the picture that can be read, then you probably will be asked about it. Therefore, look for these most common "readables":

   ■ Clocks
   ■ Signs
   ■ Calendars
   ■ License plates

4. **SEARCH FOR ODDITIES.** Test writers do not write questions about things that appear usual; they write questions about things that are unusual. The following are some of the unusual things to look for:

   ■ Weapons
   ■ Contraband
   ■ Things that are out of place in the scene

5. **USE ASSOCIATIONS TO REMEMBER.** Earlier we spoke a great deal about the use of associations to help you remember things. Now, as you observe key facts, you can apply the association technique to them.

6. **COUNT OBJECTS.** If there are fewer than a dozen separate items in the picture, count them. Examiners often frame questions based on the number of objects. Similarly, if there is more than one of the same type of object, count them. Finally, if money is pictured, count the money.

7. **DO NOT BREAK YOUR CONCENTRATION.** Do not stop concentrating until all the memory questions are answered. And, do not try to observe everything the first time through the picture. Go over it in a methodical way again and again.

8. **DON'T STOP CONCENTRATING WHEN YOUR TIME TO OBSERVE THE MATERIAL HAS ELAPSED.** The time between the closing of the memory booklet and the answering of the questions is the most critical time of all. It is imperative that you maintain your concentration during this time. This is the time when untrained candidates let their minds wander with the result that they forget some of what they observed.

STRATEGIES FOR RECALLING NARRATIVE MATERIAL

> **NARRATIVE QUESTION STRATEGIES**
> Become part of the story.
> Relate the unknown to the known.
> Don't try to memorize.
> Use associations.
> Concentrate.

These questions are not as difficult as you may think because the written story is never a complicated one to understand. Perhaps more than any other test area, your performance in this area can be improved upon significantly by practice. So, if you work hard and follow the following guidelines, you will be able to do very well on this part of your examination.

1. **DON'T JUST READ THE STORY; BECOME PART OF IT!** When you are reading the story, you must clear your head of everything else except what you are reading. You must concentrate. The kind of intense concentration that is needed is best achieved by "putting yourself in the story." Create a mental picture of what is happening.

2. **RELATE THE UNKNOWN TO THE KNOWN.** You will find it easier to put yourself into the story if you create mental images involving persons, places, and things that you know and are familiar with. For example, if the story involves people, try to associate each person in the story with someone you know.

3. **DON'T TRY TO MEMORIZE THE ENTIRE NARRATIVE.** Some students attempt to memorize the entire story verbatim. For most of us, this is an impossible task. The trick is to identify the key facts in the story and to remember them. And, don't be concerned if the story seems incomplete; it will not necessarily have a conclusion. All the test writer is interested in is giving you enough information to test your memory.

4. **USE ASSOCIATIONS TO REMEMBER.** As with the pictorial format, do NOT try to use brute memory. Instead, use the association techniques we discussed previously.

5. **DO NOT BREAK YOUR CONCENTRATION.** Do not stop concentrating until all the memory questions are answered. And, do not try to remember everything the first time you read the story. Go over it in a methodical way again and again.

6. **DON'T STOP CONCENTRATING WHEN YOUR TIME TO OBSERVE THE MATERIAL HAS ELAPSED.** As mentioned previously, the time between the closing of the memory booklet and the answering of the questions is the most critical time of all. It is imperative that you maintain your concentration during this time. This is the time when untrained candidates let their minds wander with the result that they forget some of what they have read.

PRACTICE EXERCISE

20-Minute Time Limit

Directions: For 5 minutes study the following illustration, which depicts items taken from two defendants immediately after they were arrested. Try to remember as many details as possible. Do not make written notes of any kind during this 5-minute period. After the 5 minutes are up, you have an additional 15 minutes to answer the 10 questions that follow immediately. When answering the questions, do NOT refer back to the illustration.

ITEMS TAKEN FROM DEFENDANT ANN SMITH

DRIVER'S LICENSE #642 ANN SMITH 246 MAIN ST. BAYSIDE

TWENTY FIVE 25¢ CENTS

KEY

PEN

PERFUME

CIGARETTES

FIVE 5¢ CENTS

TWENTY FIVE 25¢ CENTS

COMB

KEY

KEY

TEN DOLLARS

TEN 10¢ CENTS

TEN 10¢ CENTS

ITEMS TAKEN FROM DEFENDANT JOHN BROWN

FIFTY 50¢ CENTS

KNIFE

KEY

TWENTY FIVE 25¢ CENTS

KEY

COMB

PENCIL

ASPIRIN

TEN 10¢ CENTS

FIVE DOLLARS

DRIVER'S LICENSE #731 JOHN BROWN 31 7th AVE BAYSIDE

DO NOT PROCEED UNTIL 5 MINUTES HAVE PASSED

Answer questions 1–10 solely on the basis of this illustration. Do not refer back to the scene when answering these questions. You have 15 minutes to complete all 10 questions.

1. Ann Smith's address is . . .

   (A) 246 Main Street.
   (B) 264 Main Street.
   (C) 462 Main Avenue.
   (D) 246 Main Avenue.   Ⓐ Ⓑ Ⓒ Ⓓ

2. Ann Smith's driver's license number is . . .

   (A) 731.
   (B) 642.
   (C) 462.
   (D) 371.   Ⓐ Ⓑ Ⓒ Ⓓ

3. Both Ann Smith and John Brown have . . .

   (A) perfume.
   (B) cigarettes.
   (C) a knife.
   (D) something to write with.   Ⓐ Ⓑ Ⓒ Ⓓ

4. Together, Ann Smith and John Brown possessed . . .

   (A) two keys.
   (B) three keys.
   (C) four keys.
   (D) five keys.   Ⓐ Ⓑ Ⓒ Ⓓ

5. Both Ann Smith and John Brown had . . .

   (A) car registrations.
   (B) a pen.
   (C) eyeglasses.
   (D) a $5 bill.   Ⓐ Ⓑ Ⓒ Ⓓ

6. Which of the defendants probably was experiencing headaches?

   (A) Ann Smith
   (B) John Brown
   (C) neither of them
   (D) both of them   Ⓐ Ⓑ Ⓒ Ⓓ

7. Which of the defendants clearly possessed a weapon?

   (A) Ann Smith
   (B) John Brown
   (C) neither of them
   (D) both of them   Ⓐ Ⓑ Ⓒ Ⓓ

8. What was John Brown's driver's license number?

   (A) 642
   (B) 731
   (C) 137
   (D) 317   Ⓐ Ⓑ Ⓒ Ⓓ

9. What is John Brown's address?

   (A) 31 7th Avenue
   (B) 317 Main Street
   (C) 3 17th Avenue
   (D) 31 Main Street   Ⓐ Ⓑ Ⓒ Ⓓ

10. What do Ann Smith and John Brown have in common?

   (A) They are the same age.
   (B) They were arrested for the same crime.
   (C) They live in the same town.
   (D) They drive the same make car.   Ⓐ Ⓑ Ⓒ Ⓓ

ANSWER KEY

1. **A**		6. **B**
2. **B**		7. **B**
3. **D**		8. **B**
4. **D**		9. **A**
5. **C**		10. **C**

ANSWERS EXPLAINED

Please note that in giving the answers we will suggest associations that could have been made to recall the information needed to answer the questions. But our associations are only suggestions to help give you an idea of how associations can be made. You must remember that the development of associations is a personal matter. What works best for you is what you should follow.

1. **(A)** 2-4-6 is certainly easy enough to remember. Hopefully you recalled it was Main Street and not Main Avenue.

2. **(B)** If you noticed that Ann Smith's driver's license number is the reverse of her house address, 642 and 246, you would have developed an association that helped you answer questions 1 and 2. Remember that associating one item to be remembered with another item to be remembered always pays big dividends.

3. **(D)** Ann Smith had a pen, and John Brown had a pencil.

4. **(D)** Ann Smith had three keys, and John Brown had two keys. Remember to count similar items.

5. **(C)** When you see this format, always notice items that both defendants possess.

6. **(B)** Assumptions can be made in these questions if they are based on facts. In this case, John Brown had aspirin. That fact can support the assumption that John Brown was probably experiencing headaches.

7. **(B)** John Brown had a knife.

8. **(B)** Choice A is Ann Smith's driver's license number. Notice the similarity among Choices B, C, and D. Be careful.

9. **(A)** If you noticed the association between John Brown's driver's license number and his address, you would have earned two sure points. Always try to relate one thing in the illustration with another.

10. **(C)** Both defendants live in Bayside. There is no support in the illustration for any of the other choices.

Understanding and Applying Court Officer Directives, Procedures, and Regulations | 3

→ **UNDERSTANDING PROCEDURES QUESTIONS**
→ **APPLYING PROCEDURES TO SITUATIONS QUESTIONS**

Court officers, like other law enforcement officers, often work alone and not under the direct supervision of their supervisors. As such, they find themselves in difficult situations that call for them to use discretion while making their decisions. To help and guide them in these situations, they are given procedures to follow. These procedures, which act as guidelines, are, of course, in keeping with the overall policies of the agency. These guidelines and procedures are usually in written form and are made available to the court officers. Therefore, part of the job of a court officer is to read and understand these guidelines and procedures and also to apply them correctly to job-related incidents.

For example, it may become evident that a need exists for better detection of weapons hidden on persons seeking admission to courthouses. A court officer would probably then receive new guidelines for searching for such weapons. The officer would be expected to read and understand the new guidelines. However, the officer would also be expected to be able to apply these guidelines correctly to situations involving the detection of weapons on persons seeking admission to courthouses. Because no two incidents are exactly alike and each involves a different and specific set of circumstances, the officer involved must be able to apply the general guidelines to specific situations. The questions in this chapter will develop your ability to read, understand, and apply procedures that might be typically given to court officers.

Two main types of questions used to test a candidate's ability to read, understand, and apply procedures are known as understanding procedures and applying procedures to situations.

UNDERSTANDING PROCEDURES QUESTIONS

In the understanding procedures question type, a candidate is given a procedure similar to what a court officer might typically receive on the job. After reading and understanding the procedure, the candidate then must answer questions about the procedure. Here a candidate's ability to understand such procedures is tested. Generally this question type requires the candidate to identify accurate or inaccurate statements about the procedure. The candidate may refer back to the procedure as often as the candidate needs.

Example of an Understanding Procedures Question

EXAMPLE

Answer question Q1 based solely on the following procedure.

When handcuffing a prisoner, court officers shall always handcuff the prisoner with the prisoner's hands behind his back. This is known as rear cuffing. However, when, in the opinion of, and with permission of, the court officer's supervisor, it would be safe to handcuff a prisoner with the prisoner's hands in front, then a prisoner may be front cuffed. In those instances when authorized to front cuff a prisoner, under no circumstances will court officers leave such prisoner unattended.

Q1.   Based solely on the information in this procedure, which of the following statements is most appropriate?

(A) Only the court officer's supervisor may front cuff a prisoner.

(B) A court officer may never front cuff a prisoner.

(C) At times a prisoner who has been front cuffed may be left unattended if the permission of the court officer's supervisor is obtained.

(D) A court officer may front cuff a prisoner under certain circumstances.

A Strategy for Answering Understanding Procedures Questions

1.   **SCAN THE PROCEDURE.** The first step you should take is to read the material quickly to get an idea of what the procedure is about. A quick scan of the procedure in this example tells you that usually court officers are not allowed to front cuff prisoners. However, it also tells you when and by whose authority a court officer might be allowed to front cuff a prisoner. Finally the procedure indicates that a prisoner who has been front cuffed may never be left unattended.

2.   **SCAN THE STEM AND THE CHOICES.** You should read the stem of the question and the choices quickly. By doing this, for the example given, you should have been able to determine that the question concerned itself with the use of handcuffs on prisoners by court officers. The question asks you to select the most appropriate statement concerning the procedure.

> **STRATEGIES**
> Scan the procedure.
> Scan the stem.
> Read the procedure.
> Use a mental picture.
> Select your answer.

3.   **NOW CLOSELY READ THE PROCEDURE.** By closely reading the procedure, you should have determined that a court officer's supervisor could authorize a court officer to front cuff a prisoner. Also the procedure very clearly states that under no circumstances should a prisoner who has been front cuffed be left unattended.

4.   **USE A MENTAL PICTURE.** Imagine yourself in the situation that the procedure and the question are describing. In the example given, think of a situation where you are a court officer who has arrested and rear cuffed a dangerous felon. Then imagine a situation where you are given permission to front cuff such a prisoner. Who, according to the procedure, is allowed to give you such permission? All the while you are remembering that you are not permitted to leave a prisoner who has been front cuffed unattended. Put yourself into the situation that is being described to develop a mental image of what is occurring.

5. **SELECT YOUR ANSWER.** Selecting your answer involves a process of elimination. For example, in this practice question, Choice A is inappropriate because a court officer's supervisor is not the only officer who may front cuff a prisoner. A court officer could also do it with the permission of the officer's supervisor. Therefore, an X should be placed through Choice A and Choice B, which is inappropriate for the same reason. Choice C is inappropriate and should receive an X through it because a prisoner who has been front cuffed may never be left unattended. Choice D is the most appropriate choice because a court officer could front cuff a prisoner under certain circumstances. Choice D is, therefore, the answer.

APPLYING PROCEDURES TO SITUATIONS QUESTIONS

In the applying procedures to situations type of question, the candidate is given a typical court officer procedure. The candidate is given a story or narrative describing an incident or situation that an officer could be expected to encounter. In some instances, the candidate is then asked to identify the most appropriate (or inappropriate) course of action for the court officer to take in the situation described based on the procedure provided. The procedures remain available and may be referred back to by the candidates if necessary to answer the question. In other instances, the candidate is required to identify what action the officer should take next based on the procedure provided and the facts of the narrative or situation described. Both variations of this type of question are designed to test a candidate's ability to apply procedures to situations.

Example of an Applying Procedures to Situations Question

EXAMPLE

Answer question Q2 based solely on the following procedure.

A court officer is required to prepare the form ACCIDENT REPORT when, as an operator of an official vehicle, the court officer is involved in a motor vehicle accident. A motor vehicle accident is defined as one that occurs on a public highway or on a public street between building lines. Regarding accidents involving official vehicles that occur on private property or on property to which the public does not have access, the form ACCIDENT REPORT shall not be prepared by the operator of the official vehicle because such incidents shall not be considered motor vehicle accidents. Instead, the officer acting as the operator of the official vehicle shall notify the officer's supervisor.

Q2. Court Officer Bill Roe is driving an agency car to the agency's motor pool. Also assigned to the same vehicle is Court Officer Frank Long. Officer Long is present because he will be required to drive back another vehicle from the motor pool to the courthouse. While entering the private parking lot of the agency's motor pool, which is not accessible to the public, Officer Roe accidentally hits a chain link fence causing some damage to the car he is driving. Based solely on the preceding information, it would be most appropriate for . . .

(A) Officer Roe to prepare the form ACCIDENT REPORT.
(B) Officer Long to prepare the form ACCIDENT REPORT.
(C) Officer Long to notify the supervisor.
(D) Officer Roe to notify the supervisor.

A Strategy for Answering Applying Procedures to Situations Questions

1. **SCAN THE PROCEDURE.** Get a quick idea of what the procedure is about. What is the intent of the procedure? What is it describing? To whom does it apply? When should it be used? The intent of the procedure given in this example is to identify who is responsible for preparing a certain form, when that form should be prepared, and what should be done when the form is not prepared.

   You should highlight and/or underline the important parts of the procedure, such as the names of the forms involved, the circumstances under which they should be prepared, the persons charged with the responsibility of preparing them, and what should be done if the form is not required.

   > **STRATEGIES**
   > Scan the procedure.
   > Scan the narrative.
   > Scan the question.
   > Reread the procedure.
   > Reread the narrative.
   > Pick your answer.

2. **SCAN THE NARRATIVE.** Quickly looking over the narrative in this example reveals that an agency car is damaged in a parking lot not accessible to the public. The incident occurs while the operator and another court officer are responding to the agency's motor pool.

3. **SCAN THE QUESTION.** By looking at the stem of the question and the choices, it should be clear that the question asks whether or not a form should be prepared, and if not, what should be done and by whom. This should sensitize you as to what to focus on when performing the next step of the strategy.

4. **CLOSELY REREAD THE PROCEDURE.** This part of the strategy should not be time-consuming because you have already underlined and/or highlighted the procedure when you previously scanned it. Now knowing what part of the procedure will be asked about by the question that you have just scanned, it is an easy task to focus on the relevant part(s) of the procedure.

5. **CLOSELY REREAD THE NARRATIVE.** While now reading the narrative closely, it is recommended that you put yourself into the narrative. Pretend, as in the example, that you are the driver of the vehicle and that the damage to the vehicle occurred while you were driving. Should this be considered a motor vehicle accident? If it should, what must you do? If it's not, what should you do?

6. **PICK YOUR ANSWER.** You must now closely examine the questions and consider all choices. For example, in this question, Choice A is inappropriate because the form ACCIDENT REPORT is not required because the incident did not occur on a public highway or on a public street between building lines. By definition, a motor vehicle accident has not occurred. The incident occurred on property to which the public does not have access. Choice B is inappropriate because whenever it is appropriate for the form ACCIDENT REPORT to be prepared, it is the job of the operator of the vehicle to prepare the necessary form. Officer Long is not the operator. Thus, Choice C is inappropriate because it is the job of the operator to notify the supervisor when an accident involving an official vehicle occurs on private property. The answer is Choice D. Choice D, which calls for Officer Roe to notify the supervisor, is correct because the incident is not considered a motor vehicle accident, and in such instances, the operator of the vehicle is required to notify the supervisor.

10 Questions — Time Allowed 20 Minutes

> **Directions:** Answer questions 1–10 based solely on the following information.

The general procedures for handling prisoners are as follows:

A court officer upon making an arrest shall:

A. Request the Prisoner Detention Unit to assign cell space and determine the method of transportation to an activated detention facility.

B. Comply with the instructions given by the Prisoner Detention Unit.

C. Permit the prisoner to be interviewed by the following properly identified persons when they are on official business:

    a. A supervisory officer of the County Police

    b. A member of the County Police Detective Bureau

    c. The state attorney general or a county prosecutor or their representative

    d. The Chief Medical Examiner or a representative

    e. The prisoner's legal representative (but only if the interview is conducted in the presence of a supervisor of the court officer)

    f. An official of a state or county agency if the prisoner is an employee of that agency

    g. A federal or other properly identified local law enforcement officer

    h. Clergyman (but only upon request by the prisoner)

    i. A state division of parole officer (but only to serve parole violation papers)

D. Prepare an ARREST REPORT.

E. Prepare an ARREST REPORT SUPPLEMENT when an attorney interviews a prisoner while the prisoner is still in the court officer's custody.

F. Permit parents or legal guardian to visit a prisoner between the ages of 16 and 21, for not longer than 20 minutes in the presence of the court officer. However, the prisoner must first have been in custody more than four (4) hours before any such visit can take place.

G. Advise the prisoner of telephone privileges and permit the prisoner to make use of telephone privileges. Only three local calls are permitted. Long distance calls may be made in place of local calls if the party receiving the call will accept the charges for the call. No one call shall be longer than 5 minutes.

Note: A female prisoner with a nursing baby shall not be confined in a detention cell.

1. When a court officer makes an arrest, the court officer shall request which of the following units to assign cell space?

    (A) the County Police Detective Bureau
    (B) the state attorney general
    (C) the Prisoner Detention Unit
    (D) the state division of parole   Ⓐ Ⓑ Ⓒ Ⓓ

2. A prisoner has been arrested by a court officer. The prisoner may be interviewed by a parole officer from the state division of parole on official business . . .

(A) only if the prisoner consents.
(B) anytime the parole officer deems it necessary.
(C) only to serve parole violation papers.
(D) only with permission of the court officer's supervisor.

Ⓐ Ⓑ Ⓒ Ⓓ

3. The preparation of an ARREST REPORT is the job of . . .

(A) the court officer making the arrest.
(B) the county prosecutor or a representative.
(C) a member of the county police department.
(D) a federal law enforcement officer who interviews the prisoner.

Ⓐ Ⓑ Ⓒ Ⓓ

4. When a prisoner's legal representative interviews a prisoner who has been arrested by a court officer, the interview . . .

(A) must be overheard by a member of the county police.
(B) can be no longer than 20 minutes.
(C) must be conducted in the presence of the court officer who made the arrest.
(D) must be conducted in the presence of a supervisor of the court officer.

Ⓐ Ⓑ Ⓒ Ⓓ

5. If a youth who is 17 years old is arrested at 10:00 A.M., which of the following is the earliest time that his parents would be allowed to visit him?

(A) 11:01 A.M.
(B) 12:01 P.M.
(C) 1:01 P.M.
(D) 2:01 P.M.

Ⓐ Ⓑ Ⓒ Ⓓ

6. If the parents of an 18 year old who has been arrested are appropriately permitted to visit with the 18 year old prisoner and if the visit began at 11:00 A.M., then the latest the visit could last is . . .

(A) 11:10 A.M.
(B) 11:20 A.M.
(C) 1:00 P.M.
(D) 3:00 P.M.

Ⓐ Ⓑ Ⓒ Ⓓ

7. A clergyman appears at a location where a prisoner who has been arrested by a court officer is being detained and asks to interview the prisoner. In such an instance, after establishing that the clergyman is requesting to visit in his official capacity, it would be most correct if the court officer . . .

(A) immediately allowed the clergyman to interview the prisoner.
(B) politely told the clergyman that it is against policy to allow prisoners to be interviewed before they are arraigned.
(C) told the clergyman to obtain permission from the court officer's immediate supervisor.
(D) asked the prisoner if he requested the clergyman to appear. Ⓐ Ⓑ Ⓒ Ⓓ

8. Regarding the use of a telephone by a prisoner who has been arrested by a court officer, which of the following statements is least accurate?

(A) The court officer shall advise the prisoner of telephone privileges.
(B) The maximum number of local calls that are permitted is three.
(C) The prisoner can talk as long as desired as long as the prisoner absorbs any additional costs.
(D) If long distance calls are made, they shall be considered made in place of local calls. Ⓐ Ⓑ Ⓒ Ⓓ

9. It would be most correct to prepare which of the following forms when an attorney on official business interviews a prisoner while the prisoner is still in the court officer's custody?

(A) an ARREST REPORT
(B) an ARREST REPORT SUPPLEMENT
(C) an AIDED REPORT
(D) a COURT AFFIDAVIT Ⓐ Ⓑ Ⓒ Ⓓ

10. Upon making an arrest, a court officer may permit the prisoner to be interviewed by all the following properly identified persons when they are on official business except . . .

(A) any member of the County Police.
(B) the state attorney general.
(C) the Chief Medical Examiner.
(D) an official of a county agency if the prisoner is an employee of that agency. Ⓐ Ⓑ Ⓒ Ⓓ

ANSWER KEY

1. **C**	6. **B**
2. **C**	7. **D**
3. **A**	8. **C**
4. **D**	9. **B**
5. **D**	10. **A**

ANSWERS EXPLAINED

1. **(C)** Scanning the question stem and the choices before closely reading the procedure would have helped you to answer this question quickly and accurately.

2. **(C)** The importance of words such as *only* and *anytime* can be seen here. A prisoner may be interviewed by a parole officer from the state division of parole on official business, not anytime, but only when serving parole violation papers.

3. **(A)** When reviewing procedures, it is always important to determine to whom the tasks are assigned. In this instance, all the tasks are assigned to the court officer making the arrest.

4. **(D)** When examining procedures, give special attention to what are known as qualifiers. They are statements that change a previously made statement. As in this example, obviously a prisoner may be interviewed by his attorney but notice the qualifier—the interview must be conducted in the presence of the supervisor of the court officer.

5. **(D)** A prisoner between the ages of 16 and 21 years must be in custody for more than four (4) hours before the parents can visit with the prisoner.

6. **(B)** The time limit for the visit is no longer than 20 minutes. If you selected Choice D, then possibly you confused the time limit for the visit with the 4-hour period required before a visit with such a prisoner can take place.

7. **(D)** This is a good example of having to base your answer on the procedure that has been provided. Although it might seem logical to simply allow a clergyman to interview a prisoner, it is not to be done unless the prisoner requests the clergyman.

8. **(C)** Note that in this question you are looking for the least accurate (or false) statement. The maximum length of time for one phone call is 5 minutes.

9. **(B)** As stated in paragraph E of the procedure, an ARREST REPORT SUPPLEMENT is needed when an attorney interviews a prisoner while the prisoner is still in a court officer's custody.

10. **(A)** Not any member of the County Police, but a supervisory officer of the County Police or a member of the County Police Detective Bureau is permitted to conduct such an interview. Remember to review carefully statements that have words such as *only* and *any*.

Understanding Legal Definitions

4

→ **THE THREE SIGNALS**
→ **DIRECT LEGAL DEFINITION QUESTIONS**
→ **INDIRECT LEGAL DEFINITION QUESTIONS**

Court Officers, similar to other law enforcement officers, are often called upon to make split-second decisions regarding whether or not they should take legal action. To make such decisions properly, two things are required. First the court officer must know and understand what the law defines as legal and illegal, and then the court officer must be able to measure ongoing situations against what he or she knows and understands to be the law. So much of what a court officer does calls for determining whether a violation of law has occurred. This requires knowledge of the law and analysis of the existing situation.

This chapter is designed to help a candidate to deal with questions that determine whether the candidate can understand and apply the law when it is represented as legal definitions. The definitions found in this chapter are of the type that men and women working as court officers would use while performing their duties. Sometimes the definitions that appear in this chapter are exactly as they are written in the law. At other times, they are not. This is to make you aware that often on civil service examinations the definitions have been slightly changed by exam writers to make it easier for them to ask questions about the law. This is important to understand because most legal definition questions ask the candidate to answer such questions based solely on the basis of the information provided by the examination question. Therefore, unless specifically directed to do so, a candidate answering legal definition questions appearing in a court officer examination should not rely on anything that the candidate might already know about the law. If the question directions clearly instruct the candidate to answer the legal definition questions based solely on the information given, prior knowledge of the law is not needed.

THE THREE SIGNALS

When a candidate is examining a legal definition question, three specific signals send a message alerting the candidate as to what the examiner will specifically ask about the legal definition.

The First Signal

First, are there any numbers such as distances, weights, ages, or other numerical amounts mentioned in the legal definition? If there are, then you should pay specific attention to them because they usually will be the focus of at least one question.

It is first-degree rape if someone who is at least 16 years of age has sexual intercourse with someone who is less than 10 years old.

Q1. Based solely on this information, of the following persons, who would be most likely to be charged with first-degree rape?

(A) Don who is 16 years of age has sexual intercourse with April who is 12 years of age.

(B) Mark who is 15 years of age has sexual intercourse with June who is 8 years of age.

(C) Tom who is 17 years of age forcibly has sexual intercourse with May who is 10 years of age.

(D) Frank who is 16 years of age has sexual intercourse with Sherry who is 9 years of age.

Answer: (D) Note that there were two numbers mentioned in the definition, and you should note them when you review the definition. They were the age requirements to be met for a charge of first-degree rape, namely the age of the perpetrator of the rape, at least 16 years of age, *and* the age of the victim, less than 10 years of age. Also note that, although in most jurisdictions a use of force as described in Choice C would result in a charge of first-degree rape, such a situation was not mentioned in the definition. The question indicated that the answer was to be based solely on the information given. Therefore, any prior knowledge of the law should not have been used in answering the question.

The Second Signal

The second signal that sends a message to a candidate answering legal definition questions is the use of the word *and*. Law makers use the word and to indicate that more than one circumstance is required before a violation of a particular law has occurred. Therefore, when the word *and* is used, before a person is considered to have violated a certain law, more than one element must be present to turn a person's conduct into a criminal act.

The Third Signal

The third signal is the use of the word *or*. At times one of two or more situations can turn someone's conduct into a criminal act. Unlike the use of the word *and*, where one element is needed in conjunction with another element for the crime to have been committed, the use of the word *or* indicates that only one of two or more elements is all that is needed for the crime to have been committed.

The crime of criminal mischief is committed when a person intentionally damages the property of another *OR* when a person recklessly damages the property of another *and* the resulting damage is more than $250.

Q2.　Based solely on this information, which of the following statements is most correct?

(A) Criminal mischief can be committed only when a person intentionally damages the property of another.

(B) Criminal mischief can be committed only when someone recklessly damages the property of another.

(C) Criminal mischief is committed whenever a person recklessly damages the property of another.

(D) Criminal mischief occurs when someone acts recklessly and causes more than $250 in damages to the property of another.

Answer: (D) Note that the use of the word *OR* indicates that criminal mischief can be committed either by a person damaging property intentionally or recklessly. Therefore, Choices A and B are incorrect. Also note that Choice C is incorrect because of the use of the word *AND* in the part of the definition describing what is required for a criminal mischief to occur when a person recklessly damages the property of another. Specifically, a person must recklessly damage the property of another *and* the resulting damage must be more than $250. You must make sure that you understand how the words *and* and *or* can change a legal definition.

In summary, use caution and stay particularly alert when you see any of these three signals used in legal definition questions:

1.　numbers
2.　the word *or*
3.　the word *and*

DIRECT LEGAL DEFINITION QUESTIONS

This type of legal definition question is known as a direct legal definition question because, in this type of question, a candidate is presented one or several legal definitions to review and then *directly* asked a question or questions about the legal definition(s). No additional information is given nor required to answer the question. For example, the candidate is required to select accurate or inaccurate statements about the legal definition(s) or to select which of several incidents offered by the choices is the best example of criminal conduct according to the legal definition(s). The instructions usually tell the candidate to answer questions based *solely* on the information contained in the legal definitions that have been provided. While answering the questions, the candidate is permitted to go back and review the legal definitions.

Strategies for Answering Direct Legal Definition Questions

STRATEGIES

Scan the definitions.
Scan the stem and choices.
Fully read the definitions.
Reread and answer the questions.

1. **QUICKLY READ AND SCAN THE LEGAL DEFINITION(S) WITH YOUR PENCIL.** This is done to understand what crimes or situations are being described by the legal definition(s). Is this the definition of a robbery, or bribery, or is this the definition of what is considered an assault? While scanning, you should identify important parts of the definition(s) and key words such as *and* and *or* by underlining them. In addition, numerical amounts such as ages, dollar amounts, weights, and times should be noted because they are favorite areas for test writers. Look at the following examples of how to underline while scanning legal definitions:

   A person is guilty of robbery in the third degree when such person <u>forcibly steals</u> the <u>property</u> of <u>another</u>.

   A person is guilty of grand larceny when <u>he steals</u> the <u>property of another</u> <u>and</u> the <u>property</u> is taken <u>directly</u> <u>from</u> the <u>person</u> of the owner who is <u>less than 21</u> years of age.

2. **READ THE STEM AND CHOICES QUICKLY.** The stem is the part of a multiple-choice question that comes before the choices. By reading the stem quickly, you can determine what part or parts of the legal definitions will be asked about. Also take a quick look at the choices for the same reason. The stem of the question and its choices will alert you as to what part of the definition you will be asked about. The test writer will not ask you about all the parts of the legal definition. Time prohibits this. Therefore, it's a waste of effort for you as the candidate to try to remember all the parts of a legal definition. It is much better to focus mainly on what the test writer might ask you about. And this is done by quickly reading the stems of the questions and their choices. Remember that you do this to get an idea about what parts of the legal definition the exam writer intends to test.

3. **FULLY READ THE LEGAL DEFINITION(S).** As you now carefully read the definitions, you should be focusing in on those parts of the definitions that the test writer will ask you about, which you have already discovered by your previous quick reading of the stems and their choices. Now, when you recognize those parts of the definitions that you will probably be asked about, you should circle them.

4. **REREAD AND ANSWER THE QUESTIONS.** As you again read the questions along with their choices, you should go back to those parts of the definitions that you circled and underlined based on your previous scanning efforts. Finally, select the correct answer to each question.

Answer question Q3 based solely on the following legal definition.

The crime of assault occurs when a person causes a physical injury to another person. A physical injury occurs when a victim experiences substantial pain.

Q3. Based solely on this information, which of the following is the most correct statement concerning the crime of assault?

(A) If Tom kicks Pat, an assault occurs.

(B) If May punches Ray, an assault occurs.

(C) If Don intends to punch Frank but misses and strikes June causing substantial pain, an assault occurs.

(D) If Don becomes frustrated and pounds his fist on a table and substantially hurts his own hand, an assault has occurred.

Here you were given a legal definition and then directly asked a question about the legal definition with no additional information offered or required to answer the question. You should have arrived at Choice C as an answer, if you followed our strategy of

- quickly reading, scanning and underlining the legal definition with your pencil,

  For example: The crime of assault occurs when a <u>person causes</u> a <u>physical injury</u> to <u>another</u> person. A <u>physical injury</u> occurs when a <u>victim</u> experiences <u>substantial pain</u>.

- reading the stem quickly and taking a quick look at the choices,
- fully reading the legal definition, and
- rereading and answering the questions.

Don caused substantial pain, a physical injury, to another person, namely June. Choices A and B are incorrect because no substantial pain occurred. Choice D is incorrect because, for a physical injury to occur, substantial pain to another, not oneself, must result.

INDIRECT LEGAL DEFINITION QUESTIONS

The indirect legal definition type of question presents one or more legal definitions similar to the direct legal definition question. However, in addition, a brief story or narrative, which usually describes some type of criminal conduct, is added. The candidate is then asked to answer questions that require him or her to apply the details of the narrative to the legal definitions that have been provided. Thus, you are asked indirect questions about the legal definition(s).

Strategies for Answering Indirect Legal Definition Questions

1. **QUICKLY SCAN THE LEGAL DEFINITIONS.** Look for and underline the elements that make up the law being described. Actually visualize what is being described and underline key words.

2. **QUICKLY SCAN THE NARRATIVE TO SEE HOW THE NARRATIVE RELATES TO THE LEGAL DEFINITIONS.**

> **STRATEGIES**
> Scan the definitions.
> Scan the narrative.
> Scan the stem and choices.
> Closely read the definitions.
> Closely read the narrative.
> Answer the questions.

3. **SCAN THE STEMS AND THEIR CHOICES.** In this way, when you take another look at the definition(s) and the narrative, you will be able to focus mainly on what is pertinent. You'll know what parts of the narrative the question(s) are asking about.

4. **CLOSELY READ THE DEFINITIONS.** Zero in on those parts you have previously underlined, and circle those parts that you now recognize as relating to the narrative and the questions.

5. **CLOSELY READ THE NARRATIVE, ESPECIALLY THOSE IMPORTANT PARTS OF THE NARRATIVE THAT YOU NOW RECOGNIZE AS RELATING TO THE DEFINITIONS AND THE QUESTION(S).**

6. **ANSWER THE QUESTIONS.** Remember that in this type of legal definition question, you are permitted to refer back to both the definitions and the narrative.

EXAMPLE

Answer question Q4 based solely on the following legal definition.

The crime of robbery occurs when a <u>person</u> takes <u>permanent possession</u> of the <u>physical property of another</u> by the use of <u>force</u> or the <u>threat of force against another</u>. The <u>force</u> used must <u>be more than</u> that needed merely to <u>wrench or pull</u> the <u>property</u> away <u>from its owner</u>.

One night while walking home, May is approached by Pat who forcefully pulls May's purse from under her arm and runs away with May's purse. Court Officer North sees the incident and gives chase. A few blocks away, Pat is apprehended by the officer. A search of Pat reveals that he is carrying an unloaded pistol concealed in his jacket. May arrives on the scene and tells the officer that her purse was just purchased at a department store and is completely empty of any contents.

Q4. Based solely on the preceding information, Pat . . .

(A) has committed a robbery, mainly because he was carrying a concealed pistol.

(B) has committed no crime, mainly because the purse was empty.

(C) has committed a robbery, mainly because he used some degree of force to remove the purse from May.

(D) has possibly committed some crime, but not robbery mainly because the kind of force required for a robbery was not used.

Here you were given a legal definition plus a narrative. You were then indirectly asked a question about the legal definition when you were asked to apply the narrative to the legal definition. If you followed our strategy, you should have

- quickly scanned and underlined the legal definitions,
- quickly scanned the narrative to see how the narrative relates to the legal definitions,
- scanned the stem and its choices,
- closely read the underlined definitions and circled those parts now known to be important,
- closely read those parts of the narrative that relate to the definitions and questions, and
- answered the questions.

In this case you should have arrived at Choice D as the answer. The kind of force used was to merely pull the purse away from the victim. As indicated in the legal definition, that is not the force that is required for a robbery.

PRACTICE EXERCISE

10 Questions — Time Allowed 20 Minutes

> **Directions:** Answer questions 1–10 based solely on the content of the legal definitions given. Do not use any other knowledge of the law that you might have. You may refer to the definitions when answering the questions.

a. Petit larceny—A person commits petit larceny when he takes the property of another without such other person's consent and intends to permanently keep the property for himself or another and the property is worth $1000 or less. Petit larceny is a misdemeanor.

b. Criminal impersonation—A person commits criminal impersonation when, with intent to have another submit to his authority, he pretends to be a public servant such as a court officer. Criminal impersonation is a misdemeanor.

c. Arson—A person commits arson when he intentionally burns a building or a motor vehicle by causing an explosion or starting a fire. If the damage to a building is more than $50,000, or the damage to a motor vehicle is more than $15,000 it is second-degree arson. If someone is injured as a result of the arson, it is first-degree arson. All other arsons are third degree. All arsons are felonies.

d. Robbery—A person commits robbery when he forcibly takes the property of another. Forcibly taking includes the use or threatened use of force against the owner of the property or another. The illegal force exhibited in robbery must be to prevent or overcome resistance to the illegal taking of the property. Robbery is always a felony.

e. Bribe giving—A person commits bribe giving when with intent to influence the future official action of a public servant, he gives, offers to give, or agrees to give a benefit to some other person. Bribe giving is a felony.

f. Bribe receiving—A person commits bribe receiving when with intent that the future official action of a public servant will be influenced, he asks for, receives, or agrees to receive a benefit. Bribe receiving is a felony.

g. Burglary—A person commits burglary in the third degree when he knowingly enters or remains unlawfully in a building and intends to commit a crime in such building. Burglary becomes second degree when he injures a nonparticipant in the burglary either during the burglary or during immediate flight therefrom. A person commits burglary in the first degree when the building is a private dwelling. All burglaries are felonies.

h. Simple assault—A person commits simple assault, a misdemeanor, when he intentionally causes a physical injury to another. If a person intentionally causes a serious physical injury to another, or intentionally causes any injury to another by means of a deadly weapon, or the assault is carried out through the efforts of more than one person, it is felonious assault, which is a Class C felony. A person, however, causing injury to another while in an act of self defense is not considered to have committed assault.

1. Which of the following statements concerning petit larceny is most accurate?

   (A) If the property stolen is worth $1000, it is not petit larceny.
   (B) If Don borrows Tom's motor scooter worth $800 without Tom's permission, it is petit larceny.
   (C) Petit larceny is a misdemeanor.
   (D) Petit larceny is a felony.

   Ⓐ Ⓑ Ⓒ Ⓓ

2. Don is in a bar and strikes up a conversation with several female patrons. Seeking to impress them, Don tells them he is a famous court officer assigned to the state supreme court. In reality, Don is an unemployed golf instructor. In this instance, Don . . .

   (A) has committed criminal impersonation, mainly because he intended to impress the female patrons.
   (B) has not committed criminal impersonation, mainly because he did not intend to have the female patrons submit to his authority.
   (C) has committed criminal impersonation, mainly because he did pretend to be a court officer.
   (D) has not committed criminal impersonation, mainly because he never showed any false identification.

   Ⓐ Ⓑ Ⓒ Ⓓ

3. Ray intentionally burns down a building he owns. The building is worth less than $50,000. Ray did not want to collect any insurance but rather he wanted to put up a new building. However, unknown to Ray, a homeless person was sleeping in the building and was injured as a result of the fire. Ray has committed . . .

   (A) third-degree arson.
   (B) second-degree arson.
   (C) first-degree arson.
   (D) no arson because Ray owned the building.

   Ⓐ Ⓑ Ⓒ Ⓓ

4. Frank is seated in his auto with his girlfriend waiting for a signal light to change. Suddenly Jay approaches the car and demands that Frank turn the auto over to him. Frank refuses but Jay motions to his pocket where what appears to be the outline of a pistol is easily seen by Frank. Jay tells Frank that if Frank does not do as Jay wants, he will shoot Frank's girlfriend. Frank and his girlfriend exit the auto and Jay drives off with the auto. Jay has committed . . .

   (A) robbery, mainly because he forcibly took the property of another.
   (B) larceny, mainly because no weapon was actually displayed.
   (C) assault, mainly because he threatened injury to another person.
   (D) some crime but not robbery, mainly because the owner of the property was not directly threatened.

   Ⓐ Ⓑ Ⓒ Ⓓ

5. Jack damages a car worth $15,000 by setting fire to it. Jack has committed . . .

   (A) first-degree arson.
   (B) second-degree arson.
   (C) third-degree arson.
   (D) no arson because no building was damaged.   Ⓐ Ⓑ Ⓒ Ⓓ

6. Waters is a public servant working as a state building inspector. One day after inspecting a building he finds that no violations are present and that everything has been built properly according to building code regulations. As he is about to leave, Mark, the building contractor, approaches Waters and hands him $50 and tells Waters that he appreciates the fine job Waters has done. Mark has committed . . .

   (A) bribe giving because money was offered.
   (B) bribe giving because Waters is a public servant.
   (C) bribe giving, but only a misdemeanor, because only $50 was offered.
   (D) possibly some crime but not bribe giving because the offering was not given to influence Waters' future official actions.   Ⓐ Ⓑ Ⓒ Ⓓ

7. Ray and Jay burglarize a factory. While inside the factory, Ray argues with Jay about the value of some tools in the factory. During the argument, Ray strikes Jay and causes an injury to Jay. Ray has committed . . .

   (A) third-degree burglary.
   (B) second-degree burglary.
   (C) first-degree burglary.
   (D) only assault.   Ⓐ Ⓑ Ⓒ Ⓓ

8. May strikes Tab over the head with a deadly weapon causing an injury to Tab. May has committed . . .

   (A) felonious assault.
   (B) either felonious or simple assault depending on whether a serious physical injury or merely a physical injury has resulted.
   (C) a misdemeanor.
   (D) simple assault but only if it can be shown that it was an act of self defense.   Ⓐ Ⓑ Ⓒ Ⓓ

9. Court Officer Mack observes Hank stealing a late model auto belonging to Judge Drake. The officer takes no action. The next day Mack sees Hank and tells him that he could have arrested him but chose not to and thinks that he should be rewarded by Hank for what he did yesterday. Hank agrees and offers the officer $500. Based on these circumstances, which of the following statements is most correct?

(A) Court Officer Mack should be charged with bribe receiving.
(B) Hank should be charged with bribe giving.
(C) They should both be charged with both bribe receiving and bribe giving.
(D) Court Officer Mack should not be charged with bribe receiving, and Hank should not be charged with bribe giving.   Ⓐ Ⓑ Ⓒ Ⓓ

10. Jay enters a sports arena building after legitimately purchasing a ticket to see a basketball game. After the game, Jay hides in the rest room awaiting an opportunity to steal some professional sports equipment located in the building. Jay has committed . . .

(A) third-degree burglary.
(B) second-degree burglary.
(C) first-degree burglary.
(D) no burglary because he legally entered the stadium.   Ⓐ Ⓑ Ⓒ Ⓓ

ANSWER KEY

1.	**C**	6.	**D**
2.	**B**	7.	**A**
3.	**C**	8.	**A**
4.	**A**	9.	**D**
5.	**C**	10.	**A**

ANSWERS EXPLAINED

1. **(C)** Petit larceny is a misdemeanor. Choice A is incorrect because stealing property worth $1000 or less is petit larceny. Choice B is incorrect because borrowing property means that there is no intent to keep another person's property permanently; therefore, it is not a petit larceny.

2. **(B)** To commit criminal impersonation, it is not necessary to show the identification of a public servant, but it is necessary to intend to have someone submit to your authority.

3. **(C)** Regardless of who owns the building, according to the definition provided, damaging a building by a fire is arson and becomes first-degree arson if a person is injured as a result of the arson.

4. **(A)** Forcibly taking the property of another includes using or threatening the use of force against the owner of the property or another, in this instance Frank's girlfriend. According to the information provided, there is no requirement for a weapon to be

shown for a robbery to occur. Also it cannot be an assault because no one suffered any injury. It is a robbery as suggested in Choice A.

5. **(C)** A building or a motor vehicle may be the object of an arson. To become second-degree arson, the damage to the motor vehicle must be more than $15,000. Remember the importance of numbers when answering legal definition questions.

6. **(D)** Although it is true that Waters is a public servant, bribe giving has not taken place because the benefit is not being offered to influence the future actions of the public servant. It is offered to recognize proper work done in the past. This may be some crime, as Choice D suggests, but it is not bribery.

7. **(A)** It is not a private dwelling so Choice C is incorrect. It is third-degree burglary. The fact that one participant injured another participant does not raise the degree of the burglary to second degree. For the crime to become second-degree burglary, the injury must be to a nonparticipant in the burglary.

8. **(A)** A person who intentionally causes any injury to another by means of a deadly weapon commits felonious assault. Thus Choices B and C are incorrect. In addition, a person causing injury to another while in an act of self defense is not considered to have committed assault. This eliminates Choice D, leaving Choice A as the answer.

9. **(D)** The intent in both bribe receiving and bribe giving is that the future actions of a public servant be influenced. In this situation, a benefit ($500) was being offered for the past improper action of the court officer. Possibly some other crime was committed but not bribe receiving nor bribe giving.

10. **(A)** This question underscores the importance of the word *OR*. Burglary can be committed both by entering or remaining unlawfully. In this instance, Jay remained unlawfully in a building with the intent to commit a crime in such building. There were no further aggravating circumstances so the crime is burglary in the third degree.

Clerical Ability Questions

5

- → **DISTINGUISHING BETWEEN SETS OF INFORMATION QUESTIONS**
- → **CODING QUESTIONS**

A large part of a court officer's job involves processing and reviewing forms. On a daily basis while reviewing such forms, court officers are required to examine closely and compare sets of names, letters, and numbers for accuracy by determining which are alike and which are not. In addition to distinguishing between pieces or sets of information, court officers are also called upon to read, combine, and manipulate written information, which sometimes appears in the form of tables. This type of question is sometimes referred to as coding questions.

To test this required task of court officers, which we refer to as clerical ability, examiners use two basic question types. One is called distinguishing between sets of information questions and the other is known as coding questions.

DISTINGUISHING BETWEEN SETS OF INFORMATION QUESTIONS

In the distinguishing between sets of information question, written material in the form of sets of numbers and words are usually presented in three columns. In the question, you are required to compare the information, including the punctuation, in the three sets and determine the similarities and/or dissimilarities among the sets. For example, you might be directed to

- **A.** select Choice A if sets 1 and 2 are exactly the same but set 3 is not the same,
- **B.** select Choice B if sets 1 and 3 are exactly the same but set 2 is not,
- **C.** select Choice C if sets 2 and 3 are exactly the same but set 1 is not, and
- **D.** select Choice D if all or none of the sets of information is exactly the same.

A variation in the way this question is presented requires the candidate to compare three sets of information to determine whether each is the same, or not the same, as a model set of information.

Example of a Distinguishing Between Sets of Information Question

EXAMPLE

Q1. Compare the information in the three sets of information presented here in three columns and search for any differences. If any differences exist consider that set different. Choose your answer in accordance with the following:

(A) Select Choice A if sets 1 and 2 are exactly the same but set 3 is different.
(B) Select Choice B if sets 1 and 3 are exactly the same but set 2 is different.
(C) Select Choice C if sets 2 and 3 are exactly the same but set 1 is different.
(D) Select Choice D if all or none of the sets of information is exactly the same.

Column 1	Column 2	Column 3
Rocco Roofing	Rocco Roofing	Rocco Roofing
Asbestos Removed	Asbestos Remove	Asbestoes Removed
1498 Hinsale Ave.	1498 Hinsale Ave.	1498 Hinsale Ave.
Harrison County	Harrison County	Harrison County
1-917-555-7678	1-917-555-7768	1-917-555-7768

Obviously there are countless variations in the way that this question type can be asked in terms of instructions for selecting your answer. However, certain guidelines should be followed as part of an overall strategy to deal with this type of clerical ability question.

Strategies for Distinguishing Between Sets of Information

1. **READ AND ACTUALLY MEMORIZE THE SPECIFIC INSTRUCTIONS FOR ANSWERING THE SPECIFIC QUESTION.** Otherwise, looking back and forth by returning and rereading instructions on how to select the answer for each of the clerical ability questions, which typically appear on such examinations, would waste a great deal of time.

2. **IF YOU FIND ANY DIFFERENCES AT ALL IN A SET OF INFORMATION WHEN COMPARED TO THE OTHER SETS OR THE SAMPLE SET, CONSIDER SUCH SET AS BEING DIFFERENT.** In other words, only one difference constitutes enough of a dissimilarity to qualify that set of information as being different. You do not have to continue to examine that set of information for additional differences. Move on and examine the next set of information.

3. **WHEN YOU FIND A DISSIMILARITY IN AN ITEM OF INFORMATION, MARK THE PART THAT YOU HAVE IDENTIFIED AS BEING DIFFERENT.** In this way, when you check your work, you can quickly establish why you identified that item of information as being different.

4. **IF THERE ARE SEVERAL ITEMS IN A SET, EXAMINE THE SAME ITEM IN EACH OF THE SETS OF INFORMATION.** For example, if a telephone number appears in each of the sets of information, examine the telephone number in each of the sets. Do not examine all the items in the set at once. Examine one item in one set 1 with the same item in another set.

STRATEGIES

Read and memorize specific instructions.
Recognize differences.
Mark the difference.
Examine the same item across sets.
Divide long series of numbers into segments and compare similar segments.
Softly whisper the manageable segment to yourself.
Look for similarities.
Look for differences.
Look for specific patterns.
Look for tricky letters and words.

5. **WHENEVER A LONG SERIES OF NUMBERS IS GIVEN, DIVIDE THAT ITEM OF INFORMA-TION INTO MANAGEABLE SEGMENTS AND COMPARE THAT SEGMENT OF THAT ITEM OF INFORMATION WITH SIMILAR SEGMENTS APPEARING IN THE SAME ITEMS FOUND IN OTHER SETS OF INFORMATION.**
   For example, if you were comparing

   (1) XYT9694ABT   (2) XYT9694ABT   (3) XYT9694ATB

   first examine the first three letters in each of the items,
   XYT   XYT   XYT

   then check the four numbers that follow next
   9694   9694   9694

   and finally compare the last three letters in each of the items
   ABT   ABT   ATB
   Note the difference in the last three letters of set 3.

6. **WHEN COMPARING MANAGEABLE SEGMENTS OF INFORMATION WITH CORRESPOND-ING SEGMENTS APPEARING IN OTHER SETS OF INFORMATION, SOFTLY WHISPER THE MANAGEABLE SEGMENT TO YOURSELF AS YOU COMPARE EACH OF THE SETS.** In this way, you not only rely solely on your sight but also on your sense of hearing to help you identify dissimilar information.

7. **LOOK FOR SIMILARITIES.** If set 1 is the same as set 2, and set 1 is the same as set 3, then there obviously is no need to examine sets 2 and 3 to see if they are the same. Under such circumstances, sets 2 and 3 must also be the same.

8. **LOOK FOR DIFFERENCES.** If set 1 is the same as set 2, and set 1 is different from set 3, then there obviously would be no need to examine sets 2 and 3 to see if they are different from each other. Under such circumstances, sets 2 and 3 must also be different from each other.

9. **HINTS REGARDING NUMBERS:** Be on the lookout for:
   a. Omission of repeated numbers

   (1) 96945500002   (2) 9694550002   (3) 96945500002

   Note that in set 2, one of the zeros was omitted.

   b. Addition of repeated numbers

   (1) 96945500002   (2) 969455500002   (3) 96945500002

   Note that in set 2, an additional five (5) was included.

   c. Number reversals

   (1) 96945500002   (2) 96945500002   (3) 96495500002

   Note that in set 3, the numbers nine (9) and four (4) were reversed.

10. HINTS REGARDING LETTERS:

a. All in the family—Be careful of letters that are different but look alike, such as m and n, s and z, p and q, and d and b. For example,

to<u>m</u>e/to<u>n</u>e   torre<u>s</u>/torre<u>z</u>   pe<u>q</u>uot/pe<u>p</u>uot   bo<u>d</u>kan/bo<u>b</u>kan

b. Letter switching—Examiners often engage in letter switching with the letters e and i. For example,

rec<u>ei</u>ving station   rec<u>ie</u>ving station

c. Two accepted spellings—Although there may be two acceptable ways of spelling the same word, remember that, in this type of question, you are seeking only to determine if the items in the set are the same. It is not important that both may be acceptable spellings of the same word. For example,

practi<u>c</u>e   practi<u>s</u>e

d. Silencers—Examiners realize that many candidates, when reading the words in the choices, actually sound out the words. Be careful of words that contain silent letters. They may sound the same when you say them, but they are not the same. For example,

kelly   kell<u>ey</u>

e. Doubles of the same letter—Be careful when examining words that contain double letters in the sample word but omit one of the double letters in the other words found in the choices. For example,

mississippi   missi<u>s</u>ippi

Answer to Example of a Distinguishing Between Sets of Information Question

Regarding question Q1, if you used the strategy for dealing with silencers, you should have discovered that the word *asbestoes* appearing in column 3, even though it may sound the same when you say it to yourself as the word *asbestos* appearing in the other two columns, actually contains an additional *e*. Therefore, the set of information in column 3 is different from the sets of information in columns 1 and 2. In addition, a circle should be put around the difference you have discovered (e.g., a s b e s t o(e)s).

Continuing to examine the sets of information in columns 1 and 2, you should have discovered number reversal with the telephone numbers,

1-917-555-7678   1-917-555-7768.

Thus, remembering the instructions, you should have selected Choice D because none of the sets of information is exactly the same.

CODING QUESTIONS

The second common variation of clerical ability questions is what we refer to as coding questions. The ability to answer coding questions is the ability that court officers need when they are called upon to read, combine, and manipulate written information, which sometimes appears in the form of tables.

There are an infinite number of types and variations of coding questions. To review each type of coding question would be impossible. However, coding questions do have some basic similarities. They usually have

- a reference table,
- specific instructions, and
- the actual questions that require you to use the table and follow the directions given.

Example of a Coding Question

In the following reference table, you will find a series of letters that have been associated with a series of numbers. For example, the letter R is associated with the number 1, and so forth.

				REFERENCE TABLE					
R	O	Y	G	B	I	V	X	W	Z
1	2	3	4	5	6	7	8	9	0

EXAMPLE

Directions: Select the choice that correctly spells the word identified in the question.

Q2. Using the reference table, which of the following choices most accurately spells VIGOR?

(A) 76241
(B) 76412
(C) 76421
(D) 47621

Strategies for Answering Coding Questions

1. **SCAN THE REFERENCE TABLE.** Get a quick idea of what is being coded. In our example, numbers are being associated with letters.

2. **SCAN THE DIRECTIONS.** What is expected of you? Try to get a sense of what the examiner wants you to do. This is so important and is actually the key to answering coding questions.

For example, will the questions ask you to determine whether numbers suggested in an answer choice accurately, according to the reference table provided, represent certain letters. In another variation you might be asked to identify, based on a reference table, whether sets of numbers accurately represent properly alphabetized letters. The variations are endless, and therefore the specific instructions should always be carefully read and clearly understood.

In our example, you should have determined that you are to select the choice that correctly spells the word identified in the stem of the question. In other words, you would be spelling a word by using individual numbers representing different letters

> **STRATEGIES**
> Scan the reference table.
> Scan the directions.
> Scan the question.
> Read the directions.
> Look again at the reference table.
> Answer the questions.

according to a previously given reference table. To spell the word, you had to use a reference table, which acts like a coding device. Hence, we see where the name for this type of question comes from. It is a coding question.

3. **SCAN THE QUESTION.** Take a quick look at the actual question and choices. Familiarize yourself with what you will be asked to do. In our example question, you were asked to select the choice that most accurately spelled the word *vigor*.

All the steps so far should be completed fairly quickly and are done so that you can begin to point your thinking in the right direction.

4. **READ THE DIRECTIONS CLOSELY.** Note that you do not return to the reference table yet. The directions are the key to answering this question. You must understand them clearly. You must know what it is that you are seeking to accomplish. In short, you must know how to use the reference table that has been provided. If you do not fully understand the directions, you will find yourself going back to the directions again and again. This will use up a lot of your time.

5. **TAKE ANOTHER LOOK AT THE REFERENCE TABLE.** The purpose of looking at the reference table again is to see if you understand how to use it based on the directions. Even though there is no need to memorize the reference table, you should be prepared to have it ready to answer the questions.

6. **ANSWER THE QUESTIONS.** From scanning the stem of the sample question and its choices, you should have been able to ascertain that the word to be represented by the numbers was *VIGOR*. Note that Choice D is the only choice that does not begin with the number 7. It begins with the number 4, which according to the reference table represents the letter G. Choice D can be quickly eliminated. Choice B is the only remaining choice that does not end with the number 1. It ends in 2, which represents the letter O. Choice B can be eliminated. The difference between the remaining Choices A and C lies in the third and fourth number of each choice. Examination of Choice A reveals that its third number is a 2, which represents the letter O and that is not the third letter of the word *VIGOR*. After you verify the remaining Choice, which is C, with the reference table, you should determine that Choice C is the answer.

It should be apparent that in doing Coding questions it is sometimes necessary to eliminate the inappropriate choices by comparing one choice against another. Then after you decide upon an answer, you should check or verify it using the reference table.

PRACTICE EXERCISE

10 Questions — Time Allowed 20 Minutes

Directions: For questions 1–3, compare the information appearing in each of the three columns and select your answer as follows:

 A. Select Choice A if all or none of the sets of information is exactly alike.
 B. Select Choice B if only the first and second sets of information are exactly alike.
 C. Select Choice C if only the second and third sets of information are exactly alike.
 D. Select Choice D if only the first and third sets of information are exactly alike.

Indicate your answer in the space provided after the information.

1.
Set 1	Set 2	Set 3
800049320000497	80004932000497	800049320000497
.32 cal. A9JQ342	.32 cal. A9JQ342	.32 cal. A9JQ342
Springfield, Il.	Springfield, Il.	Springfield, Il.
Judge Capresans	Judge Capresans	Judge Capresans
Special Sess#49821	Special Sess#49821	Special Sess#49821

1. Answer ____

2.
Set 1	Set 2	Set 3
Magistrate Schmidt	Magistrate Schmidt	Magistrate Schmidt
Indict. #B438627	Indict. #B438627	Indict. #B438627
c/o People vs. Ray	c/o People vs. Ray	c/o People vs. Ray
Pr clk#C627963B42	Pr clk#C627963B42	Pr. clk#C627963B42
Court Officer Ruiz	Court Officer Ruis	Court Officer Ruiz

2. Answer ____

3.
Set 1	Set 2	Set 3
St. Pol. ID#6Z296A4	St.Pol. ID#6Z296A4	St. Pol. ID#6Z296A4
Trper H. J. Clarke	Trper H. J. Clarke	Trper H. J. Clark
Capital St. Div.	Capital St. Div.	Capital St. Div.
Rochdale 11372	Rochdale 11372	Rochdale 11372
Gr. Larceny 2nd	Gr. Larceny 2nd	Gr. Larceny 2nd

3. Answer ____

Answer questions 4 and 5 based on the following instructions.

Directions: Compare the three sets of information that follow the sample set of information.

Select Choice A if only set 1 is exactly like the model set.
Select Choice B if only set 2 is exactly like the model set.
Select Choice C if only set 3 is exactly like the model set.
Select Choice D if none or more than one of the sets are exactly like the model set.

The order of the information is not relevant and should not be considered when making your selection. Indicate your answer in the space provided after the information.

---

4. Model set
   Steven Bisciotti
   ID#9104-30-3356
   147-25 Lois Lane
   1-713-555-9623
   Zip Code: 00695

Set 1	Set 2	Set 3
Steven Bisciotti	Zip Code: 00695	1-713-555-9623
147-25 Lois Lane	1-713-555-9623	147-25 Luis Lane
1-713-555-9623	147-25 Lois Lane	ID#9104-30-3356
Zip Code 00695	Steven Bisciotti	Zip Code: 00695
ID#9104-30-3356	ID#9104-30-3356	Steven Bisciotti

4. Answer _____

5. Model set
   Barry Decievedo
   Docket# 47265
   c/o P v. Miranga
   dob 01-05-72
   crim id#5205186

Set 1	Set 2	Set 3
Barry Deceivedo	dob 01-05-72	c/o P v. Miranga
Docket# 47265	c/o P v. Miranda	dob 01-05-72
c/o P v. Miranga	Barry Decievedo	crim id no 5205186
dob 01-05-72	crim id#5205186	Docket# 47265
crim id#5205186	Docket# 47265	Barry Decievedo

5. Answer _____

Answer questions 6–10 based on the following directions.

> **Directions:** In Reference Table 1, numbers have been associated with letters. The same has been done in Reference Table 2. First use Table 1 to determine the numbers represented by the model letters given in each of questions 6–10. Then use Table 2 to translate those numbers back to letters and select the choice that matches the model letters.

REFERENCE TABLE 1

Z	E	N	I	T	H		B	R	A	G
1	2	3	4	5	6		7	8	9	0

REFERENCE TABLE 2

C	A	P	T	U	R	E		D	O	G
1	2	3	4	5	6	7		8	9	0

6. Which of the following choices is most accurately associated with the model letters T-H-E?

   (A) TRA
   (B) URA
   (C) GOD
   (D) PAR

7. Which of the following choices is most accurately associated with the model letters N-A-G?

   (A) DOT
   (B) EUA
   (C) POG
   (D) RAC

8. Which of the following choices is most accurately associated with the model letters R-I-B?

   (A) PUE
   (B) TEC
   (C) ODE
   (D) DTE

9. Which of the following choices is most accurately associated with the model letters H-A-Z?

   (A) ROC
   (B) OCA
   (C) PET
   (D) RGO

10. Which of the following choices is most accurately associated with the model letters G-E-T?

(A) GUA
(B) GRC
(C) GAU
(D) GOU

ANSWER KEY

1.	**D**	6.	**B**
2.	**A**	7.	**C**
3.	**B**	8.	**D**
4.	**B**	9.	**A**
5.	**D**	10.	**C**

ANSWERS EXPLAINED

1. **(D)** The first and third sets are exactly alike. A zero is missing in the following number appearing in set 2, 80004932000497. Remember our advice to understand the instructions completely before answering any questions.

2. **(A)** None of the three sets of information is exactly the same. The name Ruis appears in set 2. And a period appears after Pr. in set 3.

3. **(B)** Only the first and second sets are exactly the same. The letter e has been omitted from the name Clark in the third set.

4. **(B)** Only set 2 is exactly like the model set. There is a colon missing after Code in set 1, and the name Luis is spelled differently in set 3. Note that the instructions for questions 4 and 5 specified that the order of the information is not relevant and should not be considered when making your selection.

5. **(D)** None of the sets is exactly like the sample set. In set 1 the name Deceivedo is spelled differently. In set 2 the name Miranda is spelled differently. In set 3 the abbreviation no is substituted for #, the number sign.

6. **(B)** The letters THE from Reference Table 1 represent the number 562, which when represented by the letters in Reference Table 2 are URA, as in Choice B.

7. **(C)** The letters NAG from Reference Table 1 represent the number 390, which when represented by the letters in Reference Table 2 are POG, as in Choice C.

8. **(D)** The letters RIB from Reference Table 1 represent the number 847, which when represented by the letters in Reference Table 2 are DTE, as in Choice D.

9. **(A)** The letters HAZ from Reference Table 1 represent the number 691, which when represented by the letters in Reference Table 2 are ROC, as in Choice A.

10. **(C)** The letters GET from Reference Table 1 represent the number 025, which when represented by the letters in Reference Table 2 are GAU, as in Choice C.

The Oral Interview

6

- → **THE IMPORTANCE OF TRUTHFULNESS**
- → **UNDERSTANDING THE PROCESS**
- → **ADVANCE PREPARATION—THE KEY TO SUCCESS**
- → **INTERVIEW DAY**
- → **A FINAL WORD**

There is a growing trend to use oral interviews as part of the process used in selecting court officers. Therefore, candidates who are seeking employment with a state or local court agency that uses the oral interview as a formal component of its entry level selection process must attach great importance to the information presented in this chapter. We believe the information in this chapter is of importance to you even if the agency you are interested in does not have a formal oral interview component, because the qualities measured in a formal oral interview are always evaluated. If they are not specifically evaluated in a structured oral interview, then they are evaluated as part of the probationary period. Said another way, court agencies know the profile of their ideal candidate. They know what they want their officers to be like and how they want them to behave. In some cases they use a formal process to determine if you fit that profile. In other cases, they make this determination in other, less direct ways. But they always make that determination before granting you full civil service tenure. Your job is to find out the kind of person they want you to be, and then, insofar as possible, to be that person.

THE IMPORTANCE OF TRUTHFULNESS

Sometimes candidates, in their desire to obtain employment as a court officer, will present false factual information about their background to investigators. This is a grievous and irreversible error. You must understand that the factual information about yourself that you supply will be checked. If a subsequent determination is made that you misrepresented your background in an attempt to deceive, you will be rejected. In many cases, the rejection is made even if the information you misrepresented is not cause for automatic disqualification. The bottom line is this: Be truthful and accurate about your background. You will not be judged solely on any one fact but upon the total of all the facts.

UNDERSTANDING THE PROCESS

Your chances of success on an oral interview are increased if you have a good working knowledge of the oral interview process. Please understand that we cannot describe for you the exact process as it exists in each jurisdiction. There are simply too many variations of the process. There are certain concepts, however, that are the same regardless of the exact process, and it is these concepts that you should understand.

Why Are Oral Interviews Needed?

The first thing you should understand is the reason oral interviews are needed. There are certain attitudes and abilities that a court officer must have that cannot be measured by a written examination. For example, during an oral interview, an evaluator can measure your communication abilities. In addition, your attitude, which means your approach toward law enforcement work, can also be identified during an oral interview. These attitudes and abilities are not as effectively measured on a written test.

Are Oral Interviews Part of All Selection Models?

No! Some jurisdictions do not include an oral component in their selection process. In most cases when they are not used, the reason is economics. Oral interviews are costly; therefore, they are not used in some jurisdictions, especially in larger ones where hundreds—even thousands—of prospective candidates would have to be interviewed. On the other hand, some jurisdictions rely heavily on oral interviews and not on written tests.

Who Are the Panelists on an Oral Board?

To begin with, most oral interviews are usually conducted by a panel of three people, although you might see anywhere from one to five panelists. In almost all cases you can expect to have someone on the board who has a background in the court administration field, and someone from the local personnel agency. Quite often an attempt is made to have community representation on the board, and in some instances the services of a psychologist are used. If you are furnished ahead of time with information about the composition of the board, you should display this knowledge during the interview, since it will probably help you to score better. For example, if you know the names of the board members, use them during the interview.

Are the Questions You Are Asked Standardized?

ILLEGAL QUESTIONS

**Marital status
Religious affiliation
Political beliefs**

Yes! There are mandatory questions that must be asked of each candidate. Think of the interview as being quite structured. Panelists do not ask different questions of candidates based on how the interview goes; they ask each candidate the same basic questions. These questions must, of course, be legal. For example, questions about marital status, religious affiliation, or political beliefs would be illegal. Questions must also be job related. For this reason, you should secure a copy of the job description (also known as a position description) for the court officer title in the jurisdiction where you are applying. This description is very often included as part of the job announcement (sometimes called the test announcement) that is published when the court officer test is scheduled. The job description is important to you with respect to the oral interview because it tells you those typical tasks of a court officer that are emphasized in the jurisdiction where you are applying. The persons responsible for formulating the questions asked during the oral interview almost always use the job description to develop interview questions. It is, therefore, relatively safe for you to assume that some of the questions during your oral interview will be related to those tasks that are included in the job description.

How Are Oral Interviews Scored?

Each board member is an evaluator and is trained in the scoring process. From the start of the interview until its conclusion you will probably see board members making notes as you speak. What they are doing is recording positive or negative comments about you in accordance with the guidelines that were established during their training. Immediately after each interview, the panelists independently arrive at a numerical rating within an agreed upon range, e.g., from one to ten, with, for example, one being the lowest rating and ten being the highest. Then, after each board member has arrived at a score for the interview, a group discussion is held to guard against the possibility that one of the members missed some very important negative or positive information. While consensus among the raters is not required, quite often the ratings have to fall within a certain range of each other.

Is the Scoring Process Subjective or Objective?

From the preceding discussion, it is now quite apparent to you that the scoring of oral interviews is a subjective process. Unlike a written multiple-choice examination, there is not just one correct answer to each question asked during an oral interview. Although evaluators are trained to be as objective as possible, to overlook the fact that the process is subjective is a big mistake. Therefore, you should not answer questions from your perspective of what the ideal court officer should be. Rather, your goal should be to convince the board members that you will be the kind of court officer they think is ideal. And you can rest assured that they are very traditional in their beliefs. They have a fixed idea of how a court officer should behave and also about how a court officer should present himself or herself. This includes appearance. This is why it is a good idea to find out in advance whatever you can about the composition of the board. This will be discussed in more detail later.

Would It Be Helpful to See a Sample Rating Form?

Yes. Reviewing a sample rating form allows a candidate to see at a glance the attitudes and abilities that are typically measured during an oral interview for the position of court officer. A sample oral interview rating form follows. Remember, however, when you review this form that it is only a sample of what a rating form typically looks like. It is meant to give you a general idea of what the form used in your jurisdiction might be.

COURT OFFICER CANDIDATE
ORAL INTERVIEW RATING FORM

1. **APPEARANCE AND BEARING**   SCORE _____
    Has appropriate general appearance,
    poise, confidence, level of enthusiasm.

2. **COMMUNICATION SKILLS**   SCORE _____
    Speaks with clarity of expression, good tone of
    voice; uses body language; has the ability to listen.

3. **JUDGMENT**   SCORE _____
    Statements are logical, reasonable, and
    supported by facts.

4. **UNDERSTANDING OF POSITION**   SCORE _____
    Shows a good grasp of the duties and
    responsibilities of a court officer.

5. **ATTITUDE**   SCORE _____
    Displays a service attitude and a desire to
    serve society.

6. **SELF-ASSURANCE**   SCORE _____
    Recognizes the essence of questions and
    responds with confidence.

7. **INTERPERSONAL SKILLS**   SCORE _____
    Indicates an understanding of the point of
    view of others; shows a level of tolerance
    for those with different values.

8. **PERSONAL INTEGRITY**   SCORE _____
    Answers show a high level of personal
    integrity.

9. **OBJECTIVITY**   SCORE _____
    Displays the ability to keep subjective
    feelings out of the decision-making process.

10. **EMPATHY**   SCORE _____
    Displays concern for those victimized by
    events beyond their control.

ADVANCE PREPARATION—THE KEY TO SUCCESS

In those court agencies that use a formal oral interview as part of their selection process, you will often be told by those conducting the examination that you cannot prepare for it. In some jurisdictions you will be told to simply appear at the appointed time and to be yourself. This is bad advice. The truth is that there are a number of steps you can take ahead of time that can greatly increase your chances of being selected. These steps follow:

1. **STUDY THE JOB ANNOUNCEMENT.** The court officer job announcement for your jurisdiction usually contains statements concerning the knowledge, skills, and abilities required for the job. It also contains examples of the typical tasks performed by court officers in that jurisdiction. The oral board members are very often given the job announcement as the source for the questions they develop for the interview. It, therefore, contains many clues to the type of questions you will be asked and the responses you should give. Study this announcement and anticipate questions from it, and frame tentative answers.

2. **REVIEW YOUR JOB APPLICATION.** You may very well be asked questions during your interview about information you included on your job application. You should be quite familiar with that information so that you will be able to answer promptly and coherently when asked about it. Also consider the possibility that you could be asked to elaborate on some portion of the job application at the interview. You should, therefore, be prepared to do so.

3. **LEARN ABOUT THE COURT AGENCY INVOLVED.** Make an effort to gain knowledge about the agency you want to join. Know the salary, fringe benefits, retirement policy, and promotional opportunities. Also try to gain an understanding of the current critical issues the agency is trying to deal with. As explained below, this information should be discussed during the interview if it becomes relevant to the interview, and it should.

4. **TAKE PART IN VOLUNTEER PROGRAMS.** Many court agencies use civilian volunteers to supplement the work of its paid members. Insofar as possible, you should participate in such a volunteer program.

5. **ENROLL IN A CRIMINAL JUSTICE PROGRAM.** If you have the opportunity, you should enroll in a criminal justice program at an accredited college or university. This would not only help you at the interview, but by doing so you would be taking the first step toward getting promoted after you are appointed.

6. **SPEAK TO SOMEONE WHO SUCCESSFULLY COMPLETED THE PROCESS.** Find relatives or friends who are members of the agency and discuss the process with them. Unless they are prohibited from doing so, and that is unlikely, they can give you a lot of insight and valuable information about the interview. Although the specific questions asked from test to test usually differ, the structure of the interview usually remains fixed. Find out the type of questions that are asked and then prepare yourself to answer them as discussed below.

7. **WORK ON YOUR METHOD OF ANSWERING QUESTIONS.** It is a mistake to believe that having the correct response to a question is the only thing that matters. Of course, accuracy is important, but your method of answering questions is also of great importance. Your answer must reflect organized thought. Where appropriate, introduce your answer, give your answer, and then conclude your answer. In other words, employ a format that includes an introduction, a body, and a conclusion. In addition, using the sample rating form as your guide:

   a. Present a good appearance.
   b. Show enthusiasm.
   c. Speak loudly enough to be heard, but remember to modulate your tone of voice. Candidates who speak in a monotone lose points.
   d. Use appropriate hand gestures to make a point. Don't sit with your arms crossed or with your hands folded in front of you.
   e. Maintain eye contact with the board members.
   f. Display empathy for crime victims and other unfortunate people, such as the homeless.
   g. Have tolerance for the lifestyles of others.

8. **PREPARE TO MAKE A GOOD PERSONAL APPEARANCE.** Your personal appearance at your interview is of critical importance. Board members expect you to dress in proper business attire. Any departure from that mode of dress can hurt your chances. Remember, appearance is the first thing noticed about you when you enter the interview room, and first impressions are extremely important. If you do not own appropriate business attire, borrow it, rent it, or buy it, and then be sure to wear it.

9. **LEARN SOME SUGGESTED RESPONSES.** Below we have listed some interview responses. Practice working these responses, rephrased in your own words, into the interview. Couple these responses with information gleaned from the job announcement, your job application, your volunteer efforts, your college experience, and your court officer contacts in answering general questions you might be asked. Then, ask a friend to help you and do some dry runs. With your friend acting as the interviewer, practice answering a series of general questions. To facilitate this, we have included below a list of general questions often asked during interviews of court officer candidates. We strongly urge that you videotape these dry run interviews, then listen to your answers, observe your body language, and strive to improve on the content of your answers as well as your method of delivery.

Suggested Responses

Remember, learn to use only those responses that apply to your situation.

1. I have a relative (or friend) who has been a court officer for quite a long time and over the years I have discussed court officer work a lot with him (or her). These discussions led me to admire the work being done by court officers and to want to be one myself.

2. My interest in court work led me to do volunteer work with a court agency, and/or to enroll in a college-level criminal justice program, and that experience served to increase my interest in becoming a court officer.

3. Court officers should be extremely honest and have ethical standards that are beyond reproach. I feel this way because of the fact that court officers are entrusted with a great deal of authority, which gives them an even greater responsibility to the society they serve.

4. Court officers should be mature individuals who possess a great deal of common sense. I feel this way because I realize that it is impossible to have a standard procedure for every situation encountered in court facilities.

5. If I am fortunate enough to earn the job of court officer, I will be guided by the rule that it is never appropriate to be anything except courteous and respectful to those whom I deal with in an official capacity.

6. All my life I have enjoyed helping people. It makes me feel good. And, working as a court officer is certainly a good way to help people.

7. Court officers should be able to communicate well. This certainly includes listening. A court officer who doesn't take the time to listen carefully to what others are telling him is not doing his job properly.

8. Court officers must be extremely tolerant of the viewpoints of others. They must understand that just because a person is different from them, that doesn't mean that person is not entitled to fair treatment.

9. If I were forced to choose, I would have to say that having high ethical standards is the most important characteristic a court officer should possess.

10. In my opinion, a court officer should use force only as an absolute last resort, when it is absolutely necessary to protect someone. And, even then, the amount of force used should be the minimum necessary to deal with the situation at hand.

11. The protection of life is clearly the most important responsibility of a court officer, and it takes precedence over all other matters.

12. I occasionally drink alcoholic beverages at social functions, but I would not, under any circumstances, use illegal drugs. Nor would I attend any function where illegal drugs were being used.

13. When a court officer is off duty, he or she must remain mindful of the fact that he or she is still a court officer. For this reason, a court officer's off-duty conduct must be beyond reproach.

14. If someone offered me money to violate my oath of office, I would follow the legal mandates of my agency. If the agency's policy was to make an immediate arrest, I would not hesitate to do so.

15. If I had knowledge that another court officer was involved in a criminal activity, such as taking a bribe, I would follow the policy of my department in that situation. If the policy was to make an immediate arrest, I would not hesitate to do so. In my opinion, it is doubly wrong for a court officer to commit a crime, and I simply would not tolerate it.

16. There is no question that I am interested in the salary, pension, and other fringe benefits that go with the job of a court officer, but my interest in being a court officer involves more than just these material considerations. I want a job that will give me a feeling that I am contributing to the betterment of society, and that, more than anything else, is why I want to be a court officer.

A List of General Questions

The following is a list of general questions that are often used during oral interviews for the court officer's job.

1. Tell us about your background and life experience.
2. Why do you want to be a court officer?
3. Are you prepared to be a court officer?
4. Why would you make a good court officer?
5. What is it about the court officer's job that appeals to you?
6. What kind of person should a court officer be?
7. What would you do if you were offered a bribe?
8. What would you do if a friend of yours committed a crime and you knew about it?
9. How do you feel about alcohol and drugs?
10. How should a court officer conduct himself while off duty?

INTERVIEW DAY

You have done everything possible to prepare yourself for your interview. You have learned a lot and it is now the time for all of your effort to pay off. It would be a tragedy if all of that work was wasted because of a foolish mistake you made on the day of your interview. Listed below are our recommendations for you to follow to prevent that from happening.

1. **DRESS APPROPRIATELY.** We already discussed the importance of appearance, but it is important enough to mention once again. Don't dress to be overly stylish. Dress the way the board members think you should be dressed; they want you to dress neatly and conservatively. Also, be sure to bring notes with you to use as last-minute reminders of your interview room strategy. Review them just before the interview.

2. **PLAN TO ARRIVE EARLY.** You absolutely must arrive on time for your interview. Arriving late, or even at the last minute, is a big mistake. Punctuality is the hallmark of a reliable court officer. Make sure you know the route you are going to take and how much travel time is involved in the trip to the interview site. If you are using public transportation, make sure you know the bus or train schedules for the day you are being interviewed. Remember that in other than peak rush hour times, there are fewer buses and trains running. If you are traveling by car, make sure you are aware of the traffic patterns involved at the time of your trip, and make sure you know ahead of time where you will park upon arrival. For all of the above reasons, we recommend that you make a practice run one week ahead of the day of your interview at the exact time you will be making the trip on interview day. All of this may seem excessive, but there have been many instances where people lost their opportunity because they did not take the necessary precautions against arriving late for their interview. If it turns out that you have to wait to have your interview, take that time to review your interview room strategy.

> **INTERVIEW STRATEGIES**
> Dress appropriately.
> Arrive early.
> Be professional.
> Know what to expect in the interview room.
> Listen.
> Be polite, professional, and confident.
> Thank the panelists.

3. **MAINTAIN A PROFESSIONAL DEMEANOR FROM START TO FINISH.** Be courteous and dignified from the time you walk into the interview site to the time you leave. Don't make the mistake of believing that you will be judged solely during the interview. Quite often the impression you make upon arrival and while you are waiting for your interview can help you or hurt you. Remember that first impressions are quite often lasting impressions.

4. **HOW TO START THE INTERVIEW.** When you are finally called into the interview room, here is what you can expect. You will see the board members, and they will probably be sitting down. Don't sit down until you are invited to do so. And be sure to thank whoever extends that invitation to you. You may or may not be introduced to the board members. If you are introduced, listen carefully to their names. If, during the interview, you refer to board members by their names you will enhance your chances. Expect to see a recording device on the desk, and note pads and other papers.

5. **LISTEN.** Although this may seem to be a basic recommendation, it is the most important recommendation for you to follow while you are being interviewed. Don't anticipate the question. Listen attentively and make sure you understand the question before you answer.

6. **BE GUIDED BY THE FOLLOWING SUGGESTIONS:**

   - Sit up straight.
   - Maintain eye contact with the board members.
   - Use simple but complete sentences while responding.
   - Maintain an appropriate volume of speech.
   - Inflect your voice when appropriate.
   - Use hand gestures appropriately to emphasize important points.
   - Use only words you can pronounce and fully understand.
   - Be confident but not cocky.
   - Don't display nervous mannerisms.
   - Don't fold your arms in front of you.
   - Don't make jokes.
   - Don't ever interrupt a board member.
   - Think for a moment before responding.
   - Don't be overly repetitious.

7. **THANK EVERYONE PRESENT AT THE END OF THE INTERVIEW.**

A FINAL WORD

This chapter has given you an overview of what to expect in a typical oral interview for the court officer position. We have explained concepts to follow to achieve your optimal score. But you must remain flexible on the day of the interview. Apply those concepts that are appropriate to your interview as it unfolds. Don't get flustered if the interview involves a format you are not expecting. Stay cool. Regardless of the format, if you come across as possessing the attributes we have discussed in this chapter, you should do well. Good Luck.

Test
YOURSELF

Practice Examination
One

When you took the Diagnostic Test, you took the first of five examinations we have provided for you. This is your first practice examination. Three more practice examinations follow.

Be sure to take each practice examination in one sitting. Each test contains 100 questions, which you must answer in 3½ hours. It is imperative that you become accustomed to concentrating for the length of time required to complete an entire examination. Be sure to review the test-taking strategy outlined in the Introduction before taking this practice examination, to use that strategy when doing the examination, and to record your answers on the following Answer Sheet.

ANSWER SHEET
Practice Exam One

Follow the instructions given in the test. Mark only your answers in the circles below.

WARNING: Be sure that the circle you fill is in the same row as the question you are answering. Use a No. 2 pencil (soft pencil).

BE SURE YOUR PENCIL MARKS ARE HEAVY AND BLACK.

ERASE COMPLETELY ANY ANSWER YOU WISH TO CHANGE.

DO NOT make stray pencil dots, dashes, or marks.

1. Ⓐ Ⓑ Ⓒ Ⓓ   26. Ⓐ Ⓑ Ⓒ Ⓓ   51. Ⓐ Ⓑ Ⓒ Ⓓ   76. Ⓐ Ⓑ Ⓒ Ⓓ
2. Ⓐ Ⓑ Ⓒ Ⓓ   27. Ⓐ Ⓑ Ⓒ Ⓓ   52. Ⓐ Ⓑ Ⓒ Ⓓ   77. Ⓐ Ⓑ Ⓒ Ⓓ
3. Ⓐ Ⓑ Ⓒ Ⓓ   28. Ⓐ Ⓑ Ⓒ Ⓓ   53. Ⓐ Ⓑ Ⓒ Ⓓ   78. Ⓐ Ⓑ Ⓒ Ⓓ
4. Ⓐ Ⓑ Ⓒ Ⓓ   29. Ⓐ Ⓑ Ⓒ Ⓓ   54. Ⓐ Ⓑ Ⓒ Ⓓ   79. Ⓐ Ⓑ Ⓒ Ⓓ
5. Ⓐ Ⓑ Ⓒ Ⓓ   30. Ⓐ Ⓑ Ⓒ Ⓓ   55. Ⓐ Ⓑ Ⓒ Ⓓ   80. Ⓐ Ⓑ Ⓒ Ⓓ
6. Ⓐ Ⓑ Ⓒ Ⓓ   31. Ⓐ Ⓑ Ⓒ Ⓓ   56. Ⓐ Ⓑ Ⓒ Ⓓ   81. Ⓐ Ⓑ Ⓒ Ⓓ
7. Ⓐ Ⓑ Ⓒ Ⓓ   32. Ⓐ Ⓑ Ⓒ Ⓓ   57. Ⓐ Ⓑ Ⓒ Ⓓ   82. Ⓐ Ⓑ Ⓒ Ⓓ
8. Ⓐ Ⓑ Ⓒ Ⓓ   33. Ⓐ Ⓑ Ⓒ Ⓓ   58. Ⓐ Ⓑ Ⓒ Ⓓ   83. Ⓐ Ⓑ Ⓒ Ⓓ
9. Ⓐ Ⓑ Ⓒ Ⓓ   34. Ⓐ Ⓑ Ⓒ Ⓓ   59. Ⓐ Ⓑ Ⓒ Ⓓ   84. Ⓐ Ⓑ Ⓒ Ⓓ
10. Ⓐ Ⓑ Ⓒ Ⓓ   35. Ⓐ Ⓑ Ⓒ Ⓓ   60. Ⓐ Ⓑ Ⓒ Ⓓ   85. Ⓐ Ⓑ Ⓒ Ⓓ
11. Ⓐ Ⓑ Ⓒ Ⓓ   36. Ⓐ Ⓑ Ⓒ Ⓓ   61. Ⓐ Ⓑ Ⓒ Ⓓ   86. Ⓐ Ⓑ Ⓒ Ⓓ
12. Ⓐ Ⓑ Ⓒ Ⓓ   37. Ⓐ Ⓑ Ⓒ Ⓓ   62. Ⓐ Ⓑ Ⓒ Ⓓ   87. Ⓐ Ⓑ Ⓒ Ⓓ
13. Ⓐ Ⓑ Ⓒ Ⓓ   38. Ⓐ Ⓑ Ⓒ Ⓓ   63. Ⓐ Ⓑ Ⓒ Ⓓ   88. Ⓐ Ⓑ Ⓒ Ⓓ
14. Ⓐ Ⓑ Ⓒ Ⓓ   39. Ⓐ Ⓑ Ⓒ Ⓓ   64. Ⓐ Ⓑ Ⓒ Ⓓ   89. Ⓐ Ⓑ Ⓒ Ⓓ
15. Ⓐ Ⓑ Ⓒ Ⓓ   40. Ⓐ Ⓑ Ⓒ Ⓓ   65. Ⓐ Ⓑ Ⓒ Ⓓ   90. Ⓐ Ⓑ Ⓒ Ⓓ
16. Ⓐ Ⓑ Ⓒ Ⓓ   41. Ⓐ Ⓑ Ⓒ Ⓓ   66. Ⓐ Ⓑ Ⓒ Ⓓ   91. Ⓐ Ⓑ Ⓒ Ⓓ
17. Ⓐ Ⓑ Ⓒ Ⓓ   42. Ⓐ Ⓑ Ⓒ Ⓓ   67. Ⓐ Ⓑ Ⓒ Ⓓ   92. Ⓐ Ⓑ Ⓒ Ⓓ
18. Ⓐ Ⓑ Ⓒ Ⓓ   43. Ⓐ Ⓑ Ⓒ Ⓓ   68. Ⓐ Ⓑ Ⓒ Ⓓ   93. Ⓐ Ⓑ Ⓒ Ⓓ
19. Ⓐ Ⓑ Ⓒ Ⓓ   44. Ⓐ Ⓑ Ⓒ Ⓓ   69. Ⓐ Ⓑ Ⓒ Ⓓ   94. Ⓐ Ⓑ Ⓒ Ⓓ
20. Ⓐ Ⓑ Ⓒ Ⓓ   45. Ⓐ Ⓑ Ⓒ Ⓓ   70. Ⓐ Ⓑ Ⓒ Ⓓ   95. Ⓐ Ⓑ Ⓒ Ⓓ
21. Ⓐ Ⓑ Ⓒ Ⓓ   46. Ⓐ Ⓑ Ⓒ Ⓓ   71. Ⓐ Ⓑ Ⓒ Ⓓ   96. Ⓐ Ⓑ Ⓒ Ⓓ
22. Ⓐ Ⓑ Ⓒ Ⓓ   47. Ⓐ Ⓑ Ⓒ Ⓓ   72. Ⓐ Ⓑ Ⓒ Ⓓ   97. Ⓐ Ⓑ Ⓒ Ⓓ
23. Ⓐ Ⓑ Ⓒ Ⓓ   48. Ⓐ Ⓑ Ⓒ Ⓓ   73. Ⓐ Ⓑ Ⓒ Ⓓ   98. Ⓐ Ⓑ Ⓒ Ⓓ
24. Ⓐ Ⓑ Ⓒ Ⓓ   49. Ⓐ Ⓑ Ⓒ Ⓓ   74. Ⓐ Ⓑ Ⓒ Ⓓ   99. Ⓐ Ⓑ Ⓒ Ⓓ
25. Ⓐ Ⓑ Ⓒ Ⓓ   50. Ⓐ Ⓑ Ⓒ Ⓓ   75. Ⓐ Ⓑ Ⓒ Ⓓ   100. Ⓐ Ⓑ Ⓒ Ⓓ

THE TEST

Time: 3 ½ hours
100 questions

Directions: Before answering questions 1–8 take five minutes to examine the following four wanted posters with the information that accompanies each poster. When answering the questions, do not refer back to the wanted posters.

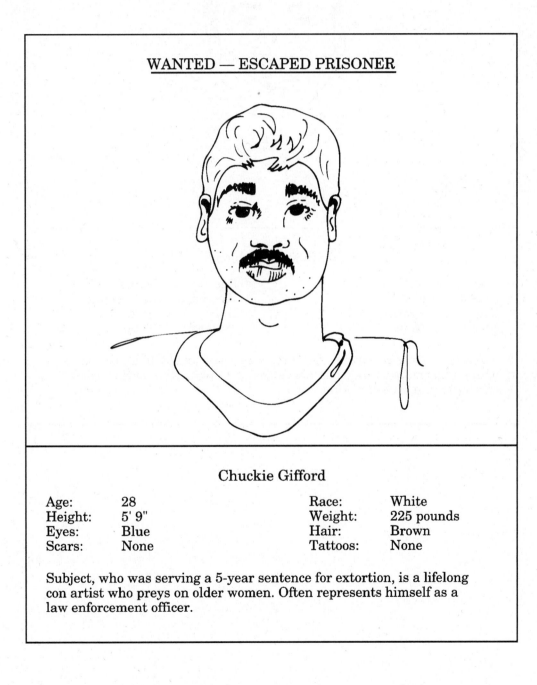

WANTED — ESCAPED PRISONER

Chuckie Gifford

Age:	28	Race:	White
Height:	5' 9"	Weight:	225 pounds
Eyes:	Blue	Hair:	Brown
Scars:	None	Tattoos:	None

Subject, who was serving a 5-year sentence for extortion, is a lifelong con artist who preys on older women. Often represents himself as a law enforcement officer.

WANTED — ESCAPED PRISONER

Samuel Youngblood

Age:	32	Race:	White
Height:	5' 9"	Weight:	200 pounds
Eyes:	Brown	Hair:	Bald
Scars:	None	Tattoos:	None

Subject, who was serving a life sentence for rape and child abuse, often wears a hairpiece as shown in above poster. Often loiters in the vicinity of schools in search of victims.

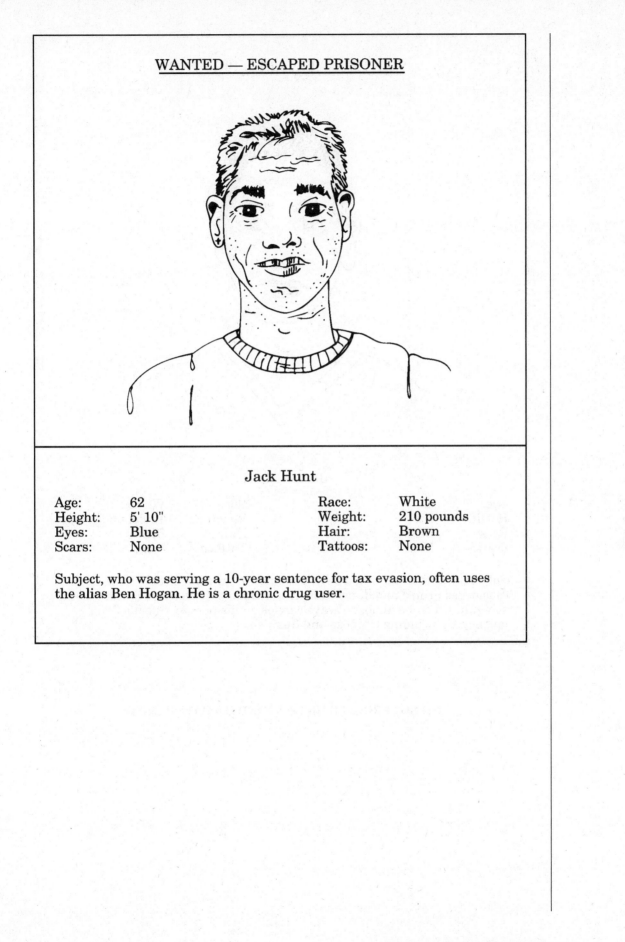

WANTED — ESCAPED PRISONER

Jack Hunt

Age:	62	Race:	White
Height:	5' 10"	Weight:	210 pounds
Eyes:	Blue	Hair:	Brown
Scars:	None	Tattoos:	None

Subject, who was serving a 10-year sentence for tax evasion, often uses the alias Ben Hogan. He is a chronic drug user.

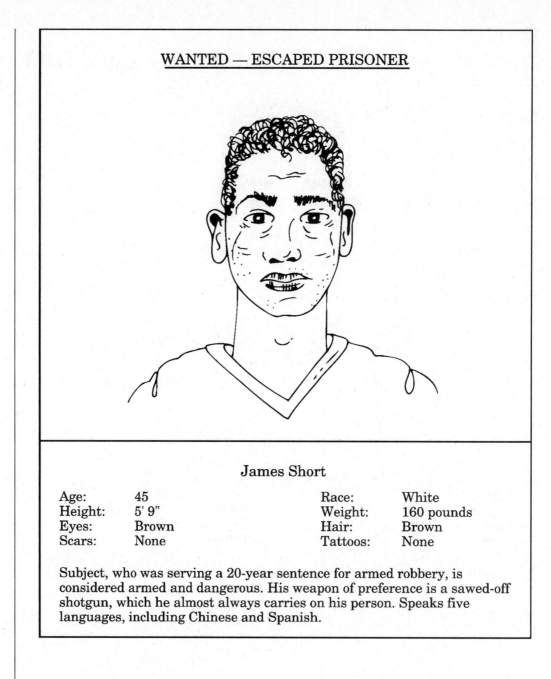

WANTED — ESCAPED PRISONER

James Short

Age:	45	Race:	White
Height:	5' 9"	Weight:	160 pounds
Eyes:	Brown	Hair:	Brown
Scars:	None	Tattoos:	None

Subject, who was serving a 20-year sentence for armed robbery, is considered armed and dangerous. His weapon of preference is a sawed-off shotgun, which he almost always carries on his person. Speaks five languages, including Chinese and Spanish.

DO NOT PROCEED UNTIL 5 MINUTES HAVE PASSED

TURN TO NEXT PAGE

1. Which of the escaped inmates illustrated in the following posters often loiters in the vicinity of schools?

    (A)

    (B)

    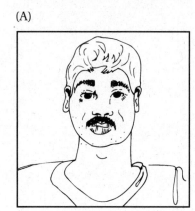 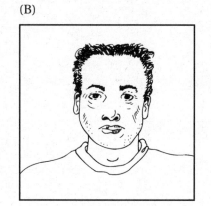

    (C)

    (D)

2. Which of the escaped inmates illustrated in the following posters often carries a sawed-off shotgun?

(A)

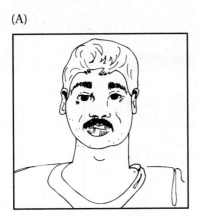

(B)

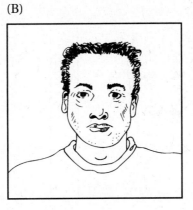

(C)

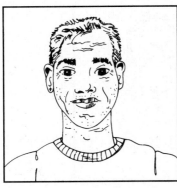

(D)

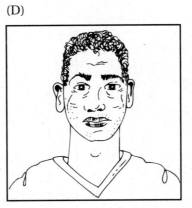

3. Which of the escaped inmates illustrated in the following posters uses the alias Ben Hogan?

(A)

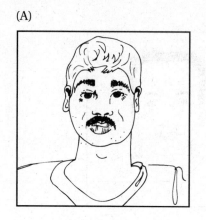

(B)

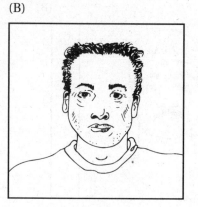

(C)

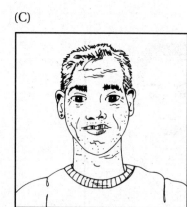

(D)

4. Which of the escaped inmates illustrated in the following posters often wears a hairpiece?

(A)

(B)

(C)

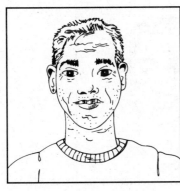

(D)

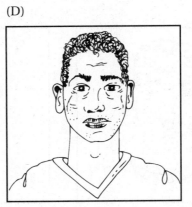

5. Which of the escaped inmates illustrated in the following posters was serving a life sentence when he escaped?

(A)

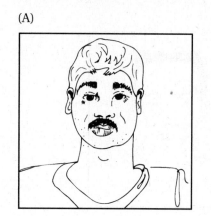

(B)

(C)

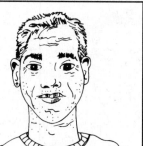

(D)

6.

The subject illustrated in this wanted poster . . .

(A) often poses as a law enforcement officer.
(B) is considered armed and dangerous.
(C) is a tax evader.
(D) is a murderer.

7.

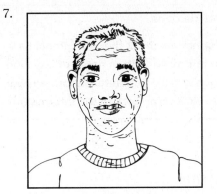

The subject illustrated in this wanted poster . . .

(A) often poses as a law enforcement officer.
(B) is considered armed and dangerous.
(C) is a chronic drug user.
(D) is a murderer.

8.

The subject illustrated in this wanted poster . . .

(A) often poses as a law enforcement officer.
(B) is not considered armed and dangerous.
(C) is a chronic drug user.
(D) speaks five languages.

> **Answer questions 9–15 based on the following instructions.**
>
> **Directions:** Study for 5 minutes the following information about the State Penal Law. Try to remember as many details as possible. Do not make written notes of any kind during this 5-minute period. After the completion of the 5-minute period, answer questions 9–15. When answering the questions, do NOT refer back to the information.

MEMORY INFORMATION
5-MINUTE TIME LIMIT

Court Officers very often must make speedy referrals to provisions of the State Penal Law. The most common sections of this law that have an impact on the court officer's job follow:

	Penal Law Article and/or Section	Subject Matter or Offense	Classification
a.	Article 10	Definitions	N/A
b.	Article 35	Defense of justification	N/A
c.	Section 120.05	Assault in second degree	Class D felony
d.	Section 120.11	Assault on peace officer	Class B felony
e.	Section 125.27	Murder in the first degree	Class A felony
f.	Article 130	Sex offenses	Various
g.	Section 140.10	Criminal trespass	Misdemeanor
h.	Section 155.25	Petit larceny	Misdemeanor
i.	Article 158	Welfare fraud	Various
j.	Section 200.03	Bribery in the second degree	Class C felony
k.	Section 210.15	Perjury in the first degree	Class D felony
l.	Section 215.00	Bribing a witness	Class D felony
m.	Section 215.40	Tampering with evidence	Class E felony
n.	Section 215.51	Criminal contempt	Class E felony

DO NOT PROCEED UNTIL 5 MINUTES HAVE PASSED.

TURN TO THE NEXT PAGE

9. Criminal trespass is a . . .

(A) Class E felony.
(B) misdemeanor.
(C) Class C felony.
(D) Class A felony.

10. Information about sex offenses can be found in . . .

(A) Article 10.
(B) Article 130.
(C) Article 35.
(D) Article 158.

11. Murder in the first degree is a . . .

(A) misdemeanor.
(B) Class C felony.
(C) Class B felony.
(D) Class A felony.

12. Criminal contempt is a . . .

(A) misdemeanor.
(B) Class E felony.
(C) Class B felony.
(D) Class A felony.

13. Information about welfare fraud can be found in . . .

(A) Article 10.
(B) Article 130.
(C) Article 35.
(D) Article 158.

14. Perjury in the first degree is a . . .

(A) misdemeanor.
(B) Class E felony.
(C) Class D felony.
(D) Class B felony.

15. The information contained in the listing that you studied comes from . . .

(A) various laws.
(B) the State Penal Law.
(C) the State Criminal Procedure Law.
(D) the State Listing of Criminal Offenses.

Most crimes fall into one of two categories, felonies or misdemeanors. Felonies are more serious than misdemeanors. They are considered serious enough to deserve severe punishment or even death. At one time, the distinction between felonies and misdemeanors was based on the fact that all felonies were capital offenses punishable by death. The present-day distinction between a felony and misdemeanor in the United States is usually based on the length of the sentence imposed. Felony convictions require a sentence of more than 1 year in prison. Misdemeanors, however, account for a great majority of arrests made. There are almost three million misdemeanor arrests made each year. A misdemeanor conviction involves a sentence of 1 year or less. Convictions for either felonies or misdemeanors can result in the assessment of a fine.

16.   Misdemeanors are . . .

(A) less serious than felonies.
(B) punishable by more than one year in prison.
(C) sometimes punishable by death.
(D) capital offenses.

17.   In the United States, the difference between felonies and misdemeanors is usually based . . .

(A) on the length of the sentence imposed.
(B) on the location where confinement takes place.
(C) on the intent of the criminal.
(D) on the amount of fine that can be imposed.

18.   Which of the following is the most accurate statement concerning fines?

(A) They may be imposed only for misdemeanor convictions.
(B) They may be imposed only for felony convictions.
(C) They may be imposed for both felony and misdemeanor convictions.
(D) They may not be imposed for felony convictions.

Directions: Answer questions 19–21 solely on the basis of the information contained in the following passage.

The criminal justice system is composed of four separate components—police, prosecutor, courts, and corrections. Each of these four components has its own specific tasks. A major problem for the overall system is that each of the four components acts independently of one another. This is so despite the fact that what happens in one component definitely has an impact on what happens in the other three. For example, an increase in arrest activity by the police always results in an increased workload for the rest of the system. And, if corrections does not do its job properly, the police become overloaded with repeat offenders. The problem is made worse by the fact that the four components of the system compete with one another for funding. By far, the component that receives the most funding is the police, and the most underfunded component is corrections. This is a difficult fact to understand because corrections has the most complex problems. Clearly, however, the most powerful component is the courts. The police, the prosecutor, and corrections are all responsible to and supervised by the courts.

19. The component of the criminal justice system that receives the most money to operate is the . . .

    (A) police.
    (B) prosecutors.
    (C) courts.
    (D) corrections.

20. The courts . . .

    (A) have the most complex problems.
    (B) receive less money than the other three components.
    (C) exercise authority over the other three components.
    (D) have fewer problems than the other three components.

21. A major problem of the criminal justice system is that . . .

    (A) there are insufficient funds available.
    (B) there are many complex problems to solve.
    (C) the amount of crime is increasing drastically.
    (D) there is a lack of coordinated action.

When a defendant in a criminal action has been found guilty, the courts have a number of sentencing options. The most commonly used sentencing option is probation. Over half of convicted felons are given a sentence of probation. Probation is defined as a sentence not involving confinement that imposes certain conditions on the convicted criminal. When a person is sentenced to probation, the courts retain the authority to resentence the offender if these certain conditions are violated. Probation has many advantages for offenders. It allows them to work, keep their families together, and avoid the stigma of going to prison. It must be remembered, however, that people on probation are not completely free to do as they choose. They remain under the supervision of a probation officer for their entire probation period. Even though probation has many critics and people on probation often create serious crime problems, it is indispensable. Society could not afford the financial cost of sending all convicted persons to prison.

22. Probation is . . .

   (A) the most frequently used sentencing option.
   (B) not an effective way to rehabilitate repeat offenders.
   (C) very expensive.
   (D) unfair to convicted felons.

23. People on probation . . .

   (A) must spend some time in confinement.
   (B) find it difficult to keep their families together.
   (C) sometimes create serious crime problems.
   (D) are completely free to do as they choose.

24. Probation is a necessary sentencing option because it . . .

   (A) allows offenders to work.
   (B) reduces the level of crime.
   (C) usually rehabilitates the offender.
   (D) is not as expensive as incarceration.

Directions: Answer questions 25–27 based solely on the following passage.

In order to carry a firearm, a court officer must have attained the age of 21 years or older. The State Court System's policy is to prohibit an officer from carrying firearms when it is determined that:

   a. The officer has engaged in misconduct involving the use or threatened use of a firearm;

   b. The officer has failed to attain a minimum score of at least 80% on the timed shooting drill administered annually by the State Police;

   c. The court officer has lost a firearm under circumstances that indicated carelessness;

   d. The officer's mental or emotional condition is such that possession of a firearm represents a clear threat to the safety of the officer or any other person(s);

   e. The officer has been arrested for and convicted of the commission of a crime;

   f. The officer is found to be intoxicated while on duty or when armed while off duty.

25. A court officer who has been arrested . . .

   (A) automatically loses the right to carry firearms.
   (B) will lose the right to carry firearms only if the arrest was for a crime of violence.
   (C) will lose the right to carry firearms only if the arrest results in a conviction.
   (D) is in no danger of losing the right to carry firearms.

26. When it has been established that a court officer has engaged in misconduct, the officer's right to carry firearms . . .

   (A) is automatically revoked.
   (B) will be revoked only if the misconduct involved the use of a firearm.
   (C) will only be revoked if the misconduct involved the use or threatened use of a firearm.
   (D) is not in any danger of losing the right to carry a firearm.

27. Which of the following will always result in the revocation of an officer's right to carry a firearm?

   (A) The officer loses a firearm.
   (B) The officer scores 78% on the State Police annual timed shooting drill.
   (C) The officer has a nervous condition.
   (D) The officer is found to be intoxicated.

28. Court Officer Smith is told to notify his supervisor immediately when he observes a dangerous condition. For which one of the following should Officer Smith notify his supervisor immediately?

(A) A motorist is stalled in the street outside of the courtroom and is causing a traffic jam.
(B) A parking sign in the courtroom parking lot has been painted over.
(C) A car alarm in the courtroom parking lot has gone off.
(D) Smoke is coming out of the first floor window of an abandoned building adjoining the court building.

29. When searching visitors to a court facility, court officers must seize legally carried items that could very easily be used as a dangerous weapon. Which one of the following objects could very easily be used as a dangerous weapon?

(A) a newspaper
(B) a nail file
(C) lipstick
(D) tissues

30. Court officers often must regulate the flow of vehicle and pedestrian traffic around a court facility. A court officer's first action at the scene of a vehicle accident is to determine if anyone requires medical assistance. The main reason for this rule is that . . .

(A) ambulances often take a long time to arrive at the scene.
(B) the protection of life is a court officer's first and most important responsibility.
(C) a court officer receives special training in the administration of first aid.
(D) the prevention of accidents is a very important responsibility of a court officer.

31. When questioning many witnesses to the same occurrence, a court officer must always separate them and question them individually. The most important reason for this rule is that

(A) many witnesses tend to be improperly influenced by what they hear other witnesses say.
(B) one of the witnesses may be the guilty party.
(C) it guarantees that each witness will tell the truth.
(D) it makes the court officer look more professional.

32. When questioning witnesses to an incident, a court officer should not ask leading questions. Questions should be framed in a manner that does not suggest the answers to them. Which of the following is the most appropriate question to ask a witness who is giving a description of a suspect?

(A) Was he about 6 feet tall?
(B) Did he walk with a limp?
(C) What was his approximate weight?
(D) Did he have blue eyes?

33. While on patrol outside the court building, an armed court officer observes what he believes to be a robbery in progress taking place in the court parking lot. It seems to the court officer that there is only one robber. The officer's first action should be to . . .

(A) draw his revolver and confront the robber.
(B) make an immediate call for assistance.
(C) take cover and wait for the robber to exit the parking lot.
(D) fire a warning shot.

34. Report writing is an essential part of the job of a court officer. The most important characteristic of a good report is . . .

(A) brevity.
(B) accuracy.
(C) subjectivity.
(D) good grammar.

35. Court officers are required to maintain a neat and clean appearance. The primary justification for this rule is that

(A) a neat and clean appearance tends to win the respect and cooperation of the public.
(B) officers can be disciplined for presenting an unkempt appearance.
(C) the directions of sloppy officers are never followed.
(D) court officers are paid to be neat and clean.

Directions: Answer question 36 based solely on the following rule.

Unless such action interferes with their prescribed duties, court officers in uniform must stand at attention and render a hand salute before speaking to a supervisor or when spoken to by a supervisor.

36. Court officers . . .

(A) must always salute their supervisors before talking to them.
(B) must always stand at attention when speaking with their supervisors.
(C) who are not in uniform are not required to salute their supervisors.
(D) who are in uniform must always salute their supervisors before speaking with them.

Court officers shall not behave with disrespect toward a supervising officer.

37. For a court officer to behave in a disrespectful way when dealing with a supervisor . . .

   (A) is never permissible.
   (B) is sometimes allowed.
   (C) is always tolerated.
   (D) may or may not be permissible.

Court officers are responsible for the proper care and maintenance as well as the serviceable condition of agency equipment and/or property issued for their use. If at any time, equipment is properly passed from one officer to another, the last officer to receive the equipment shall be responsible for it. Whenever file cabinets are made available to court officers, all official documents and records must be placed therein overnight. The last officer leaving an office is responsible for the turning off of all nonessential lights and electrical appliances. Windows must be closed overnight in all offices that are not used at night.

38. Court officers . . .

   (A) can be held responsible for the maintenance of all agency equipment.
   (B) are responsible for the serviceable condition of all agency property.
   (C) must take care of agency equipment that has been issued for their use.
   (D) are not responsible for the maintenance of any agency equipment.

39. When equipment is properly passed from one officer to another . . .

   (A) responsibility for that equipment belongs to everyone who used it.
   (B) the first officer who used it is responsible for it.
   (C) the last officer who had the equipment is responsible for it.
   (D) no officer can be held responsible for it.

40. The last officer leaving an office . . .

   (A) must always turn off all the lights.
   (B) must always turn off all electrical devices.
   (C) does not have to always close the windows.
   (D) must always close all windows.

Directions: Answer question 41 based solely on the following rule.

Court officers shall not carry packages into or from any court facility without the prior authorization of the Court Clerk or Deputy Court Clerk.

41. Court officers . . .

(A) must receive permission from the Court Clerk to take packages out of a court facility.
(B) must get permission ahead of time to carry a package into a court facility.
(C) can sometimes carry packages into or out of a court facility without anyone's permission.
(D) can never carry packages into or out of a court facility.

Directions: Answer question 42 based solely on the following rule.

Disciplinary charges may be brought against any court officer who fails to pay his or her just debts.

42. A court officer . . .

(A) may or may not be disciplined for failing to pay his or her debts.
(B) must pay anyone who claims the officer owes a debt.
(C) does not have to pay any of his or her debts.
(D) must be punished for nonpayment of any debts claimed against him or her.

Directions: Answer question 43 based solely on the following rule.

Court officers shall not accept an award or gift for departmental services without the written consent of the Court Administrator.

43. Gifts given to court officers . . .

(A) must sometimes be refused.
(B) can be accepted only with written permission of the Court Administrator.
(C) are all subject to this rule.
(D) are treated differently than awards.

Directions: Answer questions 44 and 45 based solely on the following rule.

A complaint is an allegation of an improper or unlawful act committed by a court officer provided that the act relates to the business of the court system that employs the officer. A complaint shall be thoroughly investigated by the supervisor to whom it is referred, and if the condition complained of actually exists, it shall be corrected and steps shall be taken to prevent its recurrence.

44. Complaints . . .

    (A) must involve an unlawful act.
    (B) must relate to the business of a court system.
    (C) must be promptly made.
    (D) must be made in person.

45. Complaints . . .

    (A) must be investigated by a supervisor.
    (B) cannot be made anonymously.
    (C) must all result in some form of corrective action.
    (D) do not all need to be investigated.

Directions: Answer question 46 based solely on the following rule.

Court officers shall not intercede with any court for the acquittal of or change of sentence for any defendant.

46. Court officers . . .

    (A) need permission to intercede with a court concerning the acquittal of a defendant.
    (B) are prohibited from asking a court to modify the sentence of a defendant.
    (C) can sometimes petition the courts to have a defendant's sentenced reduced.
    (D) can sometimes petition the courts to have a defendant's sentenced increased.

Directions: Answer question 47 based solely on the following information.

Most court officers are peace officers. A peace officer does not usually make arrests, but they do have special legal authority to do so. When they are working in a courtroom, court officers who are peace officers may make an arrest when they have reasonable grounds to believe that a crime has been committed and that the person being arrested committed that crime. This means that peace officers are legally entitled to make mistakes when they arrest someone provided that their mistakes are reasonable. When court officers make arrests, it is possible that they will be called upon to testify about that arrest during a criminal trial.

47. Correction officers . . .

    (A) are all peace officers.
    (B) make numerous arrests.
    (C) are legally required to be certain when they make arrests.
    (D) may sometimes have to testify in criminal court.

Directions: Answer question 48 based solely on the following information.

There is perhaps no unresolved problem in the field of criminal justice as complex as determining the ability of the death penalty to deter the commission of violent crimes.

48. The use of the death penalty . . .

    (A) clearly prevents the commission of violent crimes.
    (B) is clearly favored by the majority of law-abiding people.
    (C) may or may not prevent the commission of violent crimes.
    (D) definitely does not prevent the commission of violent crimes.

The typical chronic criminal is neither a hero nor a villain. He is a person who has lost in the game of life. He is an unsuccessful person who has failed in one venture after another. And, he is usually no better at committing crimes than he is at anything else. However, when a chronic criminal is arrested and stands trial, it is unconstitutional for the prosecutor to use evidence of the defendant's prior criminal record unless the defense attorney attempts to establish the good character of his client.

49. The typical chronic criminal . . .

   (A) is like everyone else.
   (B) usually fails in his criminal endeavors.
   (C) usually avoids detection.
   (D) is very often successful.

50. When a chronic criminal stands trial, it is . . .

   (A) never permissible for prosecutors to introduce evidence of his or her prior criminal record.
   (B) always permissible for prosecutors to introduce evidence of his or her prior criminal record.
   (C) sometimes permissible for prosecutors to introduce evidence of his or her prior criminal record.
   (D) up to the judge to determine whether prosecutors can introduce evidence of his or her prior criminal record.

> **Directions:** Answer questions 51–65 solely on the basis of the following legal definitions. Do not base your answers on any other knowledge of the law you may have. You may refer to the definitions when answering the questions.

a. An offense is either a felony, a misdemeanor, or a violation.

b. A violation is an offense for which a person upon conviction shall receive a sentence of imprisonment of no more than 15 days.

c. A misdemeanor is an offense for which a person upon conviction shall receive a sentence of imprisonment of no less than 16 days and up to and including 1 year.

d. A felony is an offense for which a person upon conviction shall receive a sentence of imprisonment of more than 1 year. Felonies are classified as A, B, C, D, or E felonies. The most serious felonies, which receive the most severe penalties, are A felonies, followed by B felonies, and so on.

e. A crime is either a misdemeanor or a felony.

f. A deadly weapon is any loaded gun, capable of firing a shot that can cause death or other serious physical injury; or a billy, blackjack, metal knuckles, dagger, switchblade knife, metal knuckle knife, or gravity knife or pilum ballistic knife.

g. A dangerous instrument is any article or substance (including a vehicle) that depending on how it is used, attempted to be used, or threatened to be used, is capable of causing death or serious physical injury.

h. A physical injury is an injury that causes substantial pain or physical impairment.
   A serious physical injury is a physical injury that causes a substantial risk of death, a protracted injury or disfigurement, or an impairment of an organ.

i. Hindering prosecution in the second degree is a misdemeanor. A person is guilty of hindering prosecution in the second degree when such person renders criminal assistance to another knowing that such other person has committed a misdemeanor.
   Hindering prosecution in the first degree is a felony. A person is guilty of hindering prosecution in the first degree when such person renders criminal assistance to another knowing that such other person has committed a felony. A person renders criminal assistance when such person

i. harbors or conceals a criminal perpetrator or

ii. warns such perpetrator of discovery or apprehension

51. Which of the following felonies is most likely to have the least severe penalty?

   (A) A felony
   (B) B felony
   (C) C felony
   (D) D felony

52. An offense is . . .

(A) always a felony.

(B) always a misdemeanor.

(C) always a violation.

(D) either a felony, a misdemeanor, or a violation.

53. If a certain criminal act is a misdemeanor, then the act . . .

(A) is more serious than a felony and will receive a greater penalty than a felony.

(B) will receive a lesser punishment than a violation.

(C) is always a crime.

(D) will be punished according to the age of the defendant and the defendant's past criminal record.

54. Concerning felonies, misdemeanors, and violations, it would be most accurate to state that . . .

(A) they are all crimes.

(B) they are all offenses.

(C) they all have a maximum punishment stated in their respective definitions.

(D) they all have a minimum punishment stated in their respective definitions.

55. Which of the following is most likely to be considered a deadly weapon?

(A) every loaded gun

(B) any gun that is operable

(C) a razor

(D) a dagger

56. Don attempts to run over Pat with his motor vehicle. In this instance, Don's motor vehicle is . . .

(A) a deadly weapon.

(B) a dangerous instrument.

(C) both a deadly weapon and dangerous instrument.

(D) neither a deadly weapon nor a dangerous instrument.

57. If Frank kicks Pat and causes Pat to experience substantial pain, Frank has inflicted upon Pat . . .

(A) a serious physical injury.

(B) a physical injury.

(C) a serious physical injury if Pat receives any medical attention.

(D) a physical injury but only if it can be shown that Pat also experienced some type of physical impairment.

58. Tom strikes Pat over the head with an unloaded gun. Tom has used . . .

(A) a deadly weapon.
(B) a dangerous instrument.
(C) no weapon.
(D) a deadly weapon, but only if the gun is operable.

59. May recently was released from jail after serving a sentence of 13 days. In such an instance, it would be most likely that May committed some type of . . .

(A) felony.
(B) misdemeanor.
(C) crime.
(D) offense.

60. Evaluate the following statements.

1. The only way an article or substance can become a dangerous instrument is if the article or substance causes a serious physical injury.

2. Every serious physical injury is also considered a physical injury.

Which of the following statements is most accurate concerning these statements?

(A) Only statement 1 is correct.
(B) Only statement 2 is correct.
(C) Both statements 1 and 2 are correct.
(D) Neither statement 1 nor 2 is correct.

61. Evaluate the following statements.

1. Every felony is a crime.

2. Every crime is a felony.

Which of the following statements is most accurate concerning these statements?

(A) Only statement 1 is correct.
(B) Only statement 2 is correct.
(C) Both statements 1 and 2 are correct.
(D) Neither statement 1 nor 2 is correct.

62. A person who is convicted of which of the following is most likely to receive the most severe penalty?

(A) Class D felony
(B) misdemeanor
(C) violation
(D) Class E felony

63. Court Officer Collars is on duty in the courtroom of Judge Balancer. Officer Collars is leading into the courtroom four co-defendants who have been arrested for stealing an automobile. One of the defendants was found to be carrying a deadly weapon. Which of the following is most likely to be the defendant who was found to be carrying a deadly weapon?

    (A) Moss who was carrying an icepick in his coat pocket
    (B) Iris who had an unloaded .22 caliber derringer pistol strapped to her thigh
    (C) Violet who had a pair of metal knuckles secreted in the purse she was carrying
    (D) Oaks who was carrying a metal hunting knife in his belt

64. Court Officer Rivers is directed by Judge Omni to arrest Tom for contempt of court, which is a misdemeanor. Tom dashes out of the courthouse to avoid being arrested. Outside the courthouse is Mick who is just pulling away from the courthouse after paying a large fine for speeding. Tom tells Mick he is late for an appointment and asks for a ride in Mick's van. Mick drives away with Tom seated in the van, thereby prohibiting Officer Rivers from effecting the arrest. In such an instance, . . .

    (A) Mick should be charged with a misdemeanor.
    (B) Mick should be charged with a felony.
    (C) Mick should be charged with criminal contempt because he is actually an accessory after the fact to the charge of criminal contempt.
    (D) Mick should not be charged with any offense.

65. May waits on the steps of the courthouse and warns her husband Bob that the court officers assigned to the court are waiting inside the courthouse to arrest Bob for a felony he committed while previously in the courthouse on an unrelated matter. May is quite sure her husband committed the felony but does not want him to go to prison. In such an instance, . . .

    (A) May has committed a felony.
    (B) May has committed no crime because due to her relationship, it is expected that she would render assistance to her husband.
    (C) May has committed a misdemeanor.
    (D) May has committed a violation.

Directions: Answer questions 66–71 solely on the basis of the following information.

An aided case is an occurrence coming to the attention of a court officer which requires that a person, OTHER THAN A PRISONER, receive medical aid or assistance because such person is

  a. Sick or injured (except from a vehicle accident)

  b. Dead (except from a vehicle accident)

  c. Lost

  d. Mentally ill

  e. An abandoned, destitute, abused, or neglected child.

Upon arrival at the scene of an aided case, the court officer concerned shall, in this order:

  A. Render reasonable aid to a sick or injured person.

  B. Request an ambulance or doctor, if necessary.

  a. If the aided person is wearing a Medic Alert emblem indicating diabetes, heart disease, etc., notify the portable radio dispatcher and bring the emblem to the attention of the ambulance attendant. A court officer shall not remove a Medic Alert emblem.

  C. Wait in view to direct the ambulance or have some responsible person do so.

  D. Make a second call in 20 minutes if ambulance does not arrive.

  E. Make a court officer memo book entry.

  a. Include the name of person notified regarding any Medic Alert emblem.

  F. Accompany an unconscious or unidentified aided to the hospital in the body of the ambulance.

  G. Obtain name, address, and telephone number of a relative or friend for notification.

  H. Prepare an AIDED REPORT form and deliver it to the court clerk who shall have relatives/friends notified if the aided is admitted to a hospital or dies.

  66. The first action that a court officer should take at the scene of an aided case is . . .

    (A) to request an ambulance.
    (B) to render reasonable aid.
    (C) to check for a Medic Alert emblem.
    (D) to make a court officer memo book entry of the facts.

67. Court Officer Mays arrives at the scene of an aided case and appropriately calls for an ambulance at about 10:05 A.M. According to the procedure, which of the following is the earliest that a second call for the ambulance should be made?

(A) 10:40 A.M.
(B) 10:30 A.M.
(C) 10:25 A.M.
(D) 10:15 A.M.

68. According to the procedure, which of the following is least likely to be considered an aided case?

(A) a lost person
(B) a missing person
(C) an abandoned child
(D) a mentally ill person

69. While handling an aided case, Court Officer Lopez discovers a Medic Alert emblem on the aided person. In this instance, the officer should . . .

(A) notify only the portable radio dispatcher.
(B) call the hospital and notify the medical staff.
(C) remove the emblem and turn it over to the ambulance attendant.
(D) make a court officer memo book entry and include the name of the person notified about the Medic Alert emblem.

70. Which of the following incidents should be considered an aided case?

(A) any injured person
(B) any dead person
(C) a destitute child
(D) a delinquent child

71. While the court is out on recess, a witness has been injured and has been taken from the court to the hospital where he is admitted. According to the procedure, which of the following is responsible for notifying the relatives of the injured person?

(A) the shift supervisor
(B) the court desk officer
(C) the court clerk
(D) the court officer who responded to the scene

To ensure the safety of all concerned, a court officer shall adhere to the following when dealing with an emotionally disturbed person (EDP).

Maintain a zone of safety, which is the distance to be maintained between the EDP and the responding court officers. This distance may vary with each situation (e.g., type of weapon possessed, condition of EDP, surrounding area). A minimum distance of twenty (20) feet is recommended. An attempt will be made to maintain the zone of safety if the EDP does not remain stationary.

A. Upon arrival at the scene, assess the situation regarding the threat of immediate serious injury to the EDP, other persons present, or court officers.

    a. If the actions of an EDP constitute an immediate threat of serious physical injury or death to himself or others:

        i. Take reasonable action to terminate or prevent such behavior. Deadly physical force will be used only as a last resort to protect the lives of persons present.

    b. If an EDP is unarmed, not violent, and willing to leave voluntarily:

        i. The EDP may be taken into custody without the specific direction of a shift supervisor.

    c. In all other cases, if the EDP's actions do not constitute an immediate threat of serious physical injury or death to himself or others:

        i. Attempt to isolate and contain the EDP while maintaining a zone of safety until the arrival of the shift supervisor.

        ii. Do not, under these circumstances, attempt to take an EDP into custody without specific direction of the shift supervisor.

B. Request an ambulance, if one has not already been dispatched.

    a. Ascertain whether the shift supervisor is responding, and, if not, request the shift supervisor's response.

C. Establish security lines.

D. Take the EDP into custody if EDP is unarmed, not violent, and willing to leave voluntarily.

When an EDP is isolated/contained but will not leave voluntarily, the shift supervisor shall:

E. Establish firearms control.

F. Deploy protective devices such as shields.

    a. Employ nonlethal devices contained in the shift supervisor's equipment locker to ensure the safety of all present.

G. Establish security lines, if not already done.

When the EDP has been restrained, the court officer concerned shall:

H. Remove property that is dangerous to life or will aid escape.

I. Have the EDP removed to the hospital in an ambulance.

   a. Restraining equipment including handcuffs may be used if the patient is violent or resists or upon direction of a physician examiner.

   b. If unable to transport with reasonable restraint, the ambulance attendant or doctor will request a special ambulance.

   c. When possible, a female patient being transported should be accompanied by another female or by an adult member of her immediate family.

J. Ride in the body of the ambulance with the patient.

   a. At least two court officers will safeguard the EDPs if more than one patient is being transported.

   NOTE: If an ambulance is not available and the situation warrants, transport the EDP to the hospital by official department car, if able to do so with reasonable restraint. Under no circumstances will an EDP be transported to a police facility.

K. When applicable, inform the examining physician, upon arrival at the hospital of the use of nonlethal devices on an EDP.

L. Safeguard the patient at the hospital until examined by a psychiatrist.

M. Enter the details in the court officer memo book and prepare an AIDED REPORT form.

N. Deliver the AIDED REPORT form to the court desk officer.

72. In connection with the handling of EDPs, which of the following is the most accurate statement concerning a zone of safety?

    (A) A maximum of 20 feet is recommended.
    (B) A minimum of 20 feet is recommended.
    (C) The zone of safety never varies.
    (D) It is really not necessary to maintain a zone of safety if the EDP does not remain stationary.

73. At the scene of an EDP, because the EDP, who refuses to leave voluntarily, is nonviolent and unarmed, the court officer on the scene takes the EDP into custody before the arrival of the shift supervisor. In this instance, the court officer acted . . .

    (A) properly, mainly because the sooner an EDP receives treatment, the better the prognosis for recovery.
    (B) improperly, mainly because the EDP refused to leave voluntarily.
    (C) properly, mainly because an unarmed EDP can never injure anyone.
    (D) improperly, mainly because a shift supervisor must always be present before an EDP is taken into custody.

74. In handling an EDP, it became necessary for a court officer to use nonlethal devices to take the EDP into custody. According to procedure, these devices would most likely be found . . .

(A) in the shift supervisor's equipment locker.
(B) in the court officer's equipment locker.
(C) at the office of the court clerk.
(D) in the ambulance that responds to the scene.

75. At the scene of an EDP, the responsibility to establish security lines rests . . .

(A) only with the shift supervisor.
(B) initially with the court officer who responds to the scene.
(C) with the court desk officer.
(D) with ambulance personnel.

76. According to the procedure, if three EDPs are being transported in an ambulance, then the minimum number of court officers that could properly be assigned to safeguard the EDPs is . . .

(A) one.
(B) two.
(C) three.
(D) four.

77. An ambulance has been called to the courthouse, the scene of an EDP. However, information is received that an ambulance is not available. The court officer at the scene places the EDP in an official department car and transports the EDP to the nearest police station house. In this instance, the officer acted . . .

(A) properly, mainly because an EDP may be transported in an official department car.
(B) improperly, mainly because an EDP should never be transported to a police station house.
(C) properly, mainly because time is of the essence when dealing with an EDP.
(D) improperly, mainly because an EDP should always be transported in an ambulance.

78. An EDP is able to break loose from his restraints and bolt from the body of an ambulance. The assigned court officer who had been riding in the front of the ambulance with the ambulance driver was able to apprehend the EDP quickly and return him to the body of the ambulance in handcuffs. In this instance, the actions of the court officer were . . .

(A) proper, mainly because the EDP was quickly recaptured.
(B) improper, mainly because the court officer should have been riding in the body of the ambulance with the EDP.
(C) proper, mainly because the EDP was again restrained and placed in the body of the ambulance.
(D) improper, mainly because the court officer should have placed the EDP in the front of the ambulance.

79. Court Officer Regal appropriately uses a nonlethal device on an EDP. Upon arrival at the hospital, the officer should advise which of the following regarding the use of the nonlethal device?

(A) the hospital administrator
(B) the examining physician
(C) the ambulance attendant
(D) the shift supervisor

80. In connection with the handling of an EDP, after completing an AIDED REPORT form, the court officer should deliver the report to . . .

(A) the examining physician.
(B) the ambulance attendant.
(C) the court desk officer.
(D) the shift supervisor.

Directions: Answer questions 81–90 solely on the basis of the following information.

COURT OFFICER UNIFORM REGULATIONS PROCEDURES

A. An annual, in-depth uniform inspection and equipment inspection shall commence the first business day of May each year. The inspections shall be performed during the duty time, but shall not be conducted on the 0800–1600 hours tour.

B. Officers who are on sick leave or other authorized excusal when annual uniform inspection takes place shall have their uniforms inspected within two (2) weeks after they return to duty.

C. All members of the Department shall have their hair cut to a length that allows the uniform cap to be worn.

D. Mustaches and sideburns shall be maintained in a manner that reflects a professional appearance. A member of the Department performing duty in uniform shall obtain permission from the Commanding Officer of the court to which assigned before wearing a beard.

E. The only facial jewelry that is allowed while working are earrings worn on an earlobe. Such earrings shall not extend below the earlobe for safety reasons.

F. Members shall carry their shield and identification cards at all times without exception.

G. Shields shall be worn on the outermost garment when performing duty in uniform or in civilian clothes at the scene of an emergency.

H. The Department regulation pullover sweater with official logo may be worn during winter months or during inclement weather.

I. Nameplates shall be worn on the outermost uniform garment directly over the shield. However, nameplates shall not be worn on uniform raincoats.

J. Serviceable flashlights shall be carried by all members assigned to uniform duty between the hours of 4 P.M. to 8 A.M. A serviceable flashlight shall not exceed 12 inches in length and 16 ounces in weight.

K. Members of the Department shall report the loss of their shields and/or identification cards occurring within the city limits to the ranking officer on duty at their command. In the event such loss occurs outside the city limits, the member concerned shall notify the Operations Division. In both instances, it is the duty of the member suffering the loss to notify the police authorities concerned.

81. According to the uniform regulations, which of the following statements concerning the length of a member's hair would be most accurate?

(A) Members assigned to uniform positions have different regulations than members assigned to civilian clothes positions.
(B) There are different regulations for male and female officers.
(C) The shaving of one's head is prohibited.
(D) The length of the hair must allow the uniform cap to be worn.

82. Ralph is a court officer who likes to wear an earring when he socializes off duty. According to the uniform regulations, Ralph's wearing of an earring while off duty would be . . .

(A) inappropriate regardless of the style of the earring.
(B) appropriate only if the earring did not extend below the earlobe.
(C) inappropriate only if he wore a nose ring.
(D) appropriate because the facial jewelry rule applies only to on-duty officers.

83. An annual uniform inspection would be most likely to be performed . . .

(A) always on the first of May.
(B) on off-duty time.
(C) on a 1600 3 2400 (4 P.M. to 12 midnight) tour of duty.
(D) at any time and any place selected by the shift supervisor.

84. If Court Officer Tines is scheduled to undergo annual uniform inspection at a time when she will be on vacation, she must have her uniforms inspected . . .

(A) within 2 weeks after she returns to duty.
(B) within 2 days after she returns to duty.
(C) as soon as possible after she returns to duty.
(D) before she goes on vacation.

85. Evaluate the following statements concerning uniform regulations.
1. If Officer Jones who is in uniform wishes, he may wear sideburns if they are worn in a manner that reflects a professional appearance.
2. Officer Grey who is assigned to a civilian clothes position may wear a beard without seeking prior permission.

Which of the following is most accurate concerning these statements?

(A) Only statement 1 is correct.
(B) Only statement 2 is correct.
(C) Both statements 1 and 2 are correct.
(D) Neither statements 1 nor 2 are correct.

86. It would be least appropriate to wear the uniform pullover sweater with the official logo . . .

    (A) during inclement weather in June.
    (B) anytime in February.
    (C) anytime in October.
    (D) on a sunny mild day in January.

87. According to the uniform regulations, it would be most appropriate to state that . . .

    (A) if Court Officer Homes loses his shield, he must always report the loss to the Operations Division.
    (B) whenever a shield is lost, it is the duty of the commanding officer of the member suffering the loss to report the loss to the police.
    (C) whenever an identification card is lost within the city limits, the member suffering the loss shall report the loss to the Operations Division.
    (D) if Court Officer Barns loses her identification card, she must always notify the police authorities concerned.

88. Evaluate the following statements concerning uniform regulations.

    1. Members must carry their identification cards at all times without exception.

    2. Members must carry their shields at all times except when off duty.

    Which of the following is most accurate concerning these statements?

    (A) Only statement 1 is correct.
    (B) Only statement 2 is correct.
    (C) Both statements 1 and 2 are correct.
    (D) Neither statements 1 nor 2 are correct.

89. Which of the following statements would be most appropriate according to the uniform regulations concerning serviceable flashlights?

    (A) At 4:30 P.M. all members of the department should be carrying a serviceable flashlight.
    (B) Uniform members of the Department must carry serviceable flashlights on all tours.
    (C) Serviceable flashlights shall not exceed 12 inches in length.
    (D) Serviceable flashlights shall not exceed 6 ounces in weight.

90. Evaluate the following statements concerning uniform regulations.

1. Shields shall be worn on the outermost garment when performing duty in uniform or in civilian clothes at the scene of an emergency.

2. Nameplates shall always be worn on the outermost uniform garment directly over the shield.

   Which of the following is most accurate concerning these statements?

   (A) Only statement 1 is correct.
   (B) Only statement 2 is correct.
   (C) Both statements 1 and 2 are correct.
   (D) Neither statements 1 nor 2 are correct.

Directions: Use the information in the following reference table to answer questions 91–95. In the table, each number has been associated with a letter. For each question, select the choice that contains the letters that, when associated with the numbers in the reference table, can be added together to equal the sum required by the question.

REFERENCE TABLE

B	O	G	U	S	Z
1	2	3	4	5	0

EXAMPLE

Q. Which of the following choices contains the letters that add up to 8 after they are converted to numbers?

   (A) B, O, G
   (B) B, O, S
   (C) G, U, S
   (D) O, U, S

Choice B, the answer, contains letters B, O, S, which, according to the reference table, are associated with 1, 2, 5. When added together, they equal 8.

91. Which of the following choices contains the letters that add up to 12 after they are converted to numbers?

    (A) O, G, U, G
    (B) B, U, G, S
    (C) G, O, B, S
    (D) U, S, Z, U

92. Which of the following choices contains the letters that add up to 9 after they are converted to numbers?

    (A) G, Z, U, G
    (B) U, B, O, B
    (C) S, B, Z, B
    (D) O, B, S, B

93. Which of the following choices contains the letters that add up to the greatest sum after they are converted to numbers?

    (A) S, Z, S, B
    (B) U, U, S, O
    (C) G, U, B, O
    (D) B, O, B, S

94. Which of the following choices contains the letters that add up to the lowest sum after they are converted to numbers?

    (A) G, Z, U, B
    (B) S, Z, Z, S
    (C) B, O, U, Z
    (D) U, G, U, G

95. Which of the following choices contains the letters that add up to an odd number after they are converted to numbers?

    (A) S, U, Z, G
    (B) Z, U, G, B
    (C) B, U, G, O
    (D) G, S, B, O

Directions: Use the information in the following reference table to answer questions 96–100. In the table, each number has been associated with a letter. For each question, select the choice that contains the letters that, when associated with the numbers in the reference table, can be added together to equal the sum required by the question.

REFERENCE TABLE

A	B	C	D	E	X
1	2	3	4	5	0

EXAMPLE

Q. Which of the following choices contains the letters that add up to 10 after being converted to numbers?

(A) A, C, E
(B) B, D, E
(C) A, D, E
(D) C, D, E

Choice C, the answer, contains letters A,D,E, which, according to the reference table, are associated with 1, 4, 5. When added together, they equal 10.

---

96. Which of the following choices contains the letters that add up to 6 after they are converted to numbers?

(A) A, B, D
(B) A, B, C
(C) A, B, E
(D) B, C, D

97. Which of the following choices contains the letters that add up to 14 after they are converted to numbers?

(A) D, D, E
(B) D, E, E
(C) A, B, C, D, E
(D) D, D, E, X

98. Which of the following choices contains the letters that add up to 19 after they are converted to numbers?

(A) E, D, E, X, E
(B) E, E, E, A, B
(C) A, B, C, D, E, X
(D) D, D, E, C, D

99. Which of the following choices contains the letters that add up to 11 after they are converted to numbers?

(A) A, E, B, D
(B) B, C, D, A, X
(C) X, B, E, D
(D) B, A, X, E, D

100. Which of the following choices contains the letters that add up to 17 after they are converted to numbers?

(A) X, B, E, D, C
(B) A, E, E, B, E, X
(C) C, C, X, E, D
(D) E, X, D, C, E

ANSWER KEY
Practice Exam One

1.	B	26.	C	51.	D	76.	B
2.	D	27.	B	52.	D	77.	B
3.	C	28.	D	53.	C	78.	B
4.	B	29.	B	54.	B	79.	B
5.	B	30.	B	55.	D	80.	C
6.	A	31.	A	56.	B	81.	D
7.	C	32.	C	57.	B	82.	D
8.	D	33.	B	58.	B	83.	C
9.	B	34.	B	59.	D	84.	A
10.	B	35.	A	60.	B	85.	C
11.	D	36.	C	61.	A	86.	C
12.	B	37.	A	62.	A	87.	D
13.	D	38.	C	63.	C	88.	A
14.	C	39.	C	64.	D	89.	C
15.	B	40.	C	65.	A	90.	A
16.	A	41.	B	66.	B	91.	A
17.	A	42.	A	67.	C	92.	D
18.	C	43.	A	68.	B	93.	B
19.	A	44.	B	69.	D	94.	C
20.	C	45.	A	70.	C	95.	D
21.	D	46.	B	71.	C	96.	B
22.	A	47.	D	72.	B	97.	B
23.	C	48.	C	73.	B	98.	A
24.	D	49.	B	74.	A	99.	C
25.	C	50.	C	75.	B	100.	D

DIAGNOSTIC CHART

Directions: After you score your test, complete the following chart by inserting in the column entitled "Your Number Correct" the number of correct questions you answered in each of the eight sections of the test. Then compare your score in each section with the ratings in the column entitled "Scale." Finally, to correct your weaknesses, follow the instructions found at the end of the chart.

Section	Question Numbers	Area	Your Number Correct	Scale
1	1–15	Memory (15 questions)		15 Right—Excellent 13–14 Right—Good 11–12 Right—Fair Under 11 Right—Poor
2	16–50	Reading Comprehension (35 questions)		33–35 Right—Excellent 30–32 Right—Good 27–29 Right—Fair Under 27 Right—Poor
3	51–65	Legal Definitions (15 questions)		15 Right—Excellent 13–14 Right—Good 11–12 Right—Fair Under 11 Right—Poor
4	66–90	Applying Court Officer Procedures (25 questions)		25 Right—Excellent 22–24 Right—Good 18–21 Right—Fair Under 18 Right—Poor
5	91–100	Clerical Ability (10 questions)		10 Right—Excellent 8–9 Right—Good 7 Right—Fair Under 7 Right—Poor

How to correct weaknesses:

1. If you are weak in Section 1, concentrate on Chapter 2.
2. If you are weak in Section 2, concentrate on Chapter 1.
3. If you are weak in Section 3, concentrate on Chapter 4.
4. If you are weak in Section 4, concentrate on Chapter 3.
5. If you are weak in Section 5, concentrate on Chapter 5.

Note: Consider yourself weak in a section if you receive a score other than excellent in that section.

ANSWERS EXPLAINED

1. **(B)** Hopefully, you haven't forgotten to use associations to deal with memory questions. It doesn't matter what specific type of memory question you are taking, the association technique is always applicable. In this question, the word *young* in the inmate's name would be a good way to remember that he loiters near schools (where young people attend).

2. **(D)** Sawed-off shotguns are shorter than regular shotguns. This inmate's name is Short—a perfect association.

3. **(C)** An alphabetical association suits this question just fine. Jack <u>H</u>unt uses the alias Ben <u>H</u>ogan.

4. **(B)** Once again, the *young* in this inmate's name could have helped you remember the information needed to answer the question (e.g., young people don't often wear hairpieces).

5. **(B)** Youngblood was serving a life sentence. An association like Youngblood will get old in prison would have been perfect for this association.

6. **(A)** <u>C</u>huckie Gifford is a <u>c</u>on artist who poses as a <u>c</u>op.

7. **(C)** According to the posters, Jack Hunt is a chronic drug user.

8. **(D)** Hopefully you had an association to help you remember that James Short speaks five languages.

9. **(B)** Questions 9–15 are a very difficult series of memory questions. In addition to using associations, you should engage in grouping, which is the name given to the strategy of putting similar items together. For example, criminal trespass and petit larceny are the only two misdemeanors in the entire listing, so you should remember them together.

10. **(B)** There were only four categories in the Articles and/or Sections column that listed articles only, and one of them was Article 130, sex offenses.

11. **(D)** There was only one Class A felony in the entire listing and that was murder in the first degree. Whenever an item in a listing stands alone, it will probably be the subject of a question.

12. **(B)** There were only two Class E felonies: tampering with evidence and the answer to this question—criminal contempt.

13. **(D)** Grouping Articles 130 and 158 together would have led you to this answer. Be sure to group similar items together when you review a listing such as the one in this series of questions.

14. **(C)** There are three Class D felonies in the list, and perjury in the first degree is one of them.

15. **(B)** All the material found in the memory information is fair game for a question. In this case, the answer—the New York State Penal Law—is found in the lead in to the listing of offenses.

16. **(A)** Felonies are the most serious of the two categories of crime.

17. **(A)** The present-day distinction between a felony and misdemeanor in the United States is usually based on the length of the sentence imposed.

18. **(C)** Convictions for either felonies or misdemeanors can result in the assessment of a fine.

19. **(A)** By far, the component that receives the most funding is the police.

20. **(C)** The other three components are supervised by the courts.

21. **(D)** A major problem for the overall system is that each of the four components acts independently of one another.

22. **(A)** Probation is the most commonly used sentencing option.

23. **(C)** People on probation often create serious crime problems.

24. **(D)** Society could not afford the cost of sending all convicted persons to prison. For this reason, probation is indispensable.

25. **(C)** The passage clearly states that there must be an arrest and a conviction. This question emphasizes the importance of the conjunction *and*.

26. **(C)** This question emphasizes the importance of the conjunction *or*. The threatened use of a firearm, as well as the actual use of the firearm, can cause a revocation.

27. **(B)** The required passing mark is 80%.

28. **(D)** The possibility of fire is always to be considered as an extremely dangerous situation. Fire in a building can injure or kill many people. Don't be misled by the fact that the building is abandoned. The stated rule is quite specific. It doesn't require the dangerous condition to be one that is occurring in the court building. It just has to be a dangerous condition.

29. **(B)** A nail file is a relatively sharp metal instrument that could be used as a weapon.

30. **(B)** The protection of life is always more important than the protection of property. Please note that Choice D is an excellent example of a good statement that does not respond to the question.

31. **(A)** More aggressive and outspoken witnesses almost always influence other witnesses and tend to make the other witnesses think that what they have to say might be incorrect. Note that the word *guarantees* in Choice C makes that choice too strong to be the answer.

32. **(C)** Choices A, B, and D are all leading questions in that they suggest an answer.

33. **(B)** Don't let the fact that there seems to be only one robber lead you to believe that assistance is not needed. Please note that Choice C is a good action to take, but it is not the recommended first action.

34. **(B)** A report has no value if it is not accurate. Note that each of the other choices are positive attributes of a good report, but the question asked for the most important characteristic of a good report.

35. **(A)** The use of the word *never* in Choice C rules out that choice and leaves Choice A as the only possible answer.

36. **(C)** The entire rule is aimed only at court officers who are in uniform. And, even those in uniform are not covered by the rule if saluting and standing at attention interferes with their duties, such as during an emergency.

37. **(A)** This is what we call an absolute rule. It has no exceptions. Note the similarity between Choices B and D. When you see such similarity between two choices, you must recognize that, in all probability, neither will be the answer.

38. **(C)** The key to this question is the words *issued for their use*. These were the limiting words that established the answer.

39. **(C)** If at any time, equipment is properly passed from one officer to another, the last officer to receive the equipment shall be responsible for it.

40. **(C)** Only those lights and electrical appliances that are nonessential must be turned off. Windows must be closed only in offices that are not in use overnight.

41. **(B)** Choice A is wrong because permission can also be obtained from a Deputy Court Clerk. Choice B is correct because prior permission is always required.

42. **(A)** The key word in the rule is *may*. This is a flexible rule. It would be inflexible if the word *must* or *shall* was used in place of *may*. Also, the rule deals with just debts, and not all debts.

43. **(A)** If the gift is one that is given for departmental services, and the Court Administrator does not give his written consent, then that gift must be refused. The rule applies only to gifts given for departmental services, which is why Choices B and C are wrong. But, the rule is the same for gifts as it is for awards, and that is why Choice D is wrong.

44. **(B)** Complaints can involve either improper OR unlawful acts. But, they must relate to the business of some court system. Choices C and D are not mentioned in the rule.

45. **(A)** A complaint shall be thoroughly investigated by the supervisor to whom it is referred, and if the condition complained of actually exists, it shall be corrected and steps shall be taken to prevent its recurrence.

46. **(B)** This is an absolute rule. It has no exceptions. An officer cannot intercede with a court for the acquittal of or change (modification) of sentence for any defendant.

47. **(D)** When court officers make arrests, it is possible that they will be called upon to testify about that arrest during a criminal trial. This, of course, means that they may sometimes have to testify in criminal court.

48. **(C)** This question demonstrates quite clearly the danger of using personal knowledge when answering reading comprehension questions. It is common knowledge that Choice B is in fact true, but it is not mentioned in the paragraph so it cannot be the answer. The instructions clearly state that the answer must be based solely on the information contained in the passage.

49. **(B)** The typical chronic criminal is usually no better at committing crimes than he is at anything else, and he is usually a failure in all he does.

50. **(C)** This question emphasizes the importance of the word *unless* in reading comprehension questions.

51. **(D)** The most serious felonies, which receive the most severe penalties, are A felonies, followed by B felonies, and so on. Therefore, of the choices given, a Class D felony would receive the least severe penalty.

52. **(D)** An offense can be either a felony, a misdemeanor, or a violation.

53. **(C)** The punishment for a misdemeanor is less than a felony and more than a violation; so Choices A and B are incorrect. Choice D sounds good, but you are to base your answers solely on the legal definitions that were given. Choice C is correct according to that information because a crime is always either a felony or a misdemeanor.

54. **(B)** Only misdemeanors and felonies are crimes; a violation does not have a minimum punishment stated in its definition, and the definition of a felony does not state a maximum punishment. The correct choice is B because all three are considered offenses.

55. **(D)** Every loaded gun is not necessarily a deadly weapon. It must also be operable. Every operable gun is not necessarily a deadly weapon. It must also be loaded. A dagger is mentioned in the definition of deadly weapon. A razor is not.

56. **(B)** A vehicle is never a deadly weapon, but when it is used to cause serious physical injury, it would be considered a dangerous instrument.

57. **(B)** Choice B is correct, and Choice D is incorrect because either substantial pain *OR* physical impairment may occur for a physical injury to have occurred. Note the importance of the word *OR*. Choice A is incorrect because there must be more than just substantial pain for a serious physical injury to have taken place. Choice C is not found anywhere in the definitions.

58. **(B)** A dangerous instrument is any article that depending on how it is used, attempted to be used, or threatened to be used, is capable of causing death or serious physical injury. If this gun were operable, it still would not be a deadly weapon because it is unloaded.

59. **(D)** Because of her sentence of 13 days, May most likely committed a violation that is the type of offense indicated in Choice D. Because the sentence does not fit that of a felony or a misdemeanor, Choices A and B are incorrect. And because a crime is either a felony or misdemeanor, Choice C can be eliminated.

60. **(B)** By definition, a serious physical injury is, in the first instance, a physical injury. Thus, statement 2 is correct. However, an article or substance could be considered a dangerous instrument, if, merely by the way it is threatened to be used, it is capable of causing serious physical injury. Thus statement 1 is incorrect.

61. **(A)** A crime is either a felony or a misdemeanor. Therefore, even though a felony is considered a crime, not all crimes are felonies because they could also be misdemeanors. Statement 2 is incorrect, thereby making Choice A the answer.

62. **(A)** The penalty for a Class D felony would be more severe than that of a Class E felony. The penalties for misdemeanors and violations are both less than any type of felony. Choice A is the answer.

63. **(C)** Metal knuckles represent the only weapon designated by the definitions as a deadly weapon. Regarding the pistol, remember that it must be loaded and operable.

64. **(D)** To be properly charged with hindering prosecution, a person must know that another person has committed a felony or misdemeanor and render criminal assistance to such other person. Regarding being an accessory, no mention was made of any such actions in the definitions provided.

65. **(A)** A person is guilty of hindering prosecution in the first degree, which is a felony, when such person renders criminal assistance to another knowing that such other person has committed a felony. Warning such a person constitutes rendering criminal assistance.

66. **(B)** Even though the actions indicated by all the choices should be done by the court officer on the scene, the first thing a court officer should do at the scene of an aided case is to render reasonable aid to a sick or injured person.

67. **(C)** A second call for an ambulance should be made in 20 minutes if the ambulance does not arrive.

68. **(B)** A missing person is not mentioned in the definition of what an aided case is. The other persons are part of the definition of an aided case.

69. **(D)** If the aided person is wearing a Medic Alert emblem, the court officer shall notify the portable radio dispatcher and ambulance attendant. A court officer shall not remove a Medic Alert emblem but shall make a court officer memo book entry that includes the name of the person notified regarding any Medic Alert emblem. Therefore, Choices A, B, and C are incorrect, and Choice D is correct.

70. **(C)** Choices A and B are incorrect because the use of the word *any* would include injured and dead persons as a result of a vehicle accident, which are not aided cases. Choice D is not found in the definition of an aided case. Choice C is the correct answer.

71. **(C)** The court clerk shall have relatives/friends notified if the aided is admitted to a hospital or dies.

72. **(B)** Choice A is incorrect because a minimum distance of 20 feet is recommended. Choice C is incorrect because this distance may vary with each situation. Choice D is incorrect because an attempt will be made to maintain the zone of safety if the EDP does not remain stationary.

73. **(B)** Before an EDP may be taken into custody without the specific direction of a shift supervisor, the EDP must be not only unarmed and not violent, but also willing to leave voluntarily.

74. **(A)** Nonlethal devices are contained in the shift supervisor's equipment locker.

75. **(B)** Choice A is incorrect because the shift supervisor will establish security lines, if it has not already been done by the court officer who responds to the scene. Therefore, the responsibility to establish security lines does not rest only with the shift supervisor. Choice B is correct.

76. **(B)** The procedure states that at least two court officers will safeguard the EDPs if more than one patient is being transported. This would certainly include three EDPs which obviously is more than one EDP. Therefore in safeguarding three EDPs a minimum of only two court officers is required.

77. **(B)** Under no circumstances will an EDP be transported to a police facility. When you review a procedure, anytime you see absolute expressions such as *always, never*, and *under no circumstances*, pay particular attention to them. The concepts tied to these expressions often become the basis of questions.

78. **(B)** According to the procedure, the court officer should have been riding in the body of the ambulance with the patient.

79. **(B)** The court officer concerned shall inform the examining physician, upon arrival at the hospital, of the use of nonlethal devices on an EDP.

80. **(C)** As stated in the procedure, the court officer concerned shall deliver an AIDED REPORT to the court desk officer.

81. **(D)** This is an example of basing an answer solely on the information provided. Even though Choices A, B, and C might all seem probable, they are not mentioned in the uniform regulations, which were provided and upon which you must base your answers.

82. **(D)** According to the regulation dealing with facial jewelry such as earrings, the restrictions apply only when an officer is working.

83. **(C)** Choice A might have been selected if you did not read carefully. It is the first business day in May and that is not always the same as the first of May.

84. **(A)** As stated in the regulation, she has 2 weeks.

85. **(C)** If you followed our strategy and had scanned the question and the choices, you would have had no problem recognizing which parts of the regulations were going to be asked about. It is those parts that you should have been underlining when you reread the procedures.

86. **(C)** The uniform pullover sweater may be worn in the winter months and during inclement weather. Because October is in the fall, wearing it anytime in October would not always be appropriate.

87. **(D)** It is the individual member's duty to notify the police authorities.

88. **(A)** Both the shield and ID card must be carried at all times without exception.

89. **(C)** Choice A is inappropriate because it would include members of the Department who are in civilian clothes and therefore not required to carry a flashlight. Choice B is inappropriate because uniformed members are not required to carry serviceable flashlights on all tours, only from 4 P.M. to 8 A.M. Choice D is inappropriate because serviceable flashlights may not exceed 16 ounces.

90. **(A)** Nameplates shall not be worn on a raincoat, which could be the outermost garment that an officer might wear.

91. **(A)** According to the reference table the letters O, G, U, G are associated with the numbers 2, 3, 4, 3, which when added together yield the sum of 12, the number sought by the question.

92. **(D)** This is as indicated by use of the reference table. This kind of question can be time-consuming because each choice must be examined.

93. **(B)** This is as indicated by use of the reference table. Here each choice had to be examined in order to determine which choice yielded the greatest sum.

94. **(C)** Choice A yields a sum of 8; Choice B yields a sum of 10; and Choice D yields a sum of 14; but Choice C yields the lowest sum of 7.

95. **(D)** Choice D yields 11, whereas choices A, B, and C yield the even-numbered sums of 12, 8, and 10 respectively.

96. **(B)** The letters A, B, and C are associated respectfully with the numbers 1, 2, and 3 which when added together equal 6, the number sought by the question.

97. **(B)** Choice B is the correct choice because D = 4, E = 5, and E = 5, which when added together equals 14.

98. **(A)** Choice A contains three Es, which equal 5 + 5 + 5 = 15, plus D, which has a value of 4; the sum is now 19. The letter X is valued at 0. Thus, Choice A adds up to 19.

99. **(C)** X = 0; B = 2; E = 5; D = 4. Combining all the values adds up to 11. Choice C is correct.

100. **(D)** According to the reference table, the letter X should be associated with the number 0, which adds nothing to the sum. Therefore, it can be completely ignored in this exercise.

Practice Examination Two

This is your second practice examination. Two more practice examinations follow.

Be sure to take each practice examination in one sitting. Each exam contains 100 questions, which you must answer in 3½ hours. It is imperative that you become accustomed to concentrating for the length of time required to complete an entire examination. Be sure to review the test-taking strategy outlined in the Introduction before taking this practice examination, to use that strategy when doing the examination, and to record your answers on the following Answer Sheet.

ANSWER SHEET
Practice Exam Two

Follow the instructions given in the test. Mark only your answers in the circles below.

WARNING: Be sure that the circle you fill is in the same row as the question you are answering. Use a No. 2 pencil (soft pencil).

BE SURE YOUR PENCIL MARKS ARE HEAVY AND BLACK.

ERASE COMPLETELY ANY ANSWER YOU WISH TO CHANGE.

DO NOT make stray pencil dots, dashes, or marks.

1. (A) (B) (C) (D)	26. (A) (B) (C) (D)	51. (A) (B) (C) (D)	76. (A) (B) (C) (D)
2. (A) (B) (C) (D)	27. (A) (B) (C) (D)	52. (A) (B) (C) (D)	77. (A) (B) (C) (D)
3. (A) (B) (C) (D)	28. (A) (B) (C) (D)	53. (A) (B) (C) (D)	78. (A) (B) (C) (D)
4. (A) (B) (C) (D)	29. (A) (B) (C) (D)	54. (A) (B) (C) (D)	79. (A) (B) (C) (D)
5. (A) (B) (C) (D)	30. (A) (B) (C) (D)	55. (A) (B) (C) (D)	80. (A) (B) (C) (D)
6. (A) (B) (C) (D)	31. (A) (B) (C) (D)	56. (A) (B) (C) (D)	81. (A) (B) (C) (D)
7. (A) (B) (C) (D)	32. (A) (B) (C) (D)	57. (A) (B) (C) (D)	82. (A) (B) (C) (D)
8. (A) (B) (C) (D)	33. (A) (B) (C) (D)	58. (A) (B) (C) (D)	83. (A) (B) (C) (D)
9. (A) (B) (C) (D)	34. (A) (B) (C) (D)	59. (A) (B) (C) (D)	84. (A) (B) (C) (D)
10. (A) (B) (C) (D)	35. (A) (B) (C) (D)	60. (A) (B) (C) (D)	85. (A) (B) (C) (D)
11. (A) (B) (C) (D)	36. (A) (B) (C) (D)	61. (A) (B) (C) (D)	86. (A) (B) (C) (D)
12. (A) (B) (C) (D)	37. (A) (B) (C) (D)	62. (A) (B) (C) (D)	87. (A) (B) (C) (D)
13. (A) (B) (C) (D)	38. (A) (B) (C) (D)	63. (A) (B) (C) (D)	88. (A) (B) (C) (D)
14. (A) (B) (C) (D)	39. (A) (B) (C) (D)	64. (A) (B) (C) (D)	89. (A) (B) (C) (D)
15. (A) (B) (C) (D)	40. (A) (B) (C) (D)	65. (A) (B) (C) (D)	90. (A) (B) (C) (D)
16. (A) (B) (C) (D)	41. (A) (B) (C) (D)	66. (A) (B) (C) (D)	91. (A) (B) (C) (D)
17. (A) (B) (C) (D)	42. (A) (B) (C) (D)	67. (A) (B) (C) (D)	92. (A) (B) (C) (D)
18. (A) (B) (C) (D)	43. (A) (B) (C) (D)	68. (A) (B) (C) (D)	93. (A) (B) (C) (D)
19. (A) (B) (C) (D)	44. (A) (B) (C) (D)	69. (A) (B) (C) (D)	94. (A) (B) (C) (D)
20. (A) (B) (C) (D)	45. (A) (B) (C) (D)	70. (A) (B) (C) (D)	95. (A) (B) (C) (D)
21. (A) (B) (C) (D)	46. (A) (B) (C) (D)	71. (A) (B) (C) (D)	96. (A) (B) (C) (D)
22. (A) (B) (C) (D)	47. (A) (B) (C) (D)	72. (A) (B) (C) (D)	97. (A) (B) (C) (D)
23. (A) (B) (C) (D)	48. (A) (B) (C) (D)	73. (A) (B) (C) (D)	98. (A) (B) (C) (D)
24. (A) (B) (C) (D)	49. (A) (B) (C) (D)	74. (A) (B) (C) (D)	99. (A) (B) (C) (D)
25. (A) (B) (C) (D)	50. (A) (B) (C) (D)	75. (A) (B) (C) (D)	100. (A) (B) (C) (D)

THE TEST

Time: 3 ½ hours
100 questions

Answer questions 1–8 based on the following instructions.

Directions: Study for 5 minutes the following information about the trial of defendants Don Ginty and Frank Rems. Try to remember as many details as possible. Do not make written notes of any kind during this 5-minute period. After the completion of the 5-minute period, answer questions 1–8. When answering the questions, do NOT refer back to the information.

MEMORY INFORMATION
5-Minute Time Limit

Court:	Metropolis Criminal Court
Date of Trial:	March 29th
Case:	People versus Ginty
Companion Case:	People versus Rems
Case Docket Number:	1357911
Case Docket Number	
Companion Case:	0246810
Defendant # 1:	Don Ginty
Defendant # 2:	Frank Rems
Complainant:	Bill Velanis
Charge:	140.30 of the New York State Penal Law
	Burglary in the First Degree
Date of Crime:	January 22nd
Date of Arrest:	February 1st
Date of Arraignment:	February 15th
Magistrate:	The Honorable Mary Jacobs
District Attorney:	David Allen
Defense Attorney:	Perry Johnson
Court Clerk:	Richard Allen
Court Officer # 1:	Craig Singleton
Court Officer # 2:	Theresa Carey
Arresting Officer:	Police Officer Ray Coppola

DO NOT PROCEED UNTIL 5 MINUTES HAVE PASSED.

1. What is the Case Docket Number?

   (A) 1357911
   (B) 0246810
   (C) 1375911
   (D) 0248610

2. Who is Court Officer # 1?

   (A) Craig Singleton
   (B) Theresa Carey
   (C) Ray Coppola
   (D) Richard Allen

3. What was the date of the arraignment?

   (A) January 22nd
   (B) February 1st
   (C) February 15th
   (D) March 29th

4. What is the charge against the defendants?

   (A) 140.30 of the Penal Law
   (B) 130.40 of the Penal Law
   (C) 140.40 of the Penal Law
   (D) 130.30 of the Penal Law

5. Who is the Defense Attorney?

   (A) Craig Singleton
   (B) Theresa Carey
   (C) Perry Johnson
   (D) Richard Allen

6. Who is the Arresting Officer?

   (A) Craig Singleton
   (B) Theresa Carey
   (C) Ray Coppola
   (D) Richard Allen

7. Who was the presiding Magistrate?

   (A) Mary Jacobs
   (B) Theresa Carey
   (C) Perry Johnson
   (D) Richard Allen

8. Who was the District Attorney?

   (A) David Allen
   (B) Theresa Carey
   (C) Perry Johnson
   (D) Richard Allen

Answer questions 9–15 based on the following instructions.

Directions: Study for 5 minutes the following illustration, which depicts items taken from two defendants immediately after they were arrested. Try to remember as many details as possible. Do not make written notes of any kind during this 5-minute period. After the 5 minutes are up, answer questions 9–15. When answering the questions, do NOT refer back to the illustration.

DO NOT PROCEED UNTIL 5 MINUTES HAVE PASSED.

TURN TO NEXT PAGE

9. Which of the defendants is probably a sports fan?

   (A) Ron Tonso
   (B) William Judd
   (C) neither Ron Tonso nor William Judd
   (D) both Ron Tonso and William Judd

10. Which of the following statements is most correct concerning money possessed by the defendants?

    (A) Ron Tonso had the most money.
    (B) William Judd had the most money.
    (C) They both had an equal amount of money.
    (D) Neither of them had any money.

11. Which of the defendants is probably experiencing difficulties with his private residence?

    (A) Ron Tonso
    (B) William Judd
    (C) neither Ron Tonso nor William Judd
    (D) both Ron Tonso and William Judd

12. Which of the defendants is probably planning a trip?

    (A) Ron Tonso
    (B) William Judd
    (C) neither Ron Tonso nor William Judd
    (D) both Ron Tonso and William Judd

13. Which of the defendants is probably experiencing a medical problem?

    (A) Ron Tonso
    (B) William Judd
    (C) neither Ron Tonso nor William Judd
    (D) both Ron Tonso and William Judd

14. The plate number of William Judd's car is . . .

    (A) QND 160.
    (B) 1632.
    (C) 804 QND.
    (D) not given.

15. Both Ron Tonso and William Judd had . . .

   (A) a $10 bill.
   (B) a weapon.
   (C) at least one key.
   (D) aspirins.

Directions: Answer question 16 solely on the basis of the following information.

Crime is not a problem that can be easily solved by using the same strategies and methods that allowed man to split the atom or to put an astronaut on the moon. Nor can the problems created by crime be prevented by passing law after law. In fact, it is probably true that the crime problem in this country will never be truly solved.

16. The crime problem . . .

   (A) is easily solved.
   (B) can be solved through technology.
   (C) can be solved through legislation.
   (D) is probably beyond solution.

Directions: Answer question 17 solely on the basis of the following information.

The purpose of rehabilitation of criminals is to change their behavior. The supporters of rehabilitation as a basic goal of the criminal justice system suggest that criminals can leave the criminal justice system as better people than when they entered. Those who argue against the concept of rehabilitation argue that it rarely occurs, and these people usually favor the concept of reparation. Even though the truth of the matter is unknown at this time, what is known is that reparation is being used more and more and rehabilitation is used less and less.

17. Rehabilitation . . .

   (A) is definitely working.
   (B) is better than reparation.
   (C) rarely works.
   (D) is being used less and less.

Court officers are legally entitled to use physical force upon another person when and to the extent that they reasonably believe to be necessary to defend themselves or a third person from what they reasonably believe to be the use or imminent use of unlawful physical force by such other person. Court officers may not use deadly physical force upon another person unless they reasonably believe that such other person is using or about to use deadly physical force against them or another.

18. Court officers . . .

    (A) can use force only to defend themselves.
    (B) can always use an unlimited amount of force to defend themselves.
    (C) can sometimes use force to defend others.
    (D) are not entitled to use physical force upon another person.

19. The use of deadly physical force by court officers . . .

    (A) is only legally permitted in a courtroom setting.
    (B) is sometimes legally permissible.
    (C) is never legally authorized.
    (D) is always lawful to prevent escapes.

A court officer may make an arrest of a person for a felony when she has reasonable cause to believe such person has committed a felony. But, a court officer may make an arrest of a person for a misdemeanor or for a violation only when she has reasonable cause to believe such person has committed the misdemeanor or violation in her presence.

20. A criminal offense is either a felony, a misdemeanor, or a violation. A court officer . . .

    (A) can arrest for a felony even if the officer was not present when the felony was committed.
    (B) can arrest for a misdemeanor even if the officer was not present when the misdemeanor was committed.
    (C) can arrest for a violation even if the officer was not present when the violation was committed.
    (D) is prohibited from making an arrest for any criminal offense unless the offense is committed in the presence of the officer.

The courts have ruled that a juvenile, someone under the age of 16, who has been accused of a crime, has the right to counsel. The counsel may be of the juvenile's own choosing or appointed by the court for financial or other reasons. Therefore, a court officer who finds it necessary to arrest a juvenile must give notice of the juvenile's right to counsel. This notice must be clearly understood by both the juvenile and at least one of the juvenile's parents or legal guardians. In addition, such notice must be given both verbally and in writing. Even though a waiver of the right to counsel may be made, it is not effective unless the waiver is made in writing by both the juvenile and at least one of his parents or legal guardians.

21. A lawyer who represents a juvenile who has been accused of a crime . . .

    (A) must be one who is chosen by the juvenile.
    (B) must be one who is chosen by the parents or legal guardians of the juvenile.
    (C) must be one who is appointed by the courts.
    (D) may be chosen by the juvenile or appointed by the court.

22. A juvenile who is accused of a crime . . .

    (A) must be represented by a lawyer.
    (B) can decide on his own not to have a lawyer.
    (C) can state orally that he does not want a lawyer as long as one parent or guardian also agrees.
    (D) can waive the right to a lawyer if at least one of the juvenile's parents or guardians agrees provided that their waiver is put in writing.

Court Officer Gabriella Bigi is off duty. She is shopping in a local mall. At about 1:35 P.M. she observes two males she believes might be bail jumpers. The two males are sitting on a bench watching shoppers as they pass. Officer Bigi knows that she is authorized by the court system to make off-duty arrests of bail jumpers. She also knows that when she makes an off-duty arrest she is required to notify her commanding officer by telephone within 1 hour of the arrest. In this case, Officer Bigi does not make immediate arrests because she is not really sure whether the two males are indeed bail jumpers.

At 1:40 P.M., the two males get up from the bench and start walking away. Officer Bigi decides to follow the two males because they are acting suspiciously. The first suspect is a male, white, about 35–40 years old, wearing black pants and a black jacket. The second is a male, black, about 25–30 years old, wearing brown pants and a white coat. The two suspects stop in front of a bank, which is located right next to an exit from the mall into a parking lot. Officer Bigi observes the two men as they watch people enter and leave the bank. At about 1:50 P.M., an elderly woman carrying her pocketbook in her hand leaves the bank. The two men follow her out of the mall into the parking lot. Thinking that the men were about to steal the woman's pocketbook, Officer Bigi follows them out of the mall.

Sure enough, when the officer spots the two men in the parking lot, they are holding up the old lady. The male with the black jacket has a gun, and the other male is removing cash from the lady's pocketbook. Fearing for the victim's safety, the officer waits for the two robbers to finish their crime before she takes any action. At 1:55 P.M., when the robbers are fleeing the scene of the crime, Officer Bigi, with gun drawn for her own safety, catches them by surprise and arrests them.

Officer Bigi then notifies the local police about her arrests. When the police sergeant arrives on the scene and hears the story, he tells Officer Bigi that she should have notified the local police sooner and that it was a mistake for her to take police action against armed perpetrators without sufficient backup.

23. Officer Bigi did not arrest the two males at 1:35 P.M. because . . .

   (A) she is not authorized to make any off-duty arrests.
   (B) she is required to obtain the permission of her commanding officer before making an off-duty arrest.
   (C) she wasn't sure if they were bail jumpers.
   (D) she wanted to wait to get backup assistance.

24. Why did Officer Bigi decide to follow the two males at 1:40 P.M.?

   (A) They were escaped bail jumpers.
   (B) They were acting suspiciously.
   (C) They were going to steal an old lady's pocketbook.
   (D) They were armed.

25. The suspect who had the gun was . . .

   (A) a white male.
   (B) about 25–30 years old.
   (C) a black male.
   (D) wearing brown pants.

26. The officer waited for the crime in the parking lot to be completed before taking any action because . . .

   (A) she was waiting for backup assistance.
   (B) she was concerned for the safety of the victim.
   (C) she wanted to gather evidence.
   (D) she wasn't sure what to do.

27. The police sergeant believed Officer Bigi made a mistake by . . .

   (A) making an off-duty arrest.
   (B) following the suspects.
   (C) acting alone.
   (D) unholstering her gun.

28. How long does Officer Bigi have to notify her commanding officer about the arrests?

    (A) until 2:55 P.M.
    (B) until the next day.
    (C) until 4:00 P.M.
    (D) until midnight.

Directions: Answer questions 29–31 based solely on the information contained in the following passage.

From state to state, and even from county to county, the definition of what exactly constitutes a missing person varies. In some states, any unaccounted for person under the age of 21 is considered a missing person regardless of whether or not the absence is voluntary. In other jurisdictions, a requirement still exists that, in order for a person to be classified as missing, a certain time period must elapse. Properly, however, more and more jurisdictions have come to realize that no time requirement should be a factor in determining whether a person is to be considered a missing person. After all, a person missing 16 hours is no less missing than the same person will be in 24 hours. This is especially evident when the person missing might have been considering suicide.

What has really changed regarding missing persons is the perception of the public that the number of missing persons in our nation is growing at an epidemic rate. Adults, teenagers, and young children alike seem to be disappearing in alarming numbers. However, some experts feel that this perception on the part of the public is actually the result of a heightened sense of awareness on the part of the public of an already existing problem. These same experts maintain that what has raised the public sense of awareness of this problem is the attention to the problem given by the media and also federal law enforcement recognizing that in order to find such missing persons law enforcement actions must be federally coordinated.

The media's attention to the problem has been seen in everything from missing persons posters appearing on milk containers to weekly investigative programs. The efforts of law enforcement range from technical assistance in the conducting of missing persons investigations to information stored at the National Crime Information Center.

29. Which of the following statements is most correct concerning the nation's missing person problem?
    (A) There is definitely no missing person problem.
    (B) What makes a missing person investigation easy are the total similarities in tactics among all law enforcement jurisdictions.
    (C) How long a person is missing should not determine whether a person should actually be considered a missing person.
    (D) Persons considering suicide should not be considered missing persons.

30. What has really changed regarding missing persons is . . .

   (A) that only adults seem to be disappearing in large numbers.
   (B) the perception of the public that the number of missing persons in our nation is growing at an epidemic rate.
   (C) that only teenagers seem to be disappearing in large numbers.
   (D) that young children seem to be disappearing in alarming numbers faster than any other segment of our population.

31. Some experts maintain that the public's current feeling toward the state of the nation's missing persons problem is . . .

   (A) that there really is no problem.
   (B) the same as it has always been.
   (C) really the result of a heightened sense of awareness.
   (D) that the problem is less today than in years gone by as a result of the increased efforts of law enforcement.

Directions: Answer questions 32–41 based solely on following passage.

At 9:05 A.M. on Monday, May 15th, Court Clerk Green called the Metropolis Criminal Court to order and ordered all present to stand for the presiding judge, the Honorable Mark Brown.

The first case called was People versus White. According to the indictment in this case, Marvin White, a 32-year-old white male, did, on March 29th, forcibly steal property worth over $1000.00 from the Metropolis Museum of Art. Marvin White's attorney, Felix Green, requested an adjournment of 10 days to further consult with his client, and Judge Brown granted this request.

Thirty-five minutes after the court was called to order, the only bailiff on duty for the day, Sam Thompson, called the case of People versus Goodson. The allegation in this case is that on April 3rd, at 5:30 P.M., the defendant, Tom Goodson, did commit a felonious assault on the person of Allen Boston, a tourist from Australia. At 9:45 A.M., the District Attorney, John O'Hara, informed the judge that the victim in this case was still in the hospital and was unable to appear in court. Upon hearing this information, Judge Brown adjourned the case for an indefinite period of time pending the release of the victim from the hospital. Because of the apparent seriousness of the injury to the complainant in this case, the judge revoked the defendant's bail and remanded him to the Metropolis Prison.

The next case called was People versus Loughlin. This case involved a retired police officer, Sam Loughlin, who now stands accused of forgery. Upon his arraignment on May 1st, Mr. Loughlin pleaded not guilty and was released without bail. The judge's decision to release the defendant without bail was primarily a result of the fact that the defendant had no previous criminal record. After the Loughlin case, the bailiff announced a 1-hour lunch break.

At 1:20 P.M., as scheduled, the afternoon session of the court was called to order. The only item left on the day's calendar was a trial by jury of Pat Teachers, a 41-year-old white female, charged with driving while intoxicated. It seems that on October 12th of last year, the car that

Ms. Teachers was driving struck and killed a pedestrian. The rest of the afternoon was taken up with jury selection for this trial. After the jury was selected, the judge sent the jurors home with instructions to come back in 2 days for the trial of Pat Teachers.

32. Prior to May 15th, Marvin White was . . .

   (A) free on bail.
   (B) under indictment.
   (C) not represented by counsel.
   (D) incarcerated.

33. Attorney Green's request for an adjournment was granted so that Attorney Green could . . .

   (A) get additional information from his client.
   (B) find additional witnesses.
   (C) conduct his own criminal investigation.
   (D) question the victim in the case.

34. The case of People versus Goodson was called at . . .

   (A) 9:05 A.M.
   (B) 10:05 A.M.
   (C) 9:40 A.M.
   (D) 9:45 A.M.

35. Who announced the lunch break?

   (A) Green
   (B) Brown
   (C) Thompson
   (D) O'Hara

36. Why was the case of People versus Goodson adjoined?

   (A) The defendant was not available.
   (B) The defense attorney needed more time.
   (C) The people were not ready for trial.
   (D) The victim was in the hospital.

37. Prior to May 15th, Tom Goodson was . . .

   (A) free on bail.
   (B) under indictment.
   (C) not represented by counsel.
   (D) incarcerated.

38. The trial of Pat Teachers was scheduled for . . .

    (A) May 17th.
    (B) a Thursday.
    (C) May 19th.
    (D) a Friday.

39. The case of Tom Goodson was . . .

    (A) put off until some time in the future.
    (B) dismissed.
    (C) scheduled for May 17th.
    (D) sent to the grand jury.

40. Why was Mr. Loughlin released on bail?

    (A) He was a retired police officer.
    (B) His crime was a nonviolent one.
    (C) He pleaded not guilty.
    (D) He had no prior criminal record.

41. Who was the alleged victim of a felonious assault?

    (A) A retired police officer
    (B) A tourist
    (C) A white female
    (D) A white male

> **Directions:** Answer questions 42–50 based solely on the following criminal court case.

Shortly after a taxicab driver, who had been robbed by a man wielding a sawed-off shotgun, identified a picture of Innis as being that of his assailant, a peace officer saw Innis, who was unarmed at the time, on the street. The officer placed him under arrest and advised him of his rights under the Miranda decision, which is the landmark Supreme Court decision requiring law enforcement personnel to inform an arrested person of his or her constitutional rights to remain silent and to have an attorney. When police officers arrived at the scene in response to a call for assistance from the peace officer, Innis was twice again advised of his Miranda rights. Innis said that he understood his rights and wanted to talk to a lawyer. He was then placed in a police car to be driven to a police station in the company of three officers who were instructed not to question him or to intimidate him in any way. While enroute to the station house, two of the officers engaged in conversation about the shotgun, which was missing. One of the officers said, "There were a lot of handicapped children running around this area because a school for such children was located nearby and, God forbid, one of these children might find a weapon with shells and hurt themselves."

Innis, hearing this exchange, told the officers to turn around so he could show them where the gun was located. Upon returning to the scene of the arrest, where a search for the shotgun was in progress, Innis was readvised of his Miranda rights. He said that he understood these rights but that he wanted to get the gun out of the area because children were in the proximity of the school. He then led police to the shotgun.

The municipal trial court denied Innis' motion to suppress the shotgun and the statements he made to the police connected to its discovery. The trial court ruled that he had voluntarily waived his Miranda rights and, thus, he was subsequently convicted. Nevertheless, the State Supreme Court involved set aside the conviction, holding that Innis was entitled to a new trial, concluding that he had invoked his Miranda rights to counsel and that, contrary to Miranda's mandate that in the absence of counsel all custodial interrogation must cease, the police officers in the vehicle had "interrogated" Innis without a valid waiver of his right to counsel.

After the State Supreme Court issued its decision, the local prosecutor appealed the case to the U.S. Supreme Court. The U.S. Supreme Court held that Innis had not been interrogated and, thus, the fact that he did not waive his right to counsel was not important.

The Miranda safeguards come into play whenever a person in custody is subjected to either express questioning or anything similar to express questioning. The term *interrogation under Miranda* refers not only to express questioning but also to any words or actions on the part of law enforcement personnel (other than those normally attendant to arrest and custody, such as pedigree) that are reasonably likely to get an incriminating response from the suspect. (Note that pedigree refers to factual information regarding a person's name, age, date of birth, gender, and race.) Indeed, with respect to whether words or actions on the part of police or peace officers are likely to result in a person making an incriminating statement, it is less important whether the police or peace officers involved intend to get the suspect to speak than whether the suspect believes the words or actions were meant to induce him to speak.

Clearly, when questions are directed to a suspect in custody (express questioning), that is interrogation. However, when two or more police or peace officers talk to each other in a suspect's presence, but do not direct their conversation to the suspect, and the suspect responds because of what the officers said to each other, it is not always clear whether that is the same as questioning.

The key, as far as peace or police officers are concerned, is whether they should have known when talking to each other that their conversation was reasonably likely to produce an incriminating statement from the suspect. If the officer intends to get a response, or hopes for a response, by his conversation with his fellow officers, then any statement made by the suspect who has not waived his rights or for some reason cannot waive his rights (e.g., lawyer not present), would not be admissible in evidence. This would constitute interrogation because it is the equivalent of express questioning.

Even if a response is not intended but the officer is aware that the suspect is emotionally upset or would likely be touched by an appeal to his conscience (in this case the safety of handicapped children), then any conversation about the case would likely produce a response from the suspect and would be considered interrogation.

The Supreme Court of the United States indicated that there was no express questioning of Innis; the conversation between the officers did not seek a response from Innis. It could not be said that the officers should have known that their conversation was reasonably likely to cause Innis to make an incriminating statement.

42. Throughout the entire story, how many times was Innis advised of his Miranda rights?

(A) twice
(B) three times
(C) four times
(D) five times

43. Express questioning is not . . .

(A) interrogation
(B) an action by the police that is designed to make a person make an incriminating statement.
(C) a question directed to a suspect in custody.
(D) the obtaining of a person's pedigree by the police.

44. Conversation between peace or police officers about a case involving a suspect who is present and who the officers know is emotionally upset would . . .

(A) not be considered an interrogation under any circumstances.
(B) not be considered an interrogation unless the officers intended to get a response from the suspect.
(C) be considered an interrogation even if the peace or police officers did not intend to get a response from the suspect.
(D) be considered an interrogation because the courts have ruled that any conversation between enforcement personnel and a suspect is interrogation.

45. Innis was arrested after . . .

(A) the victim spotted him in the street.
(B) he was picked out of a lineup.
(C) his victim identified him from a photograph.
(D) he surrendered to a peace officer.

46. With respect to whether words or actions on the part of police or peace officers are likely to result in a person making an incriminating statement, which is more important?

(A) the intention of the officers
(B) the beliefs of the suspect
(C) the motives of the officers
(D) the age of the suspect

47. The municipal trial court based its decision on the fact that . . .

(A) Innis had not been interrogated.
(B) Innis had voluntarily waived his Miranda rights.
(C) Innis did not have a lawyer.
(D) Innis gave up the information of his own free will.

48. The U.S. Supreme Court based its findings on the fact that . . .

    (A) Innis had not been interrogated.
    (B) Innis had waived his right to counsel.
    (C) Innis was not emotionally upset when the incident occurred.
    (D) Innis was asked if he wanted a lawyer.

49. When three peace officers have a conversation with each other in the presence of a suspect but the officers do not direct the conversation to the suspect, . . .

    (A) it is considered questioning only if the suspect joins the conversation.
    (B) it is never considered questioning even if the suspect responds to the officers.
    (C) it is unclear whether it is the same as questioning even if the suspect responds to what the officers are saying.
    (D) it is not considered questioning even if the suspect joins in the conversation as long as the suspect has been informed of his Miranda rights.

50. Which of the following is an incorrect statement concerning the findings of the U.S. Supreme Court in this case?

    (A) No express questioning was involved.
    (B) The officers should have known that their conversation was reasonably likely to cause Innis to make an incriminating response.
    (C) Innis had not been interrogated.
    (D) The term interrogation under Miranda refers to more than just express questioning.

Directions: Answer questions 51–65 solely on the basis of the following legal definitions. Do not base your answers on any other knowledge of the law you may have. You may refer to the definitions when answering the questions.

  I. **Assault in the third degree**—A person is guilty of assault in the third degree when:

    A. With intent to cause a physical injury to another person, he causes a physical injury to such person or a third person; or

    B. He recklessly causes physical injury to another person; or

    C. With criminal negligence, he causes physical injury to another person by means of a deadly weapon or a dangerous instrument.

    Assault in the third degree is a misdemeanor.

  II. **Assault in the second degree**—A person is guilty of assault in the second degree when:

    A. With intent to cause serious physical injury to another person, he causes a serious physical injury to such person or to a third person; or

B. With intent to cause physical injury to another person he causes a physical injury to such person or to a third person by means of a deadly weapon or a dangerous instrument; or

C. With intent to prevent a court officer from performing a lawful duty, he causes physical injury to such court officer; or

D. He recklessly causes serious physical injury to another person by means of a deadly weapon or a dangerous instrument.

Assault in the second degree is a Class D felony. Felonies carry a greater punishment than misdemeanors.

III. Assault in the first degree—A person is guilty of assault in the first degree when:

A. With intent to cause serious physical injury to another person, he causes serious physical injury to such person or to a third person by means of a deadly weapon or a dangerous instrument; or

B. With intent to maim or scar another person, he causes such injury to such person or a third person.

Assault in the first degree is a Class C felony, which carries a greater punishment than a Class D felony.

IV. Aggravated assault upon a court officer—A person is guilty of aggravated assault upon a court officer when, with intent to cause serious physical injury to a person whom he knows or reasonably should know to be a court officer engaged in the course of performing his official duties, he causes a serious physical injury to the court officer by means of a deadly weapon or dangerous instrument. Aggravated assault upon a court officer is a Class B felony, which carries a greater punishment than a Class C or D felony.

V. Gang assault in the second degree—A person is guilty of gang assault in the second degree when, with intent to cause physical injury to another person and when aided by two or more other persons actually present, he causes serious physical injury to such person or to a third person. Gang assault in the second degree is a Class C felony.

VI. Gang assault in the first degree—A person is guilty of gang assault in the first degree when, with intent to cause serious physical injury to another person and when aided by two or more other persons actually present, he causes serious physical injury to such person or to a third person. Gang assault in the first degree is a Class B felony.

51. Ray intends to injure May by giving her a black eye. Ray strikes May in the face, but the blow does not result in a black eye as intended. Instead, May suffers a swollen lip, which is also a physical injury. In this instance, the most serious charge against Ray is . . .

    (A) assault in the third degree.
    (B) assault in the second degree.
    (C) assault in the first degree.
    (D) no crime because Ray did not intend to give May a swollen lip, the physical injury that actually resulted.

52. Don has never gotten along with his cousin, Court Officer Marks. During a family gathering, Don, who wants to seriously injure Court Officer Marks, strikes him over the head with a dangerous instrument, a beer bottle. Marks suffers a serious physical injury in the form of a concussion. In this instance, the most serious charge against Don is . . .

    (A) assault in the third degree.
    (B) assault in the second degree.
    (C) assault in the first degree.
    (D) none of the above.

53. May is being given a subpoena by Court Officer Digest. Intending to prevent the officer from issuing her the subpoena, May kicks the officer in the shins causing the officer to wince as a result of the pain of the physical injury. The most serious charge against May is . . .

    (A) assault in the third degree.
    (B) assault in the second degree.
    (C) assault in the first degree.
    (D) aggravated assault upon a court officer.

54. A person acting with criminal negligence would be most likely to commit which of the following?

    (A) only assault in the third degree
    (B) only assault in the second degree
    (C) only assault in the first degree
    (D) all the above

55. Pat intends to seriously injure Jack. Pat attempts to shoot Jack with a rifle, which is a deadly weapon; however, the rifle jams. Pat then uses the rifle as a dangerous instrument to beat Jack over the head, seriously injuring Jack. In this instance, the most serious charge against Pat . . .

    (A) is assault in the first degree.
    (B) is assault in the second degree.
    (C) is assault in the third degree.
    (D) cannot be assault because the rifle failed to fire properly.

56. Hank is still infatuated with Court Officer June Flowers, whom he had dated socially in the past. Hank follows her home one night and makes his feelings known to her. When the court officer rebuffs his advances, Hank strikes her with a blackjack, which is a deadly weapon, causing her serious injuries about the face and neck. In this instance, the most serious charge against Hank is . . .

    (A) assault in the third degree.
    (B) assault in the second degree.
    (C) assault in the first degree.
    (D) aggravated assault upon a court officer.

57. Regarding the various degrees of the crime of assault, which of the following statements is most correct?

    (A) All degrees of assault require some type of injury to result.
    (B) There is no way to commit an assault without the use of some type of deadly weapon or dangerous instrument.
    (C) Every type of assault must be committed intentionally.
    (D) All degrees of assault are felonies.

58. Tom intended to seriously injure Frank through the use of a deadly weapon but instead causes a serious physical injury to June through the use of the deadly weapon. The most serious charge against Tom is . . .

    (A) assault in the third degree.
    (B) assault in the second degree.
    (C) assault in the first degree.
    (D) not assault because the person intended to be injured was not injured.

59. Don is doing some construction on the roof of the courthouse. At quitting time, Don leaves some tools dangling dangerously from the roof. Court Officer Frank sees what Don has done and warns Don that a serious injury might occur if his tools, which under the circumstances are actually dangerous instruments, should fall and strike someone. Don in an act of recklessness decides to disregard Court Officer Frank's advice and goes home. During the night the tools fall and slightly injure a passerby. In this instance, the most serious charge against Don is . . .

    (A) assault in the second degree, mainly because he acted recklessly.
    (B) assault in the third degree, mainly because only a physical injury resulted.
    (C) assault in the first degree, mainly because the injury was caused by the tools, which are considered dangerous instruments.
    (D) no crime at all, mainly because Don was not present when the injury took place.

60. Evaluate the following statements.

1. For an assault to result in a felony charge, the victim must suffer a serious physical injury.

2. Anytime a court officer is assaulted, the charge is a felony.

Which of the following statements is most accurate concerning these statements?

(A) Only statement 1 is correct.
(B) Only statement 2 is correct.
(C) Both statements 1 and 2 are correct.
(D) Neither statement 1 nor 2 is correct.

61. Louie is angry at his landlord for having him evicted. At an eviction hearing in court, Louie throws acid at his landlord intending to scar him. However, Louie misses and strikes the judge, causing substantial scarring. In this instance, the most serious charge against Louie is . . .

(A) not assault, mainly because he injured someone other than the person whom he intended to injure.
(B) assault in the second degree, mainly because a physical injury resulted from his action.
(C) assault in the first degree, mainly because his actions caused someone to be scarred.
(D) assault in the third degree, mainly because he acted recklessly.

62. Moe, Larry, and Curly approach Tom, and each of them, intending to cause Tom a physical injury, punch him with their fists, causing Tom to suffer a physical injury. In such an instance, the most serious charge against Moe, Larry, and Curly is . . .

(A) assault in the first degree.
(B) assault in the second degree.
(C) assault in the third degree.
(D) gang assault in the second degree.

63. Joe and Harry decide to go on a "wilding spree" where innocent persons are beaten for no reason. Intending to cause serious physical injury to some senior citizens, Joe and Harry actually cause serious physical injury to seven senior citizens by punching and kicking them. When arrested, the most serious charge against Joe and Harry would be . . .

(A) assault in the first degree.
(B) assault in the second degree.
(C) assault in the third degree.
(D) gang assault in the first degree.

64. Evaluate the following statements.

1. The main difference between gang assault in the first degree and gang assault in the second degree is the number of persons actually present involved in assaulting someone.

2. Gang assault in the first degree is the same level of crime as aggravated assault on a court officer.

Which of the following statements is most accurate concerning these statements?

(A) Only statement 1 is correct.
(B) Only statement 2 is correct.
(C) Both statements 1 and 2 are correct.
(D) Neither statement 1 nor 2 is correct.

65. Huey, Dewey, and Louie wait for Court Officer Drake to enter his car as he goes off duty and leaves work. They are angry at the court for having given them long probation sentences and want to strike back at the system. As Officer Drake enters his private vehicle, he is assaulted with metal knuckles, which are considered a deadly weapon. Luckily he receives only minor physical injuries. In such an instance, the most serious charge against Huey, Dewey, and Louie is . . .

(A) assault in the first degree, mainly because a deadly weapon was used.
(B) assault in the second degree, mainly because a physical injury resulted from the use of a deadly weapon.
(C) aggravated assault upon a court officer.
(D) gang assault in the first degree.

Directions: Answer questions 66–74 solely on the basis of the following information.

Whenever a firearm comes into possession of a court officer, the court officer shall:

A. Unload any ammunition from the chamber or magazine.

NOTE: Do not handle unnecessarily to prevent possible destruction of fingerprints or other evidentiary matter. If the firearm is difficult to unload, safeguard it in its original condition and notify the court desk officer.

B. Scratch an identifying mark on the side of the cartridge case of any ammunition removed. A spent bullet shall be marked on its base.

C. Place the ammunition removed from the firearm in an envelope and seal the envelope.

D. Mark "Ammunition Removed From Firearm" across the face of the envelope, include the serial number of the firearm, or if there is no serial number, the number of the security lead seal placed on the firearm from which cartridges were removed.

E. Place additional ammunition other than that removed from the firearm, in a separate envelope and cross-reference it to the firearm.

NOTE: Do not mix ammunition removed from a firearm with that removed from clothing.

F. Deliver firearm(s) and ammunition to the court desk officer.

G. Prepare a CLERK'S INVOICE WORKSHEET.

    a. Describe the firearm(s) fully (calibre, make, model, type, and serial number).

    b. Affix a security lead seal if no serial number is distinguishable.

H. Mark initials on the flat surface of the firearm frame in evidence cases.

I. Prepare two copies of a PISTOL INDEX CARD for each handgun with serial number.

J. Notify the State Police Stolen Property Section when a firearm, with a distinguishable serial number, is seized in connection with an arrest, or is obtained under circumstances requiring investigation.

K. Enter on CLERK'S INVOICE WORKSHEET:

    a. Identity of the member notified at State Police Stolen Property Section

    b. Information received, including:

        i. "NO HIT," if there is no record.

        ii. "HIT," if there is a record.

NOTE: A court officer recovering a firearm wanted on alarm will not cancel the alarm. Cancellation of alarms will be made only by the State Police Stolen Property Section after examination of firearms by the State Police Ballistics Unit.

L. Have the court clerk type:

    a. CLERK'S INVOICE from the information on the court officer's completed CLERK'S INVOICE WORKSHEET

    b. COMPLAINT REPORT, if required

    c. REQUEST FOR LABORATORY EXAMINATION

M. Obtain a Clerk's Envelope from the court desk officer.

N. Place the firearm, bullets and shells, if any, in the envelope and seal it, in the presence of the court desk officer, to prevent loss of contents.

O. Present to the court desk officer:

    a. Clerk's envelope containing firearm

    b. CLERK'S INVOICE

    c. REQUEST FOR LABORATORY EXAMINATION

    d. PISTOL INDEX CARDS, if prepared.

Requests for gun traces concerning contraband weapons will be made to the Alcohol, Tobacco, and Firearms Bureau through the State Police Ballistics Unit. The State Police Ballistics Unit will forward a report of the results directly to the requesting court officer as well as the court's Intelligence Division.

66. According to the procedure, it would be most appropriate to make a request for a gun trace for a contraband weapon through . . .

(A) the Alcohol, Tobacco and Firearms Bureau.
(B) the State Police Ballistics Unit.
(C) the court's Intelligence Division.
(D) the court desk officer.

67. A firearm has come into the possession of Court Officer Days while the court officer was patrolling the grounds just outside the courthouse. In this instance, the court officer's first action should be . . .

(A) to look for the serial number of the firearm.
(B) to verify the owner.
(C) to unload it.
(D) to call the shift supervisor.

68. At the scene of an attempted escape by a prisoner awaiting trial, a spent bullet has been recovered by Court Officer Eaves. In such a situation, the Court Officer should . . .

(A) initial the side of the bullet.
(B) mark the base of the bullet.
(C) wrap a lead security seal around the bullet.
(D) wrap the bullet in tape.

69. Which of the following is responsible for preparing a CLERK'S INVOICE WORKSHEET?

(A) the court officer concerned
(B) the court clerk
(C) a member of the court's Intelligence Division
(D) the court desk officer

70. According to the procedure, a court officer should affix a security lead seal to a firearm if the firearm . . .

(A) has been modified.
(B) has no registered owner.
(C) has no serial number.
(D) has no firing pin.

71. According to the procedure, alarms on wanted firearms may be canceled only by . . .

(A) the court officer who recovered the firearm.
(B) the State Police Stolen Property Section.
(C) the State Police Ballistics Unit.
(D) the court desk officer.

72. A certain court officer seizes a firearm in connection with making an arrest. The firearm has no serial number. The court officer then notifies State Police Stolen Property Section. In this instance, the actions of the court officer were . . .

(A) proper, mainly because the State Police Stolen Property Section is to be notified of all firearms seized in connection with arrests.
(B) improper, mainly because the State Police Stolen Property Section is not required to be notified about recovered firearms that do not have a serial number.
(C) proper, mainly because the State Police Stolen Property Section examines recovered firearms.
(D) improper, mainly because it is never necessary to notify the State Police Stolen Property Section about firearms recovered in connection with an arrest.

73. Which of the following forms is not required in every instance to be submitted to the court desk officer by the court officer recovering the firearm?

(A) an envelope containing the firearm
(B) a CLERK'S INVOICE
(C) a REQUEST FOR LABORATORY EXAMINATION
(D) PISTOL INDEX CARDS

74. Court Officer Dawns has recovered a firearm and is attempting to unload it. The firearm is difficult to unload, so the court officer safeguards it in its original condition. In this instance, the court officer should notify . . .

(A) the State Police Ballistics Unit.
(B) the court desk officer.
(C) the shift supervisor.
(D) any member on duty at the court's Intelligence Division.

Directions: Answer questions 75–78 solely on the basis of the following information.

Upon being exposed to an infectious disease or suffering a human bite or hypodermic needle puncture wound, the affected court officer shall

A. Notify the court desk officer who shall

    a. Notify the court's Medical Unit and obtain an Exposure Report number.

    b. Make an official court log entry of the information including the Exposure Report number in the court log entry.

    c. Notify the Department of Health physician of the facts involved.

    d. Contact the court officer involved and advise of necessary treatment.

B. Comply with the directions of the Department of Health physician.

C. Make a court officer memo book entry of the facts involved including the Exposure Report number.

ACCIDENTAL SPILLS OF BLOOD OR BODY FLUIDS

A supply of household bleach will be maintained at all courthouses. Accidental spills of blood or body fluids on floors, detentions cells, department cars, or other surfaces, other than clothing or fabric, may be cleaned by applying a freshly mixed solution of one part household bleach with ten parts water. It is imperative that the preceding mixture be carefully followed. Household bleach is not to be mixed with any solution other than water, and it must be freshly mixed for each use.

Court officers are reminded that this mixture of bleach and water will cause damage if used to clean uniforms. Uniform items soiled with blood or body fluids can be effectively cleaned by routine laundering or dry cleaning procedures. Bleach should not be used to cleanse hands. In addition, bleach mixed with any substance other than water may cause a toxic gas. Therefore, disposal of bleach or bleach dilutions should be performed only in a sink (not a urinal or toilet because they sometimes contain chemical deodorizers). When preparing a bleach dilution, the container used for the diluted solution must be cleaned with water and free of any other solution.

75. According to the procedure, which of the following is least appropriate when dealing with accidental spills of blood and body fluids?

   (A) Bleach must be freshly mixed for each use.
   (B) Household bleach is not to be mixed with any solution other than water.
   (C) When mixing household bleach with water, mix ten parts of household bleach with one part water.
   (D) Bleach should not be used to cleanse hands.

76. According to the procedure, which of the following is most appropriate when dealing with accidental spills of blood and body fluids?

   (A) The container used for a diluted solution of bleach must be cleaned with water and free of any other solution.
   (B) Bleach dilutions should be performed in a urinal or toilet so that any excesses can be easily flushed away.
   (C) Bleach dilutions should not be performed in a sink.
   (D) Mixtures of bleach and water should be used to clean uniforms.

77. Court Officer Ray Collars suffers a human bite wound while effecting an arrest. According to the procedure, which of the following should he notify first?

   (A) the Department of Health physician
   (B) the court desk officer
   (C) the shift supervisor
   (D) the court's Medical Unit

78. According to the procedure, the Exposure Report number is to be entered . . .

(A) only in the court log.
(B) only in the memo book of the court officer involved.
(C) in both the court log and the memo book of the court officer involved.
(D) neither in the court log nor the memo book of the court officer involved.

Directions: Answer questions 79–85 solely on the basis of the following information.

When a court officer effects an arrest, the court officer shall in the following order:

A. Inform the prisoner of the authority for the arrest and the cause of the arrest, unless physical resistance or flight render such notification impractical.

B. Handcuff the prisoner with the prisoner's hands behind the prisoner's back.

C. Immediately field search the prisoner and search adjacent vicinity for weapons, evidence, and/or contraband.

D. Advise the prisoner of the prisoner's constitutional rights before questioning.

    a. If a juvenile is taken into custody, the parents/guardians will be notified immediately.

    b. When questioning a juvenile, both the juvenile and the parents/guardians, if present, will be advised of the juvenile's constitutional rights.

E. Notify the court desk officer of the court where the arresting court officer is assigned of the facts of the arrest.

F. Remove the prisoner to the police precinct of arrest and inform the police desk officer of the charge(s).

G. Notify the police desk officer if force was used to effect the arrest.

    NOTE: If an arrest is made by an off-duty court officer, the court desk officer is required to notify the on-duty shift supervisor who will respond to the location of the arrest to determine the validity of the arrest.

H. Make a thorough search of the prisoner in the presence of the police desk officer.

I. Remove the following property from the prisoner:

    a. Unlawfully carried

    b. Required as evidence

    c. Lawfully carried, but dangerous to life or would facilitate escape

    d. Can be used to deface or damage property

    e. Personal property, except clothing, if prisoner is intoxicated or unconscious

    NOTE: A prisoner's funds should be counted and returned by the arresting court officer.

J. Advise the prisoner of the right to make three (3) telephone calls within the state without charge or to make collect calls, outside the state, if toll charges are accepted.

    a. Make the telephone calls if the prisoner is incapacitated by alcohol or drugs.

K. Permit the prisoner to converse on the telephone, except where the ends of justice may be defeated or a dangerous condition may be created.

L. Notify the prisoner's relatives or friends if the prisoner is under 19 years of age, or is admitted to a hospital, or is apparently of unsound mind.

M. Prepare a MISSING PERSON REPORT and notify the police Missing Persons Squad if unable to make such notification.

N. Deliver all forms completed in connection with the arrest to the police desk officer.

NOTE: Court officers at the scene of an incident at which a prisoner is acting in a deranged, erratic manner apparently caused by a drug overdose (i.e., cocaine psychosis, angle dust, heroin overdose, etc.) will request the response of the shift supervisor, if an ambulance is not immediately available. The shift supervisor will determine whether the prisoner should be removed to the appropriate hospital by using an official department car or await the arrival of an ambulance. The prisoner is not to be brought to a police facility.

79. Court Officer Bob Carter has just arrested Don Frank for assaulting a witness in the hallway of the courthouse. After Court Officer Carter informs the prisoner of his authority and the cause of the arrest, he properly handcuffs the prisoner. According to procedure the court officer should now immediately . . .

    (A) advise the prisoner of his rights.
    (B) field search the prisoner.
    (C) notify the court desk officer.
    (D) request the response of the on-duty shift supervisor.

80. While off duty, Court Officer June White arrests a man who attempted to steal her car. She brings the suspect to the police precinct of arrest for booking purposes. While there, the validity of the arrest she has just made should be determined by . . .

    (A) the shift supervisor.
    (B) the court desk officer.
    (C) the police desk officer.
    (D) the detective on duty at the police precinct of arrest.

81. While effecting the arrest of a suspect for tampering with physical evidence, Court Officer Green uses force to subdue the suspect who is resisting arrest. According to the procedure, Court Officer Green should notify . . .

    (A) the court desk officer.
    (B) the police desk officer.
    (C) the shift supervisor.
    (D) the detective on duty at the police precinct of arrest.

82. According to the procedure, which of the following would be least correct?

(A) A prisoner's funds should be counted and returned by the arresting court officer.
(B) Unlawfully carried property should always be removed from a prisoner.
(C) Evidence should always be removed from a prisoner.
(D) Personal property should never be removed from a prisoner.

83. Tom Banks has been arrested for inciting a riot in the halls of the courthouse. At the time of his arrest, Banks is incapacitated because he is under the influence of narcotics. He asks the arresting court officer if he can make a phone call. The arresting court officer would be most correct if he . . .

(A) told Banks that he could make the calls only when Banks becomes sober.
(B) told the prisoner to give up his rights because he is incapacitated.
(C) made the calls for Banks.
(D) allowed him to make the call despite the fact that he was incapacitated.

84. An 18-year-old suspect has been arrested by Court Officer Hall. The court officer attempts to notify the prisoner's friends or relatives but is unsuccessful. In this situation, the court officer should notify . . .

(A) the court desk officer.
(B) the Missing Persons Squad.
(C) the police desk officer.
(D) the shift supervisor.

85. Pat Walker is arrested while acting in a deranged manner caused by a drug overdose. The arresting court officer is informed that an ambulance is not available. In this instance, the arresting court officer . . .

(A) should deliver the prisoner immediately to the hospital in an official department car.
(B) bring the prisoner to the nearest police precinct for arrest processing.
(C) request the response of the shift supervisor.
(D) make a second call for an ambulance.

At times at the scene of large assemblages, court officers will be required to make arrests because of nonviolent, but still illegal, conduct such as unlawfully obstructing courtrooms, building entrances, and governmental offices. The shift supervisor, after consultation with those at the scene, shall be the one to decide the next action such as effecting arrests. Warnings shall be given to those involved before any such arrest is made. Specifically, such persons shall be warned that they will face arrest if they do not cease their illegal conduct. A period of time that fits the circumstances will be allowed for such persons to move on. Any court officer attempting to move a passive resister shall, wherever possible, use stretchers to prevent injury to themselves or to any passive resister.

86. A large group of demonstrators have taken over a courtroom to show their displeasure over the recent decisions of a certain judge. Court Officer Drake determines that even though the demonstrators are not violent, their conduct is illegal. In such an instance, Court Officer Drake's first action should be . . .

   (A) to begin moving persons by stretcher.
   (B) to tell the demonstrators that they will be given a period of time that fits the circumstances to move on before any action will be taken.
   (C) to immediately arrest the demonstrators before the situation gets out of hand.
   (D) to consult with the shift supervisor.

A courtroom visit is a visit between a prisoner in the custody of the court and a person seeking to visit with such prisoner. Courtroom visits may take place only while a court is not actually in session.

   A court officer shall not permit a courtroom visit of a prisoner in custody unless directed to do so by a judge and the judge is present. A minimum of two court officers must be present during any such visit. No more than one visitor may visit with a prisoner at any one time unless the prisoner is under 21 years of age and such visitors are the parents or guardians of such prisoner. While the visit is being conducted, the court officers involved shall ensure that a physical barrier is maintained between the visitor and the prisoner, and no physical contacts shall be allowed, nor shall objects be passed, between any visitor and a prisoner. The duration of such visits shall not exceed 30 minutes and no more than a total of three visitors will be allowed any one prisoner.

87. Court Officer Grey is in the court while a prisoner is receiving a courtroom visit. In such a situation, according to the procedure, it would be most appropriate if . . .

(A) the judge left the courtroom while the visit took place.
(B) in all cases both parents of the prisoner were allowed to visit with the prisoner at the same time.
(C) Officer Grey was accompanied by at least one other court officer.
(D) Officer Grey examined all articles passed between the prisoner and visitors.

88. Evaluate the following statements concerning courtroom visits of prisoners.

1. No such visit shall exceed one-half hour.

2. No more than a total of three visitors will be allowed any one prisoner except in the case of parents visiting their 20-year-old prisoner.

Which of the following is most accurate concerning these statements?

(A) Only statement 1 is correct.
(B) Only statement 2 is correct.
(C) Both statements 1 and 2 are correct.
(D) Neither statements 1 nor 2 are correct.

89. Evaluate the following statements concerning courtroom visits of prisoners.

1. A courtroom visit is a visit between any defendant in court and a person seeking to visit with such defendant.

2. A courtroom visit may not take place unless so directed by a judge.

Which of the following is most accurate concerning these statements?

(A) Only statement 1 is correct.
(B) Only statement 2 is correct.
(C) Both statements 1 and 2 are correct.
(D) Neither statements 1 nor 2 are correct.

Security lines are often set up by court officers at the scene of emergencies in and around courthouses to protect life and property and to prevent unauthorized persons and vehicles from entering the area beyond security lines. To assist court officers in carrying out this responsibility, only the following persons and vehicles shall be permitted to cross security lines and enter the area beyond such security lines:

1. The mayor
2. U.S. mail vehicles while actually delivering the mail
3. Persons who hold unexpired press cards
4. Prison vans in the process of transporting prisoners
5. Ambulances, empty or carrying sick or injured
6. Law enforcement personnel whose duties actually involve them with the situation at hand

90. An organized crime mob assassination has taken place right on the steps of the courthouse. Security lines have been established to secure the scene. Court Officer Neil Bailes would be most correct in allowing which of the following to cross such security lines?

    (A) any U.S. mail truck
    (B) any prison van
    (C) any vehicle in which the mayor is traveling
    (D) any ambulance

REFERENCE TABLE

Y	O	U	N	G	S	T	E	R	Z
1	2	3	4	5	6	7	8	9	0

Directions: For each question use the relationship in the table and select the choice that correctly spells the word identified in the question.

91. Using the reference table, which of the following most accurately spells GROGGY?

    (A) 595221
    (B) 592551
    (C) 590551
    (D) 952991

92. Using the reference table, which of the following most accurately spells STRONG?

    (A) 679045
    (B) 679425
    (C) 679245
    (D) 679254

93. Using the reference table, which of the following most accurately spells TESTER?

    (A) 768789
    (B) 786987
    (C) 768769
    (D) 786789

94. Using the reference table, which of the following most accurately spells SNORES?

    (A) 642986
    (B) 640986
    (C) 604986
    (D) 642896

95. Using the reference table, which of the following most accurately spells TONGUE?

    (A) 724358
    (B) 704538
    (C) 724538
    (D) 704358

Directions: Use the information in the following reference table to answer questions 96–100. In the table each number has been associated with a letter. For each question you are to select the choice that contains the letters that, when associated with the numbers in the reference table, accurately depict the numerical calendar date required by the question.

REFERENCE TABLE

I	H	A	T	E	D	C	O	P	S
1	2	3	4	5	6	7	8	9	0

EXAMPLE

Q. Which of the following choices represents February 09?

    (A) SH-OP
    (B) SH-SP
    (C) OH-SH
    (D) OP-OP

Explanation: First convert the month into a numerical date. February would be 02 or, using the reference table, SH. The date of 09 would be represented by the letters SP. Therefore, February 09 would be represented as the letters SH-SP.

---

96. Which of the following choices represents January 05?

    (A) IS-ES
    (B) ES-SI
    (C) SI-SE
    (D) SI-ES

97. Which of the following choices represents August 30?

   (A) OA-SS
   (B) SO-AS
   (C) SO-ES
   (D) OS-SA

98. Which of the following choices represents October 15?

   (A) IS-IE
   (B) SI-EI
   (C) IO-IE
   (D) IE-IS

99. Which of the following choices represents December 16?

   (A) HI-DI
   (B) ID-IH
   (C) HI-DI
   (D) IH-ID

100. Which of the following choices represents July 14?

   (A) SI-TC
   (B) SC-IT
   (C) SC-TI
   (D) SI-CT

ANSWER KEY
Practice Exam Two

1.	A	26.	B	51.	A	76.	A
2.	A	27.	D	52.	C	77.	B
3.	C	28.	A	53.	B	78.	C
4.	A	29.	C	54.	A	79.	B
5.	C	30.	B	55.	A	80.	A
6.	C	31.	C	56.	C	81.	B
7.	A	32.	B	57.	A	82.	D
8.	A	33.	A	58.	C	83.	C
9.	D	34.	C	59.	A	84.	B
10.	C	35.	C	60.	D	85.	C
11.	B	36.	D	61.	C	86.	D
12.	A	37.	A	62.	C	87.	C
13.	A	38.	A	63.	B	88.	A
14.	D	39.	A	64.	B	89.	B
15.	C	40.	D	65.	B	90.	C
16.	D	41.	B	66.	B	91.	B
17.	D	42.	C	67.	C	92.	C
18.	C	43.	D	68.	B	93.	D
19.	B	44.	C	69.	A	94.	A
20.	A	45.	C	70.	C	95.	C
21.	D	46.	B	71.	B	96.	C
22.	D	47.	B	72.	B	97.	B
23.	C	48.	A	73.	D	98.	A
24.	B	49.	C	74.	B	99.	D
25.	A	50.	B	75.	C	100.	B

DIAGNOSTIC CHART

Directions: After you score your test, complete the following chart by inserting in the column entitled "Your Number Correct" the number of correct questions you answered in each of the eight sections of the test. Then compare your score in each section with the ratings in the column entitled "Scale." Finally, to correct your weaknesses, follow the instructions found at the end of the chart.

Section	Question Numbers	Area	Your Number Correct	Scale
1	1–15	Memory (15 questions)		15 Right—Excellent 13-14 Right—Good 11-12 Right—Fair Under 11 Right—Poor
2	16–50	Reading Comprehension (35 questions)		33-35 Right—Excellent 30-32 Right—Good 27-29 Right—Fair Under 27 Right—Poor
3	51–65	Legal Definitions (15 questions)		15 Right—Excellent 13-14 Right—Good 11-12 Right—Fair Under 11 Right—Poor
4	66–90	Applying Court Officer Procedures (25 questions)		25 Right—Excellent 22-24 Right—Good 18-21 Right—Fair Under 18 Right—Poor
5	91–100	Clerical Ability (10 questions)		10 Right—Excellent 8-9 Right—Good 7 Right—Fair Under 7 Right—Poor

How to correct weaknesses:

1. If you are weak in Section 1, concentrate on Chapter 2.
2. If you are weak in Section 2, concentrate on Chapter 1.
3. If you are weak in Section 3, concentrate on Chapter 4.
4. If you are weak in Section 4, concentrate on Chapter 3.
5. If you are weak in Section 5, concentrate on Chapter 5.

Note: Consider yourself weak in a section if you receive a score other than excellent in that section.

ANSWERS EXPLAINED

1. **(A)** Only two docket numbers are given, and both of them appear as choices. Also note that close variations of each number are also present as choices. If you noticed that the case docket number is comprised of odd numbers two digits apart (1 3 5 7 9 11), you had no problem with this question.

2. **(A)** If you noticed that Court Officer #1 was Singleton, and associated #1 with single, then you undoubtedly got this question correct. However, concerning associations, remember that the ones we suggest are just that, suggestions. If you had an association that worked for you, that is what matters. The important thing is realizing that associations are the key to answering memory questions correctly.

3. **(C)** There were four dates included in the information, and they all appeared as choices in this question. The date of arraignment was February 15th.

4. **(A)** 140.30 of the Penal Law is the correct charge. Note the examiner's attempt to confuse you by making all the choices quite similar. You must pay attention to detail to do well on memory questions.

5. **(C)** The Defense Attorney is Perry Johnson. The famous TV defense attorney is Perry Mason. If you made that association, this question would have been an easy one for you to handle.

6. **(C)** The Arresting Officer, or the "cop" who made the arrest, was Ray Coppola. In many cases involving names, such as this one, some association involving the name can be formed.

7. **(A)** The Magistrate was Mary Jacobs. Alphabetical associations are the easiest to develop and are quite effective.

8. **(A)** The District Attorney was David Allen.

9. **(D)** Ron Tonso was carrying a baseball schedule, and William Judd was carrying football tickets.

10. **(C)** Ron Tonso had a $20 bill and a quarter. William Judd had two $10 bills, two dimes, and a nickel. They both had $20.25.

11. **(B)** William Judd was in possession of an eviction notice. Ron Tonso was not in possession of any items that would lead one to believe he was having difficulties with his private residence.

12. **(A)** Ron Tonso had a plane ticket in his possession. William Judd was not in possession of any item that would lead one to believe he is planning a trip.

13. **(A)** Ron Tonso had a prescription and aspirin in his possession. William Judd did not possess any item that would lead one to believe he is experiencing a medical problem.

14. **(D)** William Judd did not possess any item that indicated the plate number of his car.

15. **(C)** Ron Tonso had one key. William Judd had two keys. They both had at least one key.

16. **(D)** It is probably true that the crime problem in this country will never be truly solved.

17. **(D)** Choices A, B, and C are opinions and not facts. Choice D is factual according to the information given.

18. **(C)** Court officers are sometimes legally entitled to use force to defend themselves or a third party against unlawful force.

19. **(B)** Court officers may not use deadly physical force upon another person unless they reasonably believe that such other person is using or about to use deadly physical force against them or another.

20. **(A)** The restriction that arrests can be made only if the offense was committed in the presence of the officer does NOT apply to felonies. It applies ONLY to misdemeanors and violations. This means that arrests can be made for felonies even if the arresting officer was not present when they occurred.

21. **(D)** Having the right to counsel means having a right to a lawyer. The counsel (lawyer) may be of the juvenile's own choosing or may be appointed by the court for financial or other reasons.

22. **(D)** To waive means to give up or to relinquish. Even though a waiver (a giving up) of the right to counsel may be made, it is not effective unless the waiver is made in writing by both the juvenile and at least one of the parents or legal guardians.

23. **(C)** At 1:35 P.M., even though the officer believed the two males might be bail jumpers, she wasn't sure so she did not make an arrest.

24. **(B)** Don't let what you think or assume is going on influence your choice of answers. It clearly states in the passage that the officer decided to follow the males in the first place because they were acting suspiciously.

25. **(A)** Test writers often make it necessary to relate information from one part of the passage to another. That is what happened here. The suspect with the gun had on a black jacket. Earlier in the passage it stated that the suspect with the black jacket was a white male.

26. **(B)** Fearing for the victim's safety, the officer waited for the crime to be completed before taking any action.

27. **(C)** The police sergeant felt that the officer should have called for backup assistance.

28. **(A)** The first paragraph states that commanding officers have to be notified of off-duty arrests within 1 hour of the arrest. The arrest was made at 1:55 P.M.

29. **(C)** A person missing 16 hours is no less missing than the same person will be in 24 hours.

30. **(B)** Choice B is found in the second paragraph of the passage.

31. **(C)** The public's current feeling is, as stated in the passage, actually the result of a heightened sense of awareness on the part of the public of an already existing problem.

32. **(B)** The second sentence of paragraph two clearly indicates that there was already an indictment in this case.

33. **(A)** Felix Green is Marvin White's attorney, and he requested a 10-day adjournment so that he could further consult with his client.

34. **(C)** The case of People versus Goodson was called 35 minutes after the court was called to order at 9:05 A.M.

35. **(C)** The lunch break was announced by the bailiff. The only bailiff on duty that day was Sam Thompson. You must understand that it is often necessary to go to more than one place in the passage to find the answers.

36. **(D)** The victim, Allen Boston, was still in the hospital and was unable to appear.

37. **(A)** Because of the apparent seriousness of the injury to the complainant, the judge revoked the bail of the defendant Tom Goodson and remanded him to the Metropolis Prison.

38. **(A)** The judge instructed the jurors to come back 2 days from May 15th.

39. **(A)** Goodson's case was adjourned for an indefinite period of time pending the release of the victim from the hospital.

40. **(D)** Statements A, B, and C are all factual but not responsive to the question. The primary reason why he was released on bail was because he had no previous criminal record.

41. **(B)** Allen Boston, a tourist from Australia, was the alleged victim of a felonious assault. The passage does not give any other information about Mr. Boston.

42. **(C)** Innis was advised of his rights once upon the initial arrest by the peace officer, twice again when police officers arrived, and a fourth time before he led the police to the shotgun. Note that this is the classic reading comprehension question. If you followed the strategy recommended in the reading comprehension chapter, you would have read the questions first. Then, knowing what information to look for, you could engage in sensitized reading.

43. **(D)** The decision specifically states that obtaining the suspect's pedigree is not considered to be express questioning.

44. **(C)** The key is whether the officers know that the suspect is emotionally upset, and the stem of the question clearly indicates that they have such knowledge. Such a conversation would be considered interrogation.

45. **(C)** It is stated in the first paragraph that Innis was identified from a picture.

46. **(B)** The most important factor is whether or not the suspect believes the words or actions of the officers are meant to get him to speak. Note the similarity between Choices A and C. They are too closely related to each other for either one of them to be the answer.

47. **(B)** The municipal trial court ruled that Innis had voluntarily waived his Miranda rights and, thus, was subsequently convicted.

48. **(A)** The U.S. Supreme Court held that Innis had not been interrogated and, thus, the fact that he did not waive his right to counsel was not important.

49. **(C)** The U.S. Supreme Court held that, under the circumstances described in the question, it is not always clear whether it is the same as questioning.

50. **(B)** The U.S. Supreme Court held that it cannot be said that the officers in the Innis case should have known that their conversation was reasonably likely to cause Innis to make an incriminating statement.

51. **(A)** Ray intended to give another person a physical injury and that is what resulted. The charge is assault in the third degree.

52. **(C)** Intending to seriously injure someone and then seriously injuring someone with a dangerous instrument or a deadly weapon is assault in the first degree.

53. **(B)** May intended to prevent the court officer from performing a lawful duty and in so doing caused a physical injury to such court officer. May committed assault in the second degree. It is not aggravated assault upon a court officer because May did not intend to inflict a serious physical injury on the officer nor was a deadly weapon nor dangerous instrument used.

54. **(A)** Only assault in the third degree can be committed while acting with criminal negligence.

55. **(A)** Pat intended to cause serious physical injury to another person and caused a serious physical injury to such person by means of a dangerous instrument. That is one way of committing assault in the first degree.

56. **(C)** Choice D is incorrect because Court Officer Flowers was not performing her official duties at the time of the attack. However, Jack intended to seriously injure another with a deadly weapon and actually did so. The charge would be as indicated in Choice C, assault in the first degree.

57. **(A)** Choice B is incorrect because at times, such as in assault in the third degree, an assault can be committed merely by using one's hands without the use of a deadly weapon or dangerous instrument. Choice C is incorrect because some assaults may be committed recklessly, as well as with criminal negligence. Choice D is incorrect because assault in the third degree is not a felony. It is a misdemeanor. However, as indicated in Choice A, all assaults must result in some type of injury.

58. **(C)** When a person intends to seriously injure another person by the use of a deadly weapon, and such person or a third person is seriously injured by the use of the deadly weapon, the correct charge is assault in the first degree as indicated in Choice C.

59. **(A)** A dangerous instrument, the tools, caused only a physical injury. Therefore, a physical injury was caused by a dangerous instrument as a result of someone acting recklessly. For a charge of first-degree assault to be properly lodged, a serious physical injury would have had to result.

60. **(D)** Statement 1 is incorrect because a charge of second-degree assault, which is a felony, could result when someone causes a physical injury, not a serious physical injury, to another intentionally by means of a deadly weapon or a dangerous instrument. Statement 2 is incorrect because an assault on an off-duty court officer, which resulted in only a physical injury to the court officer could bring about a charge of third-degree assault, which is a misdemeanor. Thus, both statements are incorrect.

61. **(C)** Choice D is incorrect because Louie acted intentionally according to the facts given. A person is guilty of assault in the first degree when with intent to maim or scar

another person, he causes such injury to such person or a third person. This eliminates Choices A and B. Choice C is the answer.

62. **(C)** It is not gang assault in the second degree because no serious physical injury resulted. The actions described constitute assault in the third degree, namely intending a physical injury, a physical injury resulted.

63. **(B)** It is not gang assault in the first degree because at least three persons would be required, the person committing the assault aided by two others actually present. It is assault in the second degree—that is, intending to cause serious physical injury, serious physical injury is actually caused without the use of a dangerous instrument or deadly weapon.

64. **(B)** The same number of people is required to commit gang assault in the first degree as is required to commit gang assault in the second degree. Gang assault in the first degree and aggravated assault on a court officer are both Class B felonies. Statement 1 is incorrect; statement 2 is correct.

65. **(B)** Choice C is incorrect because aggravated assault on a court officer must take place while the officer is performing his or her duties. Assault in the first degree and gang assault in the first degree must both result in a serious physical injury. Therefore, Choices A and C are incorrect. Choice B is the answer, which is assault in the second degree—that is, a physical injury resulted from the use of a deadly weapon.

66. **(B)** Requests for gun traces concerning contraband weapons will be made to the Alcohol, Tobacco, and Firearms Bureau through the State Police Ballistics Unit who will then forward a report of the results directly to the requesting court officer and the court's Intelligence Division.

67. **(C)** Safety is always important; hence, the first step is to unload the firearm.

68. **(B)** It would not be a good idea to mark a spent bullet on its side because there might be ballistic marking there from the firearm that discharged the bullet. As stated in the procedure, it should be marked on its base.

69. **(A)** As stated in the procedure, it is the job of the court officer concerned.

70. **(C)** The court officer shall affix a security lead seal if no serial number is distinguishable. Without a distinguishable serial number, its future identification is made more difficult. The placing of a security lead seal helps in identifying it in the future.

71. **(B)** Choice A is incorrect because a court officer recovering a firearm wanted on alarm will not cancel the alarm. Cancellation of alarms will be made only by the State Police Stolen Property Section after examination of firearms by their Ballistics Unit. Choice B is correct.

72. **(B)** Choice C is incorrect because the State Police Ballistics Unit examines firearms. Choices A and D are incorrect because the State Police Stolen Property Section will be notified if the firearm is seized in connection with an arrest and *in addition* has a distinguishable serial number.

73. **(D)** The procedure directs the court officer recovering a firearm to prepare two copies of a PISTOL INDEX CARD for each handgun with serial number. Hence, if a firearm without a serial number is recovered, there would be no need for two copies of a PIS-

TOL INDEX CARD to be prepared; therefore, they would not be required to be presented to the court desk officer.

74. **(B)** The procedure requires that the court desk officer be notified. It would seem somewhat logical that possibly the State Police Ballistics Unit should be notified for its help in such a situation. However, in these procedure-type questions the answer must be selected based on what is contained in the procedure.

75. **(C)** The statements in Choices A, B, and D are right out of the procedure. Choice C is incorrect because the proper mix is a solution of one part household bleach with ten parts water. Numerical amounts are favorite source areas of examiners.

76. **(A)** Choices B and C are incorrect because bleach dilutions should be performed only in a sink, not a urinal or toilet because they sometimes contain chemical deodorizers. Choice D is incorrect because a mixture of bleach and water will cause damage if used to clean uniforms.

77. **(B)** The first action for the affected court officer is to make a notification to the court desk officer.

78. **(C)** According to the procedure, the Exposure Report number is to be entered in both the court log and the memo book of the court officer involved.

79. **(B)** After properly handcuffing the prisoner, the next step the court officer should take immediately is to field search the prisoner.

80. **(A)** According to procedure, when an off-duty court officer makes an arrest, a determination of the validity of the off-duty arrest should be made by the on-duty shift supervisor.

81. **(B)** The court officer should notify the police desk officer if force was used to effect the arrest.

82. **(D)** Choices A, B, and C are as stated in the procedure. However, personal property, except clothing, may be removed if the prisoner is intoxicated or unconscious. Therefore, Choice D is incorrect.

83. **(C)** After making an arrest, the arresting court officer should make the telephone calls a prisoner is entitled to if the prisoner is incapacitated by alcohol or drugs.

84. **(B)** The arresting court officer is required to notify the prisoner's relatives or friends if the prisoner is under 19 years of age. If the court officer is unable to make this notification, the court officer shall notify the police Missing Persons Squad.

85. **(C)** Under these circumstances, the court officer is required to request the response of the shift supervisor if an ambulance is not immediately available. The shift supervisor will determine if the prisoner should be removed to the hospital by official department car or to await the arrival of an ambulance. The prisoner is not to be brought to a police facility.

86. **(D)** According to the procedure, the shift supervisor shall consult with those on the scene before arrests can be considered. Therefore, before any further action may be taken, Court Officer Drake must confer with the shift supervisor.

87. **(C)** Choice A is incorrect because the judge must remain present during the visit. Choice B is incorrect because parents would be allowed to visit at the same time only

if the prisoner was under 21 years of age. Choice D is incorrect because no object is allowed to be passed during such visits.

88. **(A)** Statement 2 is incorrect because the procedure is absolute about the total number visitors allowed prisoners during courtroom visits, namely three.

89. **(B)** Statement 1 is incorrect because it does not involve all defendants, only those in the custody of the court. Therefore, this procedure would not apply to a defendant who was free on bail. Statement 2 is correct.

90. **(D)** Choice A is incorrect because the U.S. mail vehicles must be actually delivering the mail. Choice B is incorrect because prison vans must be in the process of transporting prisoners. Choice C is incorrect because, even though the mayor would be permitted entry, there is no mention of the mayor's vehicle. Choice D is correct because ambulances, empty or carrying sick or injured, will be allowed to cross security lines. This question highlights the importance of paying particular attention to the use of words like *any*.

91. **(B)** Choice D can be immediately eliminated because it indicates that the number 9 represents the first letter of the word. That is incorrect because the reference table associates 9 with the letter R and the word in the question begins with a G. If you selected Choice C, you made a mistake often made by candidates when answering coding questions. Often candidates confuse the letter O with the number 0.

92. **(C)** Choice A is close to Choice C, but Choice A is incorrect because the fourth number should represent the letter O. Instead, the examiner tried to distract you by suggesting the number 0. Choice C is the correct answer.

93. **(D)** The letter T is associated with 7, E with 8, S with 6, T with 7, E with 8, and R with 9. Choice D, which is 786789, is correct.

94. **(A)** As indicated by the reference table, Choice A is correct.

95. **(C)** Choices B and D incorrectly suggested that O, the second letter of the word TONGUE, should be represented by the number 0. However, the number 0 was associated by the reference table with the letter Z. Therefore, after quickly eliminating Choices B and D, and comparing between the remaining Choices A and C, you should have selected Choice C as the correct choice.

96. **(C)** January 05 is the same as 01-05 or by use of the reference table, 01 is SI and 05 is SE or as indicated by Choice C, SI-SE.

97. **(B)** August 30 is the same as 08-30 or by use of the reference table, 08 is SO and 30 is AS or as indicated by Choice B, SO-AS.

98. **(A)** October 15 is the same as 10-15 or by use of the reference table, 10 is IS and 15 is IE or as indicated by Choice A, IS-IE.

99. **(D)** December 16 is the same as 12-16 or by use of the reference table, 12 is IH and 16 is ID or as indicated by Choice D, IH-ID.

100. **(B)** July 14 is the same as 07-14 or by use of the reference table, 07 is SC and IT is 14 or as indicated by Choice B, SC-IT.

Practice Examination Three

This is your third practice examination. After this, there is one more practice examination. Be sure to take each practice examination in one sitting. Each exam contains 100 questions, which you must answer in 3½ hours. It is imperative that you become accustomed to concentrating for the length of time required to complete an entire examination. Be sure to review the test-taking strategy outlined in the Introduction before taking this practice examination, to use that strategy when doing the examination, and to record your answers on the following Answer Sheet.

ANSWER SHEET
Practice Exam Three

Follow the instructions given in the test. Mark only your answers in the circles below.

WARNING: Be sure that the circle you fill is in the same row as the question you are answering. Use a No. 2 pencil (soft pencil).

BE SURE YOUR PENCIL MARKS ARE HEAVY AND BLACK.

ERASE COMPLETELY ANY ANSWER YOU WISH TO CHANGE.

DO NOT make stray pencil dots, dashes, or marks.

1. Ⓐ Ⓑ Ⓒ Ⓓ	26. Ⓐ Ⓑ Ⓒ Ⓓ	51. Ⓐ Ⓑ Ⓒ Ⓓ	76. Ⓐ Ⓑ Ⓒ Ⓓ
2. Ⓐ Ⓑ Ⓒ Ⓓ	27. Ⓐ Ⓑ Ⓒ Ⓓ	52. Ⓐ Ⓑ Ⓒ Ⓓ	77. Ⓐ Ⓑ Ⓒ Ⓓ
3. Ⓐ Ⓑ Ⓒ Ⓓ	28. Ⓐ Ⓑ Ⓒ Ⓓ	53. Ⓐ Ⓑ Ⓒ Ⓓ	78. Ⓐ Ⓑ Ⓒ Ⓓ
4. Ⓐ Ⓑ Ⓒ Ⓓ	29. Ⓐ Ⓑ Ⓒ Ⓓ	54. Ⓐ Ⓑ Ⓒ Ⓓ	79. Ⓐ Ⓑ Ⓒ Ⓓ
5. Ⓐ Ⓑ Ⓒ Ⓓ	30. Ⓐ Ⓑ Ⓒ Ⓓ	55. Ⓐ Ⓑ Ⓒ Ⓓ	80. Ⓐ Ⓑ Ⓒ Ⓓ
6. Ⓐ Ⓑ Ⓒ Ⓓ	31. Ⓐ Ⓑ Ⓒ Ⓓ	56. Ⓐ Ⓑ Ⓒ Ⓓ	81. Ⓐ Ⓑ Ⓒ Ⓓ
7. Ⓐ Ⓑ Ⓒ Ⓓ	32. Ⓐ Ⓑ Ⓒ Ⓓ	57. Ⓐ Ⓑ Ⓒ Ⓓ	82. Ⓐ Ⓑ Ⓒ Ⓓ
8. Ⓐ Ⓑ Ⓒ Ⓓ	33. Ⓐ Ⓑ Ⓒ Ⓓ	58. Ⓐ Ⓑ Ⓒ Ⓓ	83. Ⓐ Ⓑ Ⓒ Ⓓ
9. Ⓐ Ⓑ Ⓒ Ⓓ	34. Ⓐ Ⓑ Ⓒ Ⓓ	59. Ⓐ Ⓑ Ⓒ Ⓓ	84. Ⓐ Ⓑ Ⓒ Ⓓ
10. Ⓐ Ⓑ Ⓒ Ⓓ	35. Ⓐ Ⓑ Ⓒ Ⓓ	60. Ⓐ Ⓑ Ⓒ Ⓓ	85. Ⓐ Ⓑ Ⓒ Ⓓ
11. Ⓐ Ⓑ Ⓒ Ⓓ	36. Ⓐ Ⓑ Ⓒ Ⓓ	61. Ⓐ Ⓑ Ⓒ Ⓓ	86. Ⓐ Ⓑ Ⓒ Ⓓ
12. Ⓐ Ⓑ Ⓒ Ⓓ	37. Ⓐ Ⓑ Ⓒ Ⓓ	62. Ⓐ Ⓑ Ⓒ Ⓓ	87. Ⓐ Ⓑ Ⓒ Ⓓ
13. Ⓐ Ⓑ Ⓒ Ⓓ	38. Ⓐ Ⓑ Ⓒ Ⓓ	63. Ⓐ Ⓑ Ⓒ Ⓓ	88. Ⓐ Ⓑ Ⓒ Ⓓ
14. Ⓐ Ⓑ Ⓒ Ⓓ	39. Ⓐ Ⓑ Ⓒ Ⓓ	64. Ⓐ Ⓑ Ⓒ Ⓓ	89. Ⓐ Ⓑ Ⓒ Ⓓ
15. Ⓐ Ⓑ Ⓒ Ⓓ	40. Ⓐ Ⓑ Ⓒ Ⓓ	65. Ⓐ Ⓑ Ⓒ Ⓓ	90. Ⓐ Ⓑ Ⓒ Ⓓ
16. Ⓐ Ⓑ Ⓒ Ⓓ	41. Ⓐ Ⓑ Ⓒ Ⓓ	66. Ⓐ Ⓑ Ⓒ Ⓓ	91. Ⓐ Ⓑ Ⓒ Ⓓ
17. Ⓐ Ⓑ Ⓒ Ⓓ	42. Ⓐ Ⓑ Ⓒ Ⓓ	67. Ⓐ Ⓑ Ⓒ Ⓓ	92. Ⓐ Ⓑ Ⓒ Ⓓ
18. Ⓐ Ⓑ Ⓒ Ⓓ	43. Ⓐ Ⓑ Ⓒ Ⓓ	68. Ⓐ Ⓑ Ⓒ Ⓓ	93. Ⓐ Ⓑ Ⓒ Ⓓ
19. Ⓐ Ⓑ Ⓒ Ⓓ	44. Ⓐ Ⓑ Ⓒ Ⓓ	69. Ⓐ Ⓑ Ⓒ Ⓓ	94. Ⓐ Ⓑ Ⓒ Ⓓ
20. Ⓐ Ⓑ Ⓒ Ⓓ	45. Ⓐ Ⓑ Ⓒ Ⓓ	70. Ⓐ Ⓑ Ⓒ Ⓓ	95. Ⓐ Ⓑ Ⓒ Ⓓ
21. Ⓐ Ⓑ Ⓒ Ⓓ	46. Ⓐ Ⓑ Ⓒ Ⓓ	71. Ⓐ Ⓑ Ⓒ Ⓓ	96. Ⓐ Ⓑ Ⓒ Ⓓ
22. Ⓐ Ⓑ Ⓒ Ⓓ	47. Ⓐ Ⓑ Ⓒ Ⓓ	72. Ⓐ Ⓑ Ⓒ Ⓓ	97. Ⓐ Ⓑ Ⓒ Ⓓ
23. Ⓐ Ⓑ Ⓒ Ⓓ	48. Ⓐ Ⓑ Ⓒ Ⓓ	73. Ⓐ Ⓑ Ⓒ Ⓓ	98. Ⓐ Ⓑ Ⓒ Ⓓ
24. Ⓐ Ⓑ Ⓒ Ⓓ	49. Ⓐ Ⓑ Ⓒ Ⓓ	74. Ⓐ Ⓑ Ⓒ Ⓓ	99. Ⓐ Ⓑ Ⓒ Ⓓ
25. Ⓐ Ⓑ Ⓒ Ⓓ	50. Ⓐ Ⓑ Ⓒ Ⓓ	75. Ⓐ Ⓑ Ⓒ Ⓓ	100. Ⓐ Ⓑ Ⓒ Ⓓ

THE TEST

Time: 3 1/2 hours
100 questions

Answer questions 1–8 based on these instructions:

Directions: Before answering questions 1–8 take five minutes to examine the following four wanted posters with the information that accompanies each poster.

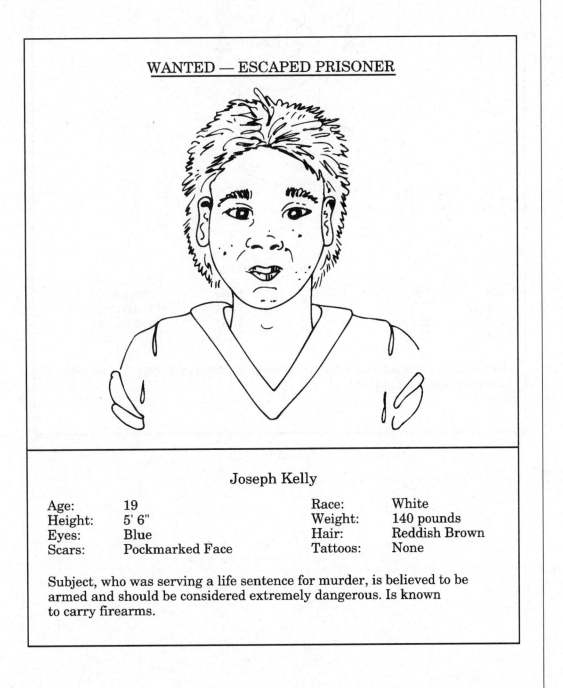

WANTED — ESCAPED PRISONER

Joseph Kelly

Age:	19	Race:	White
Height:	5' 6"	Weight:	140 pounds
Eyes:	Blue	Hair:	Reddish Brown
Scars:	Pockmarked Face	Tattoos:	None

Subject, who was serving a life sentence for murder, is believed to be armed and should be considered extremely dangerous. Is known to carry firearms.

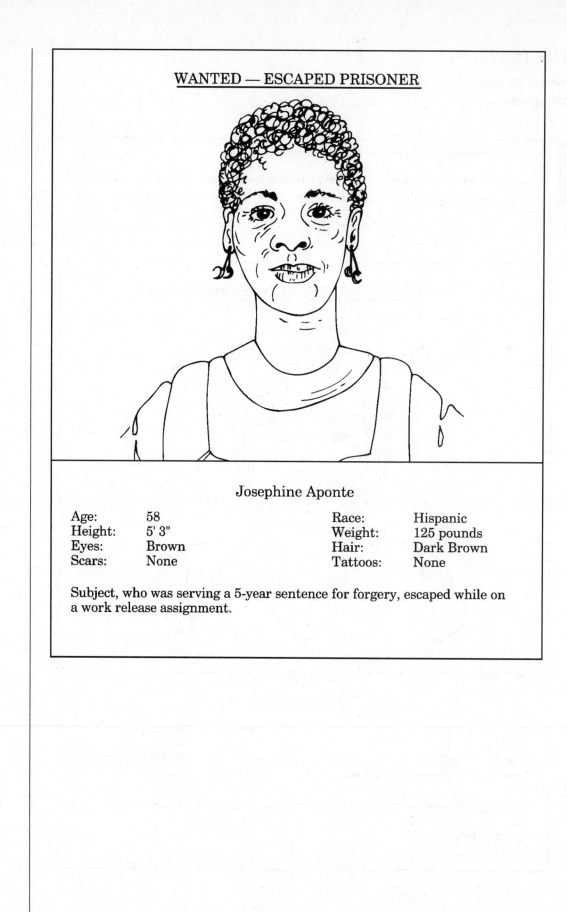

WANTED — ESCAPED PRISONER

Josephine Aponte

Age:	58	Race:	Hispanic
Height:	5' 3"	Weight:	125 pounds
Eyes:	Brown	Hair:	Dark Brown
Scars:	None	Tattoos:	None

Subject, who was serving a 5-year sentence for forgery, escaped while on a work release assignment.

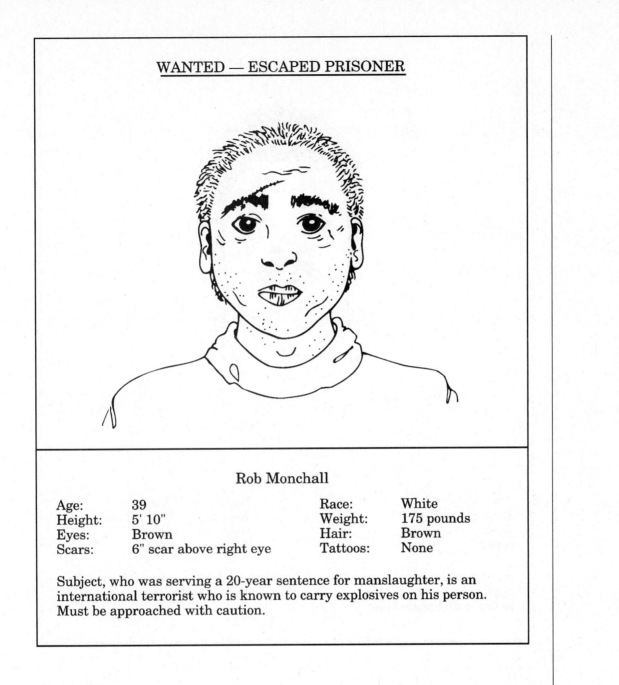

WANTED — ESCAPED PRISONER

Rob Monchall

Age:	39		Race:	White
Height:	5' 10"		Weight:	175 pounds
Eyes:	Brown		Hair:	Brown
Scars:	6" scar above right eye		Tattoos:	None

Subject, who was serving a 20-year sentence for manslaughter, is an international terrorist who is known to carry explosives on his person. Must be approached with caution.

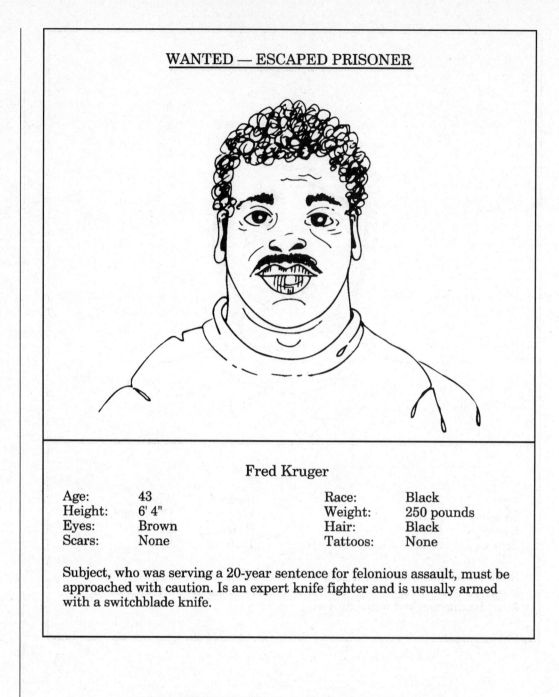

PRACTICE EXAM THREE

WANTED — ESCAPED PRISONER

Fred Kruger

Age:	43	Race:	Black
Height:	6' 4"	Weight:	250 pounds
Eyes:	Brown	Hair:	Black
Scars:	None	Tattoos:	None

Subject, who was serving a 20-year sentence for felonious assault, must be approached with caution. Is an expert knife fighter and is usually armed with a switchblade knife.

DO NOT PROCEED UNTIL 5 MINUTES HAVE PASSED.

TURN TO NEXT PAGE

1. Which of the escaped prisoners illustrated in the following posters is NOT usually armed with a weapon or explosives?

(A)

(B)

(C)

(D)

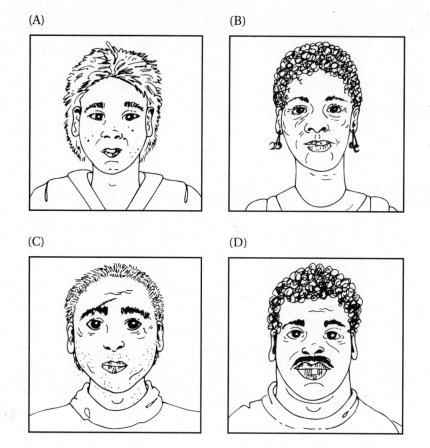

2. Which of the escaped prisoners illustrated in the following posters was serving a life sentence?

(A)

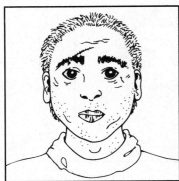

(B)

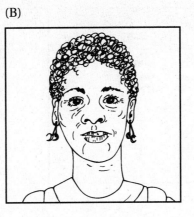

(C)

(D)

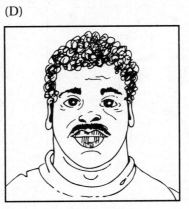

3. Which of the escaped prisoners illustrated in the following posters is the heaviest?

(A)

(B)

(C)

(D)

4. Which of the escaped prisoners illustrated in the following posters is the oldest?

(A)

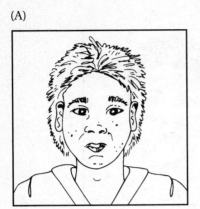

(B)

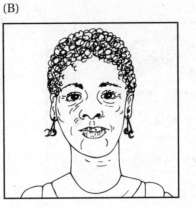

(C)

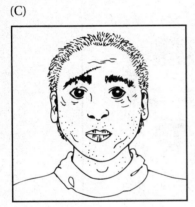

(D)

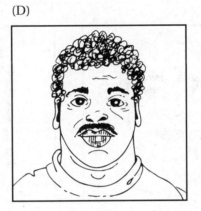

5. Which of the escaped prisoners illustrated in the following posters has blue eyes?

(A)

(B)

(C)

(D)

6.

The subject illustrated in the wanted poster directly above . . .

(A) is an expert knife fighter.
(B) is a forger.
(C) is a child abuser.
(D) is a murderer.

7.

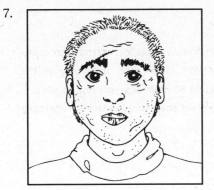

The subject illustrated in the wanted poster directly above . . .

(A) is an expert knife fighter.
(B) is an international terrorist.
(C) is a child abuser.
(D) is a murderer.

8.

The subject illustrated in the wanted poster directly above . . .

(A) is an expert knife fighter.
(B) is an international terrorist.
(C) is a forger.
(D) is a murderer.

MEMORY INFORMATION
5-Minute Time Limit

Court Officer Green, shield 1256, has just learned that four new defendants are being tried in the courtroom under his supervision. He receives the following information about the new defendants.

Defendant # 1, Bill Smith, Docket #12789, is a white male, age 46. He is an accountant by profession. He is presently charged with embezzlement. According to his pretrial report, he is a nonviolent person, and it is not anticipated that he will create any special problems for Officer Green. His only apparent vice is that he is a chronic gambler. In fact, his gambling debt caused him to engage in embezzlement. Smith is married with three children.

Defendant # 2, Peter Block, Docket # 21654, is a white male, age 26. He is a skilled auto mechanic. His criminal specialty is picking pockets. He is presently charged with larceny. Although his special skills as a mechanic make it easy for him to find employment, his salary as a mechanic is not enough to sustain his chronic drug use problem. He is single with no known relatives.

Defendant # 3, Don Hurte, Docket # 87543, is a white male, age 36. He has no special skills and has never held a legitimate job. He has lived a life of crime and has served three previous prison terms. He is presently charged with armed robbery. He is a very violent person, and during his last stay in prison he created many special problems. He is married with eight children.

Defendant # 4, Frank Wood, Docket # 33555, is a black male, age 26. He is a union carpenter, but he is also a con man. He specializes in swindling elderly people out of their life savings. He has three previous convictions for petty crimes. He is presently charged with larceny. He is a passive person who deplores violence. He is married with one child.

DO NOT PROCEED UNTIL 5 MINUTES HAVE PASSED.

TURN TO THE NEXT PAGE

Answer questions 9–15 solely on the basis of the preceding memory story.

9. Bill Smith is . . .

   (A) an accountant.
   (B) an auto mechanic.
   (C) a bank teller.
   (D) a taxi driver.

10. Of the four defendants, the one who has violent tendencies is . . .

   (A) Bill Smith.
   (B) Peter Block.
   (C) Don Hurte.
   (D) Frank Wood.

11. Peter Block is . . .

   (A) an automobile mechanic.
   (B) an accountant.
   (C) unskilled.
   (D) a carpenter.

12. Of the following defendants, which one is a black male?

   (A) Bill Smith
   (B) Peter Block
   (C) Don Hurte
   (D) Frank Wood

13. Of the following defendants, which one is not married?

   (A) Bill Smith
   (B) Peter Block
   (C) Don Hurte
   (D) Frank Wood

14. Frank Wood is . . .

   (A) an automobile mechanic.
   (B) a carpenter.
   (C) an accountant.
   (D) a lawyer.

15. The defendant who swindles elderly people is . . .

   (A) Bill Smith
   (B) Peter Block
   (C) Don Hurte
   (D) Frank Wood

As a general rule, areas inside court buildings are not permissible locations for public demonstrations. The danger of overcrowding and the potential for panic should an incident occur is much greater than outside. In courthouses, court officers are most frequently dealing with groups of people who are orderly and calm. Once in a while, cohesive groups enter the courthouse with the specific purpose of creating disruption. When such acts of disruption occur in the courtroom, the presiding magistrate has the ultimate responsibility for maintaining order and the dignity of the court. Under these circumstances, the actions of court officers should usually be based on direct instructions from the magistrate. If disruptive actions occur anywhere else in the courthouse, the order to take action must come from the court officer present who has the greatest amount of seniority as a court officer. If possible, before issuing instructions, the senior court officer present at the scene should confer with appropriate court officials.

16. Areas inside court buildings . . .

    (A) can never be used for a public demonstration.
    (B) are suitable locations for public demonstrations.
    (C) could sometimes be permissible locations for public demonstrations.
    (D) are quite often used for public demonstrations.

17. When disruptions occur in a courtroom, who has the ultimate responsibility for restoring order?

    (A) the senior court officer present
    (B) the presiding magistrate
    (C) the highest ranking court official in the courtroom
    (D) the appropriate court official

18. If disruptive actions occur in the courthouse, the source of the orders for court officers to follow to restore order . . .

    (A) depends on where in the courthouse the disruption occurs.
    (B) must always be a magistrate.
    (C) depends on the nature of the disruption.
    (D) cannot be a court officer.

Directions: Answer questions 19–22 based solely on the following information.

Confessions or admissions made by a person accused of a crime must be made voluntarily, or they cannot be used during a criminal trial. In addition, persons being interrogated by law enforcement officers may have to be advised of certain of their constitutional rights before statements they make are admissible in court at a criminal trial. The necessity to sometimes advise people accused of crimes of their constitutional rights was spelled out by the following rule, commonly known as the Miranda rule, which was established by the U.S. Supreme Court.

When a person is in custody and police or peace officers want to interrogate the person, the police or peace officer involved must advise that person of the following:

a. You have a right to remain silent.

b. You have the right to the presence of a lawyer.

c. Anything you say can be used against you in a criminal court.

d. If you cannot afford a lawyer, one will be appointed for you prior to any questioning should you so desire.

The Miranda rule does not apply to admissions or confessions made to private citizens acting on their own authority. However, if a private citizen is acting as an agent of the government, the Miranda rule would apply.

19. Confessions are not admissible in a criminal trial unless . . .

 (A) a lawyer was present when the confession was made.
 (B) the person confessing was informed of his constitutional rights.
 (C) a lawyer is appointed to represent the person confessing.
 (D) they are voluntarily made.

20. A person who cannot afford an attorney and who is being questioned by police or peace officers . . .

 (A) must be supplied with an attorney.
 (B) can make a valid confession.
 (C) must be advised of his constitutional rights.
 (D) never has to have a lawyer appointed to him.

21. The Miranda rule is a . . .

 (A) statutory rule.
 (B) judicial rule.
 (C) discretionary rule.
 (D) executive rule.

22. Private citizens . . .

    (A) are always bound by the Miranda rule.

    (B) are not subject to the Miranda rule under any circumstances.

    (C) may or may not be bound by the Miranda rule.

    (D) are not authorized to interrogate suspects in criminal cases.

Directions: Answer question 23 based solely on the following information.

Bail is something of value that is posted with a criminal court to guarantee the appearance of an accused at a later date and that is forfeited if the accused fails to appear.

23. Bail . . .

    (A) must be in the form of money.

    (B) is always returned to the person posting it.

    (C) is meant to ensure a person's future appearance in court.

    (D) can be posted in civil cases.

Directions: Answer question 24 based solely on the following information.

A bench warrant is a writ issued by a judge, which demands that a specified individual be brought before the court.

24. A bench warrant . . .

    (A) is only used to arrest criminals.

    (B) must be based on probable cause.

    (C) is valid indefinitely.

    (D) is used to secure the appearance in court of a specific person.

Directions: Answer question 25 based solely on the following information.

Entrapment is the term used to describe illegal conduct by a police officer, peace officer, or other government agent to entice a person to commit a crime that he/she would otherwise not commit.

25. Entrapment . . .

    (A) can never be legal.
    (B) can be committed by any citizen.
    (C) is a defense against a criminal charge.
    (D) is unconstitutional.

Directions: Answer questions 26–33 solely on the basis of information contained in the following court decision.

On November 10 of last year, defendant Myers and three other people were traveling north on the New York State Thruway when their car was stopped by a New York State Peace Officer for speeding. Approaching the vehicle, the officer smelled marijuana coming from within the vehicle and observed on the floor of the vehicle an envelope, which he recognized as a type commonly used in selling marijuana. The officer then ordered the occupants out of the vehicle, frisked each one, removed the envelope from the floor, and determined that it contained a small amount of marijuana.

After the marijuana was found, Myers and the three other people standing outside the car were placed under arrest for the illegal possession of marijuana. The officer reentered the vehicle, searched portions of it likely to conceal drugs, and searched the pockets of five jackets lying on the back seat. He opened the zippered pocket of one of the jackets and discovered a small amount of cocaine. The officer placed an additional charge against Myers for illegally possessing cocaine. All four prisoners were then removed to the State Police Headquarters where they were interrogated for 20 minutes.

Myers and his three accomplices engaged in plea bargaining with respect to the charges concerning possession of marijuana, but Meyers elected to go to trial with respect to the charge concerning possession of cocaine. Myers was convicted by the Trial Court, and a unanimous Appellate Division Court affirmed, holding that the warrantless search of the jacket was lawful as an incident to the defendant's arrest.

Myers appealed to the Court of Appeals. In arriving at its decision, the Court of Appeals discussed the right of privacy and the area that might be searched when an arrest is made. The Court of Appeals held that when a person is placed under arrest, there is always a danger that he/she may seek to use a weapon to effect an escape or to destroy or conceal evidence of a crime or other contraband. Accordingly, it would be reasonable (pursuant to the Fourth Amendment) for the arresting officer to conduct a prompt warrantless search of the arrestee's person and the area within his/her immediate control in order for the officer to protect himself and others and to prevent loss of evidence. The area within the arrestee's immediate control would mean any area from which he/she might reach a weapon or evidence that could be destroyed.

Both the Trial Court and the Appellate Division Court concluded that as a factual matter, the jacket was not within the exclusive control of the peace officer nor were the arrestees effectively neutralized. The Court of Appeals disagreed, holding that once the defendant Myers was arrested and removed from the vehicle, he was incapable, as were his confederates, of reentering the vehicle to attempt to obtain a weapon or destroy evidence.

26. The Court of Appeals held that it is reasonable for the arresting officer to search the person of an arrestee and the area under the arrestee's immediate control. The Court of Appeals defined immediate control as being . . .

   (A) the area within reach of the arrested persons arms.
   (B) the entire area inside the car, but not including the inside of jacket pockets.
   (C) any area from which an arrested person might gain a weapon.
   (D) any area from which an arrested person might gain evidence.

27. Which of the following can accurately be concluded from the information in this court decision?

   (A) Myers is a male.
   (B) The jacket with the cocaine belonged to Myers.
   (C) Myers was questioned alone for 20 minutes.
   (D) None of the defendants was sentenced to prison.

28. Which of the following courts ruled in favor of Myers?

   (A) only the Trial Court
   (B) only the Appellate Division Court
   (C) the Court of Appeals
   (D) both the Trial Court and the Appellate Division Court

29. Which of the following statements is most accurate concerning actual ownership of the cocaine?

   (A) Myers was the owner of the cocaine.
   (B) One of Myers' three accomplices owned the cocaine.
   (C) Someone other than Myers and his three accomplices owned the cocaine.
   (D) It is not possible to state who owned the cocaine.

30. Which of the following is the least accurate statement concerning Myers and the three accomplices?

   (A) All four were arrested for possession of marijuana.
   (B) All four engaged in plea bargaining.
   (C) All four were arrested for possession of cocaine.
   (D) All four were questioned at State Police Headquarters.

31. The Court of Appeals based its findings primarily upon which of the following?

(A) The officer smelled marijuana upon approaching the stopped car.
(B) None of the defendants could have reentered the vehicle after they were arrested.
(C) The officer acted in an unreasonable manner with respect to the Fourth Amendment.
(D) The jacket in which the cocaine was found was discovered in the car that Myers was driving.

32. As used in this court decision, the word *incident* means . . .

(A) occurrence.
(B) in connection with.
(C) unusual happening.
(D) a minor event.

33. Pursuant to the Fourth Amendment, the Court of Appeals held that searches of arrested persons are reasonable if they are made for any of the following reasons except to . . .

(A) strengthen the case of the arresting officer.
(B) prevent the arrested person from reaching a weapon.
(C) stop the arrested person from destroying evidence.
(D) prevent the arrested person from causing an injury to another.

Directions: Answer question 34 based solely on the following information.

An arraignment is the judicial process of informing an accused of the charges, of informing him/her of his/her rights, and of requiring a plea of guilty or not guilty.

34. At an arraignment, a defendant . . .

(A) is determined to be guilty or innocent.
(B) is furnished with an attorney.
(C) must plead either guilty or not guilty.
(D) must post bail.

An appeal is an official request to a higher court to review the findings of a lower court. It also refers to the act of transferring a case from a lower court to a higher court to review the findings. It may also be a case that has been so transferred.

35. Which of the following is not properly classified as an appeal?

   (A) A defendant asks the U.S. Supreme Court to review his conviction.
   (B) A defendant's case is moved from one court to a higher court.
   (C) A defendant asks the trial judge to reconsider a decision that the trial judge made.
   (D) A state court case decision is reviewed by the U.S. Supreme Court

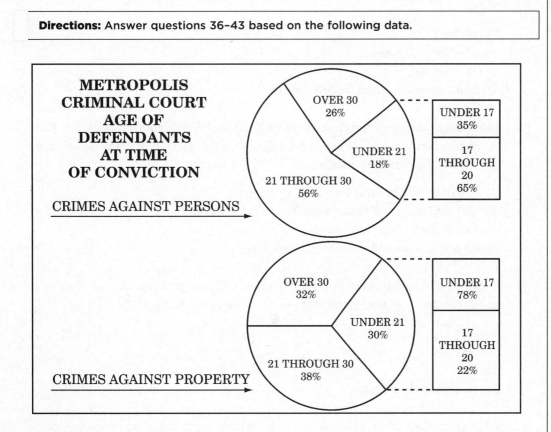

36. Most of the defendants who are convicted in Metropolis Criminal Court are . . .

   (A) under 21.
   (B) 21–30.
   (C) over 30.
   (D) of an age that cannot be determined.

37. Of the defendants who are convicted of crimes against persons, the majority of them are . . .

(A) under 21.
(B) between 21 and 30.
(C) over 30.
(D) of an age that cannot be determined.

38. Of all of the defendants under 21 who are convicted of a crime against a person, most of them are . . .

(A) under 17.
(B) 17–20 years of age.
(C) 18 years old.
(D) of an age that cannot be determined.

39. Of all the defendants under 21 who are convicted of a crime against property, most of them are . . .

(A) under 17.
(B) 17–20 years of age.
(C) 16 years old.
(D) of an age that cannot be determined.

40. Assuming that current trends concerning the age of defendants at the time of their conviction continues, if 1000 new defendants are convicted of a crime against property during the next year, then about

(A) 320 of them would be over 30 years of age.
(B) 560 of them would be between 21 and 30 years old.
(C) 180 of them would be under 21 years of age.
(D) 63 of them would be under 17 years of age.

41. If 1000 new defendants are convicted of crimes against persons, and the current trends continue, approximately how many of them would be under 17?

(A) 180
(B) 300
(C) 63
(D) cannot be determined

42. What percentage of the defendants being convicted of a crime against a person are over 21 years of age?

(A) 56%
(B) 26%
(C) 82%
(D) cannot be determined

43. On June 1st of last year, how many defendants who were convicted in the Metropolis Criminal Court were under 21 years of age?

(A) 18
(B) 30
(C) 48
(D) cannot be determined

Directions: Answer questions 44–47 based solely on the following information.

Relatives or friends over 16 years of age may visit a defendant in the court system's holding pens (jails) provided that the defendant consents to the visit. These visits must be held during normal visiting hours, which are from Monday to Friday, from 10:00 A.M. to 4:00 P.M. Children between the ages of 10 and 16 may visit defendants but only on those days that are specifically designated as family visiting days. At least three family visiting days per month will be held. Children under the age of 10 are not allowed in the holding pen area at any time. Clergy persons are allowed to visit defendants on any day of the week at any hour between 8:00 A.M. and 11:00 P.M. Such visits require the consent of the defendant. Attorneys are allowed to visit defendants but require written authorization from the defendant. Attorney visits can be held on any day of the week between the hours of 10:00 A.M. and 10:00 P.M. Police officers investigating crimes may also visit defendants on the same day and during the same times of the day that attorneys are allowed to visit. Visits from the police require written authorization from the defendant or from the court handling that defendant's case.

44. A 9-year-old child . . .

(A) could visit a parent in a holding pen on weekend family visiting days.
(B) is never allowed to visit a defendant in a holding pen.
(C) could visit a parent in a holding pen on weekdays.
(D) must be accompanied into the holding pen area by an adult.

45. Which of the following categories of visitors has the greatest number of possible visiting hours each week?

(A) relatives or friends
(B) clergy persons
(C) attorneys
(D) police personnel

46. Which of the following categories of visitors could possibly visit a defendant without the defendant's consent?

(A) relatives or friends
(B) clergy persons
(C) attorneys
(D) police personnel

47. Which of the following categories of people do not require written authorization to visit?

(A) clergy
(B) lawyers
(C) legal aide representatives
(D) police personnel

Answer questions 48–50 based solely on the following directions:

Directions: The paragraph below contains questions 48–50 in the form of three numbered blanks. Immediately following the paragraph are lists of four word choices that correspond to these numbered blanks. Select the word choice that would MOST appropriately fit the numbered blank in each question.

During his tour of duty, Court Officer Green is called to the scene of an injured civilian because he is the only court officer on duty in that area of the court house. The civilian, Mr. Tom Roe, has slipped on some water which is leaking from a public water fountain. Upon arrival at the scene, _____(Q-48)_____ calls his supervisor, Sergeant Carter, and requests that an ambulance respond to the court house to examine the injured Mr. Roe. An ambulance responds from Bayside Hospital with Emergency Medical Technician Bailes. _____(Q-49)_____ , who was injured, was taken to the hospital for treatment of a dislocated shoulder. Doctor Smith treated Mr. Roe, who was _____(Q-50)_____ later in the day and went home.

48. (A) Green
    (B) Carter
    (C) Smith
    (D) someone

49. (A) Mr. Green
    (B) Mr. Bailes
    (C) Mr. Smith
    (D) Mr. Roe

50. (A) hospitalized
    (B) released
    (C) transported
    (D) examined

Directions: Answer questions 51–58 solely on the basis of the following legal definitions. Do not base your answers on any other knowledge of the law you may have. You may refer to the definitions when answering the questions.

NOTE: The perpetrators in the definitions that follow are referred to as *he* but they actually refer to either gender. However, when the male and/or female gender is a factor in defining an offense or legal action, such distinction shall be made by the specific and appropriate use of both pronouns *he* and *she*.

a. Sexual intercourse has its ordinary meaning and occurs upon any penetration, however slight.

b. Deviate sexual intercourse means sexual conduct between persons not married to each other consisting of contact between the mouth and the penis, the penis and the anus, or the mouth and the vulva.

c. A person commits rape in the third degree when, being 21 years old or older, he or she engages in sexual intercourse with another person to whom the actor is not married and is less than 17 years old.

d. A person commits rape in the second degree when, being 18 years old or more, he or she engages in sexual intercourse with another person to whom the actor is not married and is less than 14 years old.

e. A person commits rape in the first degree when such person engages in sexual intercourse with another

   i. by forcible compulsion, or,

   ii. who is unable to consent due to being physically helpless, or,

   iii. who is less than 11 years old.

f. A person is guilty of sodomy in the third degree when being 21 years old or more, he or she engages in deviate sexual intercourse with a person to whom the actor is not married and is less than 17 years old.

g. A person commits sodomy in the second degree when, being 18 years old or more, he or she engages in deviate sexual intercourse with another person to whom the actor is not married and is less than 14 years old.

h. A person commits sodomy in the first degree when such person engages in deviate sexual intercourse with another

   i. by forcible compulsion, or,

   ii. who is unable to consent due to being physically helpless, or,

   iii. who is less than 11 years old.

i. A person commits sexual abuse in the third degree when such person engages in sexual contact with another person without the latter's consent.

j. A person commits sexual abuse in the second degree when such person submits another person to whom the actor is not married to sexual contact and such other person is less than 14 years old.

k. A person commits sexual abuse in the first degree when such person submits another person to sexual contact

    i. by forcible compulsion, or,

    ii. who is unable to consent due to being physically helpless, or,

    iii. when such other person is less than 11 years old.

l. A person commits sexual misconduct when such person engages in sexual intercourse with an animal or a dead human body.

m. A person becomes criminally responsible for his or her actions as an adult perpetrator upon reaching the age of 16 years old.

n. First-degree offenses are more serious offenses than second-degree offenses, which in turn are more serious offenses than third-degree offenses.

51. Mark is a tenth grade student at Manor High School. May is a student teacher. One afternoon Mark who is 13 years old tells May who is 21 years old and unmarried that he has a crush on her. May invites Mark to her van and engages in sexual intercourse with Mark. In this instance, . . .

(A) both Mark and May are guilty of rape in the third degree.
(B) only Mark is guilty of rape in the third degree.
(C) both Mark and May are guilty of rape in the second degree.
(D) only May is guilty of rape in the second degree.

52. Tom, who is 35 years old and is an orderly in a hospital, enters June's hospital room. Tom then has sexual intercourse with June who is 16 years old and is lying helpless in a coma. The most serious offense Tom has committed is . . .

(A) rape in the first degree.
(B) rape in the second degree.
(C) rape in the third degree.
(D) sexual misconduct.

53. Don forces his way into the apartment of Joy. At gunpoint, Don who is only 16 years old forces Joy who is 13 to perform oral sex on Don. Of the following, the most serious offense committed by Don is . . .

(A) sodomy in the third degree.
(B) sodomy in the second degree.
(C) sodomy in the first degree.
(D) none of the above because of Don's age.

54. Tab, who is 22, is riding on a crowded train during evening rush hour. He positions himself next to Mark, who is 25 years old, and with his hand, Tab begins to engage in sexual conduct by rubbing Mark's genitals. Mark does not object. In this instance, . . .

(A) both have committed sexual misconduct.
(B) both have committed sodomy.
(C) Tab has committed sexual abuse.
(D) neither have committed sexual abuse.

55. Digger works in a funeral parlor. A beautiful actress has been killed and is being prepared for her funeral by Digger who decides to, and does, have sexual intercourse with her. In this instance, Digger has committed . . .

(A) no offenses because the female was dead.
(B) sodomy in the first degree.
(C) sexual misconduct.
(D) sexual abuse in the third degree.

56. Ray who is 17 and Jay who is 21 force April into their van where they compel her to engage in anal intercourse with each of them. April is 12 years old. In this instance, Ray and Jay both committed . . .

(A) sodomy in the first degree.
(B) sodomy in the second degree.
(C) sodomy in the third degree.
(D) sexual misconduct.

57. May is 15 years old. Her aunt June is 34 years old. June invites May to the movies, and after the movie on the way home while in her car June begins to kiss May and in turn May performs oral sex on June. May does so willingly without any force or compulsion being used against her. In this instance, which of the following indicates the most serious offense(s) committed?

(A) Both have committed sexual misconduct.
(B) Both have committed sexual abuse in the third degree.
(C) May committed sodomy in the third degree.
(D) June committed sodomy in the third degree.

58. After a prom, Tucker, who is 16, has sexual intercourse with his girlfriend May, who is 17. In this instance, . . .

(A) only Tab has committed rape in the third degree.
(B) only May has committed rape in the third degree.
(C) both have committed rape in the third degree.
(D) neither has committed rape in the third degree.

Directions: Answer questions 59–65 solely on the basis of the following legal definitions. Do not base your answers on any other knowledge of the law you may have. You may refer to the definitions when answering the questions.

A. A person commits murder in the first degree when with intent to cause the death of another person, he causes the death of such person and

   a. the victim is a court officer, or correctional employee, performing his official duties, or,

   b. the perpetrator is in prison serving a life sentence, and, the perpetrator is more than 18 years of age at the time of the commission of the offense.

B. A person commits murder in the second degree when he intends to cause the death of one person, and causes the death of such person or another; or, under circumstances evincing a depraved indifference to human life, he recklessly causes the death of another; or, during the commission of a serious offense such as a robbery, rape, or kidnapping, one of the participants in the offense causes the death of a person other than a participant.

C. A person commits manslaughter in the first degree when with intent to cause serious physical injury to another person, he causes death to such person or a third person; or during the performance of an illegal abortional act on a pregnant female, a person causes the death of the pregnant female who is 24 weeks or more pregnant.

D. A person commits manslaughter in the second degree when a person intentionally aids another person to commit suicide.

E. An abortional act is any act that is done to cause the miscarriage of a female.

F. An abortional act is not considered legal unless it is done by a physician to a pregnant female before she is 24 weeks pregnant, or unless it is done by a physician anytime to a pregnant female to save her life.

G. A person commits abortion when he performs an illegal abortional act on a female who is 24 weeks or more pregnant and causes her miscarriage.

H. A female commits self abortion when, being pregnant for 24 weeks or more, she submits to, or commits, an illegal abortional act on herself, which causes her miscarriage.

59. For a proper charge of murder in the first degree . . .

   (A) the victim must be a court officer.
   (B) the victim must be a correction officer.
   (C) the perpetrator must be over 18 years of age at the time of the offense.
   (D) the perpetrator must be serving a life sentence at the time of the offense.

60. Mr. Jay is 80 years old and is angry at Mr. Burns. Jay sees Burns who is 72 years old making a pass at Jay's wife who is 78 years old while they are all having coffee in Jay's home. Jay takes a gun from a desk drawer and aims it at Burns and fires intending to kill Burns. Jay however misses and strikes and kills his wife. In this instance, the most serious charge against Jay would be . . .

   (A) murder in the first degree.
   (B) murder in the second degree.
   (C) manslaughter in the first degree.
   (D) manslaughter in the second degree.

61. Dr. Tubs gives Ms. Green, who is in excellent health and 30 weeks pregnant, a liquid to drink intended to cause her to have a miscarriage. Ms. Green knowingly and willingly drinks the liquid and as a result has a miscarriage. In this instance, Dr. Tubs has committed . . .

   (A) no crime because Ms. Green willingly drank the liquid.
   (B) murder in the second degree.
   (C) manslaughter in the first degree.
   (D) abortion.

62. In the situation described in question 61, the actions of Ms. Green would properly be classified as . . .

   (A) no crime because she followed Dr. Tubs's orders.
   (B) abortion.
   (C) self abortion.
   (D) manslaughter in the second degree.

63. In the situation described in question 61, if as a result of the actions of Dr. Tubs, Ms. Green were to die, then Dr. Tubs should be charged with . . .

   (A) murder in the second degree.
   (B) manslaughter in the first degree.
   (C) manslaughter in the second degree.
   (D) self abortion.

64. Pat wrongly believes he is suffering from an incurable disease and will die in 1 week. Pat asks Don to lend him his pistol so that Pat can kill himself. Don complies with Pat's request and lends Pat his pistol. Pat kills himself. In this instance, Don has committed . . .

   (A) no offense because Pat initiated the request for the pistol.
   (B) murder in the second degree.
   (C) manslaughter in the first degree.
   (D) manslaughter in the second degree.

65. Knuckles is an enforcer for an organized crime gang. The boss of the gang orders Knuckles to beat up Ray who has not paid money owed to the gang for gambling debts. Knuckles beats up Ray with a baseball bat. Although Knuckles only intended to break Ray's legs, a serious physical injury, he actually kills Ray. In this instance, the most serious charge against Knuckles is . . .

(A) murder in the first degree.
(B) murder in the second degree.
(C) manslaughter in the first degree.
(D) manslaughter in the second degree.

Directions: Answer questions 66–70 based solely on the basis of the following information.

A metal detector search is a search that requires a prisoner or person having business with or visiting the court to walk through a metal detector, or a search caused by a portable metal detector being passed over such persons to determine whether there are metal objects in wearing apparel or attached to the body.

A pat frisk is a search of a prisoner or person having business with or visiting the court, and a search of their wearing apparel, while such persons are clothed, except that a prisoner shall be required to remove coat, hat, and shoes. This type of search shall include searching these items of a prisoner's clothing.

A strip frisk involves a thorough visual inspection of a prisoner's armpits and oral and anal cavities as well as the spreading of the legs and the forward bending of the body.

A body cavity search is a search of a prisoner's genitals, both male and female, both internally and externally, and other body cavities. This type of search is to be performed in absolute privacy by medical personnel. Only a shift supervisor and medical personnel shall be present. However, court officers who are permitted to be present for security reasons may attend but may not observe. All such security court officer personnel present must be of the same gender as the prisoner.

66. A metal detector search is permitted to be used . . .

(A) only when performed by medical personnel.
(B) either on prisoners or visitors.
(C) only on prisoners.
(D) either by medical or court officer personnel.

67. It would be most appropriate to insist that medical personnel be present for a . . .

(A) metal detector search.
(B) pat frisk.
(C) strip frisk.
(D) body cavity search.

68. Which of the following statements is most correct concerning a pat frisk?

 (A) It may include shoes removed from a visitor.
 (B) It may include a hat removed from a prisoner.
 (C) It may only be done by a shift supervisor.
 (D) It must be done in total privacy.

69. A strip frisk shall include all the following actions except . . .

 (A) a visual inspection of oral cavities.
 (B) a visual inspection of the armpits.
 (C) the spreading of the legs and the forward bending of the body.
 (D) internally searching a female prisoner's genitals.

70. Which of the following statements concerning body cavity searches is most appropriate?

 (A) They must always be performed by males.
 (B) They must always be performed by females.
 (C) They should always be performed by medical personnel who must be the same gender as the person being searched.
 (D) They should always be conducted in the presence of the shift supervisor.

Directions: Answer questions 71–73 based solely on the following information.

All non-court-officer-department vehicles, such as delivery or service vehicles, passing through the gate to the detention area of the court shall be logged in the Gate Record of Nondepartment Vehicles by the Court Officer in charge of the gate. The log shall be maintained in the following manner and in the following order:

 a. the gate designation

 b. the name and badge number of the officer in charge of the gate, along with the names of any officers acting as relieving officers

 c. the date and time nondepartment vehicles enter and leave the detention area

 d. the name and address of the registered owner of the vehicle

 e. the name and address of the operator of the vehicle, along with the name and address of any helpers

 f. a description of the contents of the vehicles

 g. the license plate number and make and model of the vehicle

In addition to making entries in the Gate Record of Nondepartment Vehicles, the court officer in charge of the gate shall conduct a total vehicle search of all such vehicles. A total vehicle search requires that the court officer enter the vehicle and conduct a search for contraband and/or unauthorized persons. The search shall also include the undercarriage of the vehicle. The search of the undercarriage shall be conducted by the use of a mirror or a mechanic's pit if available. Any irregularities shall be immediately reported to the shift supervisor by the court officer in charge of the gate.

71. Court Officer Baker is assigned as the court officer in charge of the gate. A private vehicle not belonging to the department is attempting to enter the gate and make a delivery. Officer Baker enters the time the vehicle enters the detention area along with required preceding entries. The next entry that should be made is . . .

(A) the name and address of the registered owner of the vehicle.
(B) the gate designation.
(C) a description of the contents of the vehicles.
(D) the name and address of the operator of the vehicle, along with the name and address of any helpers.

72. A total vehicle search requires all the following except . . .

(A) that the court officer enter the vehicle.
(B) that a search be conducted for contraband.
(C) that a search be conducted for unauthorized persons.
(D) that a mechanic search the undercarriage of the vehicle by using a mirror.

73. As a result of a total vehicle search, irregularities are uncovered. Upon being made aware of such irregularities, Court Officer Baker while assigned as the court officer in charge of the gate should immediately . . .

(A) effect the arrest of the driver of the vehicle.
(B) call the owner of the vehicle.
(C) notify the shift supervisor.
(D) impound the vehicle.

Directions: Answer questions 74 and 75 based solely on the following information.

Upon arrival of a prisoner at the detention pens of the court from a correctional facility, any property removed from such prisoner, other than property involved with a criminal offense, shall be properly identified, receipted for, and safely stored in the Court Property Clerk's office. It shall remain there until returned to the prisoner upon the prisoner's release from court, or given to a friend or relative of the prisoner pursuant to the wishes of the prisoner. When so returned to a friend or relative, a receipt shall be obtained and kept on file at the Court Property Clerk's office. A prisoner may not appeal the removal of property resulting from this process. Property removed in connection with a criminal offense, such as hidden weapons, shall be turned over to the county prosecutor for appropriate action.

However a prisoner may appeal property removed as a result of a search of articles received in court from friends or relatives. Such an appeal may be made by a prisoner or a prisoner's legal counsel. Said appeals must be made within 48 hours of the seizure of such property.

74. According to these procedures, upon arrival of a prisoner at the detention pens of the court from a correctional facility, all property must . . .

(A) be returned when the prisoner is released from court.
(B) be given to any relative of the prisoner if such relative claims the property.
(C) be stored in the Court Property Clerk's office.
(D) be receipted for when returned to a friend or relative.

75. Regarding the procedure dealing with property removed from a prisoner, which of the following is least correct?

(A) A prisoner may not appeal the removal of property resulting from the processing of a prisoner delivered from a correctional facility.
(B) Property removed in connection with a criminal offense shall be turned over to the county prosecutor.
(C) A prisoner may appeal property removed as a result of a search of articles received from friends or relatives while at court.
(D) In appropriate instances, appeals about the removal of property must be made within 24 hours of the seizure of the property.

Directions: Answer questions 76–78 based solely on the following information.

When a prisoner in custody of the court requires medical/psychiatric treatment, the court officer assigned to the detention pen shall notify the shift supervisor. If necessary to take the prisoner to the hospital, an escorting officer other than the court officer assigned to the detention pen shall be assigned by the shift supervisor to escort the prisoner to the hospital. The court officer assigned to escort the prisoner shall notify the shift supervisor when the prisoner actually leaves the detention pen.

In all life-threatening situations the prisoner will be removed to the nearest hospital.

The court officer escorting the prisoner shall prepare a MEDICAL TREATMENT OF PRISONER form for each prisoner who:

a. Receives medical/psychiatric treatment (the form shall be forwarded to the City Surgeon General), OR

b. Refuses treatment after claiming injury or illness (the form shall be forwarded to the City Attorney), OR

c. May require prescribed medication (the form shall be forwarded to the City Pharmacist), OR,

d. When a prisoner in the custody of the court is in apparent need of treatment but makes no such request, the form shall be prepared by the court officer assigned to the detention pen and remain with the prisoner.

76. Ray Powers, a prisoner appearing at night court, becomes violently ill and asks for medical attention. Court Officer Best is the officer assigned to the detention pen and the shift supervisor is Sergeant Heating. The decision is made to transport the prisoner to the hospital because it is a life-threatening situation. In such an instance, . . .

   (A) Officer Best should escort the prisoner Powers to a hospital without consulting with anyone.
   (B) Sergeant Heating should select Officer Best to escort prisoner Powers to the hospital.
   (C) the prisoner Powers must be taken to the nearest hospital.
   (D) Officer Best should notify Sergeant Heating when the prisoner leaves the detention pen for the hospital.

77. One morning three prisoners are transported to a nearby hospital for treatment. While at the hospital, prisoner Cards receives medical treatment, prisoner Clubs refuses treatment after claiming an injury, and prisoner Towns has severe pain, which clearly requires prescribed medication. In such a situation, a MEDICAL TREATMENT OF PRISONER form should be prepared for . . .

   (A) only one of the prisoners.
   (B) only two of the prisoners.
   (C) all three of the prisoners.
   (D) none of the prisoners.

78. In the instance of a prisoner in a detention pen who is in apparent need of treatment but makes no such request, a MEDICAL TREATMENT OF PRISONER form should . . .

   (A) be prepared and forwarded to the City Surgeon General.
   (B) be prepared and forwarded to the City Attorney.
   (C) be prepared and remain with the prisoner.
   (D) never be prepared until help is requested by the prisoner.

Directions: Answer questions 79 and 80 based solely on the following information.

A court officer when traveling to a location outside the state while off duty shall not carry a firearm. In such a case, the court officer may choose to do any of the following:

A. deposit a personal firearm in the arsenal locker of the court command where the court officer is assigned, or

B. deposit a personal firearm in the arsenal locker of the court command that is closest to the court officer's private residence, or

C. safeguard a personal firearm at the court officer's place of residence. Note that when a personal firearm is safeguarded at a court officer's place of residence, the firearm shall be secured in such a manner so that the chance of theft is minimized as is the opportunity for tampering with the firearm by others. Because of federal regulations, the storing of a firearm in a bank safe deposit box is prohibited.

79. According to these regulations, which of the following is least correct?

(A) A court officer may never carry any firearm outside the state.

(B) A court officer going on vacation and traveling outside the state may choose to leave a personal firearm in the arsenal locker of the court officer's command of assignment.

(C) A court officer going on vacation and traveling outside the state may choose to safeguard a personal firearm at the court officer's place of residence.

(D) Under certain circumstances, a court officer could deposit a personal firearm in the arsenal locker of the court command that is closest to the court officer's private residence.

80. Court Officer Bob Knight is planning to take some time off and take a trip out of state. His wife Pat Knight, who is also a court officer with the same department, suggests that they leave their personal firearms in their bank safe deposit box. In this instance, Pat's advice is . . .

(A) good, mainly because it will be very safe there.

(B) bad, mainly because officers should always be armed.

(C) good, mainly because if any theft occurs the bank will have to replace the revolvers.

(D) bad, mainly because certain federal regulations prohibit such an action.

Directions: Answer questions 81–85 based solely on the following information.

When a death occurs for which a court officer is entitled to personal leave with pay, the court officer shall prepare a REQUEST FOR LEAVE REPORT. If the court officer is unable to make personal application, the court clerk shall prepare the REQUEST FOR LEAVE REPORT and submit it to the court officer's commanding officer. The court officer making the request shall be excused with pay for four consecutive scheduled tours of duty.

A court officer shall be entitled to such leave for the death of any of the following:

a. an immediate family member, or

b. a domestic partner, or

c. the covered relative of a domestic partner.

The immediate family shall include a spouse; natural, foster, or step parent; child; brother or sister; father-in-law, mother-in-law, or any relative residing in the household.

Domestic partners shall include two (2) persons, both of whom are twenty-one (21) years of age or older and neither of whom is married, who have a close and personal relationship including shared responsibilities, who have lived together for a period of two (2) years or more on a continuous basis at time of death, and who have registered with the City Department of Personnel as domestic partners and have not terminated the registration in accordance with procedures established by the City Department of Personnel.

A covered relative of a domestic partner includes a parent or child of such domestic partner, or a relative of such domestic partner who resides in the household.

A court officer who is turned down after seeking domestic partner status for someone and wishes to appeal must submit a written appeal within 30 days directly to the City Counsel General stating the reasons for the appeal.

81. When a death occurs for which a court officer is entitled to a personal leave, a REQUEST FOR LEAVE REPORT may be prepared by . . .

    (A) the court officer's commanding officer.
    (B) an immediate member of the court officer's family.
    (C) only the court officer seeking the leave.
    (D) the court officer seeking the leave or the court clerk.

82. When a death occurs for which a court officer is entitled to personal leave the court officer shall be excused . . .

    (A) with pay for any four tours of duty selected by the court officer.
    (B) without pay for four consecutive scheduled tours of duty.
    (C) with pay for four consecutive scheduled tours of duty.
    (D) without pay for any four tours of duty selected by the court officer.

83. A court officer would be least likely to be granted a personal leave based on the death of which of the following?

    (A) a grandmother who raised the court officer and now lives out of town
    (B) a cousin who lives in the court officer's household
    (C) a domestic partner of the same gender as the court officer
    (D) a mother-in-law of the court officer

84. Raymond who has never been married is a 24-year-old male court officer. According to the procedure, which one of the following would most qualify to become Raymond's domestic partner?

    (A) Terry, a 20-year-old female, who has never been married.
    (B) Louise, a 36-year-old female, who is presently married.
    (C) Sherry, a 23-year-old female, who is divorced and whom Raymond has lived with for 1 year.
    (D) Albert, a 24-year-old male, who is currently unmarried and whom Raymond has lived with for three years.

85. Harriet is a female court officer. She applies for domestic partner status with Roy. Her application requesting such status is turned down. She prepares a written appeal. She would be most correct if she submitted the appeal to . . .

    (A) her commanding officer within 30 days.
    (B) the court clerk within 10 days.
    (C) her commanding officer within 10 days.
    (D) the City Counsel General within 30 days.

The following general regulations shall govern the behavior of court officers.

An employee performing the duties of a court officer shall . . .

    a. Perform all duties as directed by competent authority.

    b. Remain at assigned post until properly relieved.

        i. Notify the shift supervisor and, if possible, make entry in the COURT ROOM LOG before leaving post.

        ii. Make entry in the COURT ROOM LOG upon return to post and notify the shift supervisor.

    c. Make accurate, concise entries in official records in chronological order, without delay, using BLACK ink.

    d. Sign official reports or forms with full first name, middle initial, and surname.

    e. Make corrections on official records by drawing an ink line through incorrect matter. Enter correction immediately above and initial change.

    f. Use numerals when entering dates on official forms (e.g., 1/5/96).

    g. Use abbreviation "Do" for ditto.

    h. Start serial numbers with one (1) at beginning of each year for official forms or reports, unless otherwise specified.

86. Court Officer Neil Harry Bailes is assigned to the Del Ray Courthouse. When signing an official form, Court Officer Bailes would be most correct if he signed his name in which of the following formats?

    (A) N. Bailes
    (B) N.H. Bailes
    (C) Neil H. Bailes
    (D) Neil Harry Bailes

87. Court Officer Roller is assigned to detention pen 15 as his post. The officer's assistance is required by another court officer assigned to an adjacent detention pen. Officer Roller makes an entry in the COURT ROOM LOG and then immediately leaves detention pen 15 to assist the other officer. When Officer Roller returns, the officer notifies the shift supervisor. In this situation, Officer Roller's actions were . . .

    (A) proper, mainly because an entry was made in the COURT ROOM LOG prior to leaving the detention pen.
    (B) improper, mainly because no entry is ever required in the COURT ROOM LOG prior to leaving the detention pen.
    (C) proper, mainly because the shift supervisor was notified upon return to the detention pen.
    (D) improper, mainly because the shift supervisor was not notified prior to leaving the detention pen and no entry was made in the COURT ROOM LOG upon returning to the detention pen.

88. According to regulations, which of the following statements is most correct?

    (A) Official reports must be completed in black ink and serial numbers must always begin with the number one at the beginning of the year.
    (B) Official reports may be completed in blue or black ink, and serial numbers begin with the number one at the beginning of the year unless otherwise specified.
    (C) Official reports must be completed in black ink, and serial numbers begin with the number one at the beginning of the year unless otherwise specified.
    (D) Official reports may be completed in blue or black ink, and serial numbers begin with the number one at the beginning of the year unless otherwise specified.

89. If the current date is the sixth day of June, and the year is 1998, then which of the following is the most appropriate entry when entering such a date on an official form?

    (A) June 6, 1998
    (B) June 06, 98
    (C) 06/06/1998
    (D) 6/6/98

90. Court Officer Don Goods is preparing an official form. The officer makes an error and wishes to correct one of the entries made by him. In such a situation, he would be most correct if he . . .

    (A) circled the error and entered the correction immediately below the change and initialed it.
    (B) drew an ink line through the error, entered the correction immediately below the change and initialed it.
    (C) circled the error and entered the correction immediately above the change and initialed it.
    (D) drew an ink line through the error, entered the correction immediately above the change, and initialed it.

Directions: For questions 91–100, compare the information appearing in each of the three columns and select your answer as follows:

a. Select A if only the first and second sets of information are exactly alike.

b. Select B if only the first and third sets of information are exactly alike.

c. Select C if only the second and third sets of information are exactly alike.

d. Select D if all or none of the sets of information is exactly alike.

Note that in some instances the information to be compared in each set may appear on a different line. This is not relevant in selecting your answer. Indicate your answer in the space provided after the information.

EXAMPLE FOR QUESTIONS 91–100

Set 1	Set 2	Set 3
Nick H. Bianco	Nick H. Bianco	Nick H. Bianco
3105 Park Ave.	New York, N Y	New York, N.Y.
New York, N.Y.	3105 Park Ave.	3105 Park Ave.

Answer B The information <u>NY</u> is missing periods in set 2. Hence only the first and third sets of information are exactly alike. B is the answer. Note once again that the information can appear on different lines. For these questions, the directions specify that you are comparing the information contained in each set, not where it appears in each set.

91.
Set 1	Set 2	Set 3
Paul A. Bartoszek	Paul A. Bartozsek	Paul A. Bartoszek
1-305-555-2908	1-305-555-2908	1-305-555-2908
Ford: Black	Ford: Black	Ford: Black
YM298 437 8896	YM298 437 8896	YM298 437 8896
3700 South Fork	3700 South Fork	3700 South Fork

91. Answer ____

92. Set 1
    B# 5205186
    Clay T. Davis
    Docket# 5205816
    Felony Murder
    Arraigned 06/14

    Set 2
    B# 5205186
    Docket# 5205816
    Clay T. Davis
    Felony Murder
    Arraigned 06/14

    Set 3
    B# 5205186
    Docket# 5205816
    Clay T. Davis
    Arraigned 06/14
    Felony Murder

92. Answer ____

93. Set 1
    Ron Gilbert
    Paroled 7/22
    Crim Ct# 47689
    Robbery 1st Deg.
    Judge Hangers

    Set 2
    Ron Gilbert
    Paroled 7/22
    Crim Ct# 47689
    Robbery 1st Deg
    Judge Hangers

    Set 3
    Ron Gilbert
    Paroled 7/22
    Crim Ct# 47689
    Robbery 1st Deg
    Judge Hangers

93. Answer ____

94. Set 1
    Ct. Off. Drake
    Sh # 17068
    Part 1 Sup Ct
    Appointed 6-9-97
    Smith/wesson

    Set 2
    Ct. Off. Drake
    Sh # 17098
    Part 1 Sup Ct
    Appointed 6/9/97
    Smith/wesson

    Set 3
    Sh # 17068
    Ct. Off. Drake
    Part 1 Sup Ct
    Appointed 6/9/97
    Smith/Wesson

94. Answer ____

95. Set 1
    Chris Sepe
    Probation
    Homicide
    Vin# 564739030g
    Bail voucher 699

    Set 2
    Chris Sepe
    Probation
    Homocide
    Vin# 564739030g
    Bail voucher 699

    Set 3
    Chris Sepe
    Probation
    Homocide
    Vin# 564739030g
    Bail voucher 699

95. Answer ____

96. Set 1
    .38 cal Colt
    ser# 19874563820
    Mil. Pol. Model
    Blue black finish
    Checkered grip

    Set 2
    Mil. Pol. Model
    .38 cal Colt
    Checkered grip
    Blue black finish
    ser# 19874563820

    Set 3
    .38 cal Colt
    ser# 19874653820
    Mil. Pol. Model
    Blue black finish
    Checkered grip

96. Answer ____

97. Set 1
    Atheletic Dept.
    "Racing Events"
    Ustachezkosliki
    UT489. 36S48993
    Marina del rey

    Set 2
    Atheletic Dept.
    Ustachekzosliki
    "Racing Events"
    UT489. 36S48993
    Marina del rey

    Set 3
    Atheletic Dept.
    UT489. 36S48993
    Ustachezkosliki
    Marina del rey
    "Racing Events"

97. Answer ____

98. Set 1
    NYS Pl 165.30
    Article 23A sub1
    RCA Mod#2892992911
    Brown & Biege stand
    Pr clk#Abc4362o3970

    Set 2
    Pr clk#Abc4362o3970
    NYS Pl 165.30
    Brown & Beige stand
    Article 23A sub1
    RCA Mod#2892992911

    Set 3
    NYS Pl 165.30
    Pr clk#Abc4362o3970
    Brown & Beige stand
    RCA Mod#2892992911
    Article 23A sub1

98. Answer ____

99. Set 1
    Red DuBois-Atee
    Arrested 06-09
    Det McCarthy #749
    Sp frds squad
    Adj 7/23 @9 A.M.

    Set 2
    Arrested 06-09
    Red DuBois-Atee
    Sp frds squad
    Adj 7/23 @9 A.M.
    Det MacCarthy #749

    Set 3
    Sp frds squad
    Det McCarthy #749
    Arrested 06-09
    Adj 7/23 @9 A.M.
    Red DuBois-Atee

99. Answer ____

100. Set 1
     Carmine Todo
     650 Gr Conc.
     Pt 1a spec sess ct
     St vs. TT Plastics
     Dock#85440568214

     Set 2
     Pt 1a spec sess ct
     St vs. TT Plastics
     Carmene Todo
     650 Gr Conc.
     Dock#85440568214

     Set 3
     St vs. TT Plastics
     Dock#85440568214
     650 Gr Conc.
     Pt 1a spec sess ct
     Carmine Todo

100. Answer ____

ANSWER KEY
Practice Exam Three

1. B	26. C	51. D	76. C
2. A	27. A	52. A	77. C
3. D	28. C	53. C	78. C
4. B	29. D	54. D	79. A
5. A	30. C	55. C	80. D
6. A	31. B	56. A	81. D
7. B	32. B	57. D	82. C
8. C	33. A	58. D	83. A
9. A	34. C	59. C	84. D
10. C	35. C	60. B	85. D
11. A	36. B	61. D	86. C
12. D	37. B	62. C	87. D
13. B	38. B	63. B	88. C
14. B	39. A	64. D	89. D
15. D	40. A	65. C	90. D
16. C	41. C	66. B	91. B
17. B	42. C	67. D	82. D
18. A	43. D	68. B	93. C
19. D	44. B	69. D	94. D
20. B	45. B	70. D	95. C
21. B	46. D	71. A	96. A
22. C	47. A	72. D	97. B
23. C	48. A	73. C	98. C
24. D	49. D	74. D	99. B
25. A	50. B	75. D	100. B

DIAGNOSTIC CHART

Directions: After you score your test, complete the following chart by inserting in the column entitled "Your Number Correct" the number of correct questions you answered in each of the eight sections of the test. Then compare your score in each section with the ratings in the column entitled "Scale." Finally, to correct your weaknesses, follow the instructions found at the end of the chart.

Section	Question Numbers	Area	Your Number Correct	Scale
1	1–15	Memory (15 questions)		15 Right—Excellent 13–14 Right—Good 11–12 Right—Fair Under 11 Right—Poor
2	16–50	Reading Comprehension (35 questions)		33–35 Right—Excellent 30–32 Right—Good 27–29 Right—Fair Under 27 Right—Poor
3	51–65	Legal Definitions (15 questions)		15 Right—Excellent 13–14 Right—Good 11–12 Right—Fair Under 11 Right—Poor
4	66–90	Applying Court Officer Procedures (25 questions)		25 Right—Excellent 22–24 Right—Good 18–21 Right—Fair Under 18 Right—Poor
5	91–100	Clerical Ability (10 questions)		10 Right—Excellent 8–9 Right—Good 7 Right—Fair Under 7 Right—Poor

How to correct weaknesses:

1. If you are weak in Section 1, concentrate on Chapter 2.
2. If you are weak in Section 2, concentrate on Chapter 1.
3. If you are weak in Section 3, concentrate on Chapter 4.
4. If you are weak in Section 4, concentrate on Chapter 3.
5. If you are weak in Section 5, concentrate on Chapter 5.

Note: Consider yourself weak in a section if you receive a score other than excellent in that section.

ANSWERS EXPLAINED

1. **(B)** Kelly carries firearms, Monchall carries explosives, and Kruger carries a switch-blade knife. Please note that many of the questions involving wanted posters involve comparisons among the various wanted persons.

2. **(A)** Aponte was doing 5 years, Monchall and Kruger were doing 20 years. Only Kelly was serving a life sentence.

3. **(D)** Kruger weighs 250 pounds. None of the others are over 175 pounds. Please note that once again the answer involved a comparison among the four prisoners.

4. **(B)** Aponte is 58 years old. None of the others are over 50.

5. **(A)** Kelly has blue eyes. The other three have brown eyes.

6. **(A)** Kruger is an expert knife fighter who is usually armed with a switchblade knife.

7. **(B)** Monchall is a terrorist who carries explosives on his person.

8. **(C)** Josephine Aponte was serving a 5-year sentence for forgery when she escaped.

9. **(A)** The name Bill opens the door to a number of associations, such as accountants always send you a bill. We hope that you are using associations to help you do these memory questions. The more you practice creating and using them, the better you get at it.

10. **(C)** Don Hurte's name is perfect for an association to remind you that he is violent. Hurte likes to hurt people. None of the other three defendants are linked to violence in any way.

11. **(A)** Peter Block is an automobile mechanic. One might say that Peter Block works on engine blocks.

12. **(D)** Smith, Block, and Hurte are all white males. Remember, that when one of a group of people in a memory story is different from the others, that difference is probably going to be the subject of a question.

13. **(B)** Once again, the question centered around the difference among the four defendants.

14. **(B)** Hopefully you recognized the obvious association between Frank Wood's name and his occupation. Carpenters, of course, work with wood.

15. **(D)** Frank Wood is the swindler.

16. **(C)** The rule that the area within courthouses are not permissible locations for public demonstrations is a general rule. This means, of course, that there could be exceptions to the rule.

17. **(B)** When acts of disruption occur in the courtroom, the presiding magistrate has the ultimate responsibility for maintaining order and the dignity of the court.

18. **(A)** The origin or source of orders to deal with disruptions depends on whether the disruption is in a courtroom or in some other location inside the courthouse.

19. **(D)** Confessions made by a person accused of a crime must be made voluntarily, or they cannot be used during a criminal trial.

20. **(B)** The rule does not cover all situations where a suspect is being questioned, only those situations where the person is in custody. Therefore, a person who cannot afford an attorney and who is being questioned by police or peace officers can make a valid confession.

21. **(B)** This question points out the importance of a good vocabulary. A judicial rule is one that is established by the courts, and the U.S. Supreme Court established the Miranda rule.

22. **(C)** A private citizen acting on his own authority is not bound by Miranda, but he would become subject to the rule if he was acting as an agent of the government.

23. **(C)** Bail is posted with criminal, not civil courts, and is not returned in all cases. Bail can be something of value and is not limited to money.

24. **(D)** Choice B is a correct statement but it is not the answer because it is not mentioned in the information given.

25. **(A)** Hopefully you did not choose either Choice C or D because there is no basis for those answers in the information given. It clearly describes entrapment as being illegal conduct. Therefore, it can never be legal.

26. **(C)** Choosing between C and D is the difficult part of answering this question correctly. However, in the court decision, reference to evidence is qualified by limiting it to evidence that can be destroyed, not any evidence. Get used to these kinds of qualified statements because examiners often qualify statements to make them incorrect.

27. **(A)** Myers is never specifically designated in the paragraph as a male, but in a number of instances the paragraph uses the masculine form of pronouns when referring to Myers. In the final sentence, when referring to Myers, it states when referring to Myers that "he was incapable as were his confederates, of reentering the vehicle."

28. **(C)** The Trial Court and the Appellate Division Court ruled against Myers when they held that the search was constitutional. The Court of Appeals reversed both courts by holding that the evidence was unconstitutionally obtained.

29. **(D)** Be careful of this one. Because Myers was arrested for the possession of the cocaine, you might conclude that he owns the cocaine. However, it is never stated anywhere in the decision who actually owned the cocaine. In all probability, Myers was the owner of the car. This would explain why he got arrested when the drugs were found in the jacket pocket in the back seat of the car. In any case, you can rely only on what is written, and the decision doesn't give any definitive indication of cocaine ownership.

30. **(C)** Only Myers was arrested for the possession of cocaine.

31. **(B)** See the last sentence of the decision. Please note that Choice C is factual, but it is not based on what is written.

32. **(B)** A search incident to arrest is a search that occurs in connection with an arrest. Once again, we see the value of a good vocabulary. However, if you did not know the word, you could have correctly answered the question anyway. Simply substitute the

wording of each choice for the word *incident* in the decision. *In connection with* is the only choice that makes sense when you insert it into the wording of the decision in place of *incident*.

33. **(A)** This should have been an easy one. No mention is made anywhere in the decision about strengthening the case of the arresting officer.

34. **(C)** At an arraignment, an accused (defendant) is required to enter pleas of guilty or not guilty.

35. **(C)** Appeals involve moving a jurisdiction to a higher court. In choice C, the matter remains in the same court.

36. **(B)** Remember that, as we pointed out in the reading comprehension chapter, sometimes the material you need to comprehend appears in graphic as well as written form. Questions 36–43 are examples of those kinds of questions. In question 36, you should have read from the graph that 56% of the defendants who are convicted of crimes against persons are 21–30 and 38% of those are convicted of crimes against property are between that same age. Therefore, the age category 21–30 clearly accounts for most of the convictions.

37. **(B)** 56% of the defendants who are convicted of crimes against persons are 21–30 years of age. A majority is more than half. Choice B is the answer.

38. **(B)** 65% of those under 21 who are convicted of crimes against persons are between 17 and 20 years of age. Because "most" means "more than half," Choice B is the answer. Concerning Choice C, there is no way of determining from the data any specific information about persons who are 18 years of age. 18-year-old defendants are included in the overall category of 17–20.

39. **(A)** 78% of those persons under 17 who are convicted of a crime against property are under 17.

40. **(A)** Choices B, C, and D would all be correct if the category involved was crimes against persons. However, the category was crimes against property. In the over 30 age group for the category "crimes against property," 32% of the new convictions are over 30. 1000 new convictions multiplied by 0.32 (32% in decimal form) equals 320, as indicated in Choice A.

41. **(C)** This is a difficult question because it involves making two calculations. You must first determine the approximate number of new defendants convicted of crimes against persons who are under 21. You must multiply 1000 (the total number of new defendants) by 0.18 (the decimal equivalent of 18%). By doing this, you determine that the number of new convictions under 21 convicted for a crime against a person is 180. Of that number, 35% of them are under 17 years of age. This means that 63 of them are under 17 years of age (180 multiplied by 0.35, the decimal equivalent of 35%).

42. **(C)** To determine the answer to this question, all you had to do was to pick the answer from the graph. Over 21 includes two categories, 21–30 and over 30. Because 56% are between 21 and 30 and 26% are over 30, simply add the two percentages to arrive at the answer, which is 82%, as indicated in Choice C.

43. **(D)** Once again, we have included a question that cannot be answer based on the data supplied. Test writers do this often, and we want you to be prepared. The data you were given to answer this series of questions were about the ages of defendants being convicted of crimes presented in percentages. You simply cannot use that kind of data to answer any questions about the specific number of convictions at any specific point in time.

44. **(B)** According to the passage, children under 10 are not ever allowed in the holding pen area.

45. **(B)** Clergy persons can visit 15 hours a day, 7 days a week.

46. **(D)** Police can visit if they have written authorization from the court involved.

47. **(A)** Visits by the clergy require consent but not specifically written authorization.

48. **(A)** Green is the name of the court officer who would be calling his supervisor and requesting an ambulance.

49. **(D)** Mr. Roe is the name of the injured party.

50. **(B)** After being *released*, the injured Mr. Roe went home.

51. **(D)** May is more than 18 years old and engages in sexual intercourse with Mark who is less than 14 years old. They are not married to each other. That is rape in the second degree on the part of May but not Mark.

52. **(A)** Tom has had sexual intercourse with a person who is unable to consent because she is physically helpless. The most serious charge is rape in the first degree. Although it is true that Tom could be charged with rape in the third degree because of the ages involved, the most serious offense is as indicated in Choice A.

53. **(C)** Don engaged in deviate sexual intercourse with Joy by forcible compulsion. He committed, as indicated in Choice C, sodomy in the first degree.

54. **(D)** Because of their ages Tab and Mark more than sufficiently qualify as adults. Hence no lack of consent can be due to the age of either of them. The sexual contact was not done with anyone's lack of consent, which is really the key element of sexual abuse. Hence, no sexual abuse took place.

55. **(C)** Sexual intercourse with a dead human body constitutes sexual misconduct.

56. **(A)** This is sodomy in the first degree as indicated in Choice A because force was used to engage in deviate sexual intercourse.

57. **(D)** Choice A can be eliminated because deviate sexual intercourse has occurred. Choice B can be eliminated because there was no lack of consent on the part of the 34-year-old June. Because June is obviously at least 21 years old and May is less than 17, June, but not May, commits sodomy in the third degree. This eliminates Choice C and leaves Choice D as the most serious offense.

58. **(D)** For a charge of rape in the third degree, one of the participants must be 21 or older, and the other participant must be less than 17 years old.

59. **(C)** An offense becomes murder in the first degree when someone causes the death of a victim who is either a court officer OR a correctional employee performing offi-

cial duties; or, regardless of who the victim is, the offense becomes murder in the first degree if the perpetrator is in prison serving a life sentence. However, in addition to any of these circumstances, the perpetrator must be more than 18 years old at the time of the commission of the offense. Therefore Choices A, B, and D may be eliminated, and Choice C is the answer.

60. **(B)** If a person intends to cause the death of one person, and causes the death of such person or another, the person commits murder in the second degree.

61. **(D)** When an illegal abortional act is done to a female and causes her miscarriage, the offense is abortion. In this instance, the abortional act is illegal because it was not done to save the female's life and was done to a female who was 24 weeks or more pregnant.

62. **(C)** Ms. Green committed self abortion because she submitted to an illegal abortional act that was not done to save her life while she was 24 weeks or more pregnant and that resulted in her miscarriage.

63. **(B)** If a person during the performance of an illegal abortional act on a pregnant female causes the death of the pregnant female who is 24 weeks or more pregnant, such person commits manslaughter in the first degree.

64. **(D)** By intentionally aiding another person to commit suicide, Don committed manslaughter in the second degree.

65. **(C)** Knuckles had the intent to cause serious physical injury to another person; instead, he caused death to such person. Knuckles committed manslaughter in the first degree.

66. **(B)** Choice B is correct because such a search can be performed on either subject. Choice D sounds correct, but it is not mentioned in the procedures.

67. **(D)** A body cavity search specifically requires that medical personnel perform such searches.

68. **(B)** Choice A is incorrect because the removed shoes of a prisoner and not of a visitor may be searched. Choices C and D are strictly made up and are not found in the procedure.

69. **(D)** Internally searching a female prisoner's genitals is part of a body cavity search.

70. **(D)** This type of search is to be performed in absolute privacy by medical personnel. Nothing is mentioned about the gender of the medical personnel. But, all court officer personnel present for security reasons must be of the same gender as the prisoner being searched.

71. **(A)** After entering the time the vehicle enters the detention area, the next required entry is as indicated in Choice A.

72. **(D)** Such a search is to be done by the court officer in charge of the gate.

73. **(C)** Remember to base your answers only on what is contained in the procedure.

74. **(D)** Choices A and C are incorrect because property involved with a criminal offense shall not be returned nor stored in the Court Property Clerk's office. Choice B is incorrect because the relative must be selected pursuant to the wishes of the prisoner.

75. **(D)** Choices A, B, and C are correct statements, but Choice D is incorrect and is the answer because the time frame is 48 hours.

76. **(C)** It is a life-threatening situation so the prisoner should be removed to the nearest hospital. Choice A is incorrect because the escorting officer shall be assigned by the shift supervisor. Choice B is incorrect because an officer, other than the officer assigned to the detention pen, shall be assigned to escort the prisoner. Finally, Choice D is incorrect because the officer assigned to escort the prisoner shall notify the shift supervisor when the prisoner actually leaves the detention pen.

77. **(C)** All three are examples of when such a form should be prepared.

78. **(C)** As stated in the procedure, the form shall be prepared and remain with the prisoner.

79. **(A)** Choice A is an incorrect statement because of the word *never*. A court officer is prohibited from possessing a personal firearm outside the state while off duty. Obviously, if a court officer was sent out of state on an assignment, this procedure would not apply. Choice D describes a situation where a court officer could be going out of state while off duty and wanted to leave a personal firearm in an arsenal locker of a court command, which is near home and not necessarily in the officer's command.

80. **(D)** Choice D is as stated in the procedure. Although other choices may sound logical, they are not mentioned in the procedure. Remember that this type of question is not seeking to measure your judgment. The answers are in the procedures you are given.

81. **(D)** If the court officer is unable to prepare the report, then the court clerk shall prepare it.

82. **(C)** Examiners often attempt to distract a candidate by changing one or more words of a procedure to test a candidate's ability to follow directions closely.

83. **(A)** The grandmother would have to live in the court officer's household as does the cousin in Choice B. There is no requirement that domestic partners be of the opposite gender, and a mother-in-law is considered an immediate family member according to the procedure.

84. **(D)** Terry in Choice A is too young to be a domestic partner, Louise in Choice B is still married, and Sherry in Choice C has lived with Raymond for only 1 year. Albert in Choice D meets all the criteria.

85. **(D)** The City Counsel General should get such an appeal within 30 days.

86. **(C)** The rule requires that official reports or forms be signed with full first name, middle initial, and surname.

87. **(D)** The shift supervisor must be notified before leaving and upon returning. Entries in the COURT ROOM LOG must be made, if possible, before leaving but must also be made upon return.

88. **(C)** The use of the word *always* makes Choice A incorrect. Because the ink must be black, Choices B and D are incorrect. Choice C is in keeping with the regulations.

89. **(D)** When entering such a date on an official form, only the last two digits of the year are required to be entered. Thus, Choice C is incorrect. Choice D is the answer.

90. **(D)** To correct an error, an ink line is drawn through the incorrect material, the correct entry is entered above the correction, and the change is initialed.

91. **(B)** Sets 1 and 3 are exactly alike. In set 2, Barto<u>z</u>sek is spelled differently.

92. **(D)** Although the information appears on different lines in each of the sets, the information itself is exactly alike in all three sets.

93. **(C)** Sets 2 and 3 are exactly alike. In set 1, Robbery 1st Deg<u>.</u> is different in that a period appears after Deg.

94. **(D)** None of the sets of information is exactly alike. In set 1, 6<u>-</u>9<u>-</u>97 is different; in set 2 170<u>9</u>8 is different, and in set 3 Smith/<u>W</u>esson is different.

95. **(C)** In set 1 Hom<u>i</u>cide, although it is spelled correctly, is spelled differently. Therefore, only the second and third sets of information are exactly alike. Remember that you are comparing information and are looking for differences. It is not relevant that the correct spelling of the word appears in set 1, it is not exactly like the other two sets. The answer is Choice C.

96. **(A)** The information in sets 1 and 2 is exactly alike. The ser# 19874<u>65</u>3820 is different in set 3.

97. **(B)** Only sets 1 and 3 are exactly alike. Note Ustache<u>kz</u>osliki in set 2. The fact that the word *atheletic* is not correctly spelled has no bearing on your answer.

98. **(C)** The information in sets 2 and 3 is exactly alike. The word B<u>i</u>ege is different in set 1.

99. **(B)** The information in set 2 is not exactly like the information in sets 1 and 3. See Ma<u>c</u>Carthy.

100. **(B)** The information in set 2 not exactly like the information in sets 1 and 3. See Carm<u>e</u>ne.

Practice Examination Four

This is the fourth and final practice examination for you to take.

Be sure to take each practice examination in one sitting. They each contain 100 questions, which you must answer in 3½ hours. It is imperative that you become accustomed to concentrating for the length of time required to complete an entire examination. Be sure to review the test-taking strategy outlined in the Introduction before taking this practice examination, to use that strategy when doing the examination, and to record your answers on the following Answer Sheet.

ANSWER SHEET
Practice Exam Four

Follow the instructions given in the test. Mark only your answers in the circles below.

WARNING: Be sure that the circle you fill is in the same row as the question you are answering. Use a No. 2 pencil (soft pencil).

BE SURE YOUR PENCIL MARKS ARE HEAVY AND BLACK.

ERASE COMPLETELY ANY ANSWER YOU WISH TO CHANGE.

DO NOT make stray pencil dots, dashes, or marks.

1. Ⓐ Ⓑ Ⓒ Ⓓ	26. Ⓐ Ⓑ Ⓒ Ⓓ	51. Ⓐ Ⓑ Ⓒ Ⓓ	76. Ⓐ Ⓑ Ⓒ Ⓓ
2. Ⓐ Ⓑ Ⓒ Ⓓ	27. Ⓐ Ⓑ Ⓒ Ⓓ	52. Ⓐ Ⓑ Ⓒ Ⓓ	77. Ⓐ Ⓑ Ⓒ Ⓓ
3. Ⓐ Ⓑ Ⓒ Ⓓ	28. Ⓐ Ⓑ Ⓒ Ⓓ	53. Ⓐ Ⓑ Ⓒ Ⓓ	78. Ⓐ Ⓑ Ⓒ Ⓓ
4. Ⓐ Ⓑ Ⓒ Ⓓ	29. Ⓐ Ⓑ Ⓒ Ⓓ	54. Ⓐ Ⓑ Ⓒ Ⓓ	79. Ⓐ Ⓑ Ⓒ Ⓓ
5. Ⓐ Ⓑ Ⓒ Ⓓ	30. Ⓐ Ⓑ Ⓒ Ⓓ	55. Ⓐ Ⓑ Ⓒ Ⓓ	80. Ⓐ Ⓑ Ⓒ Ⓓ
6. Ⓐ Ⓑ Ⓒ Ⓓ	31. Ⓐ Ⓑ Ⓒ Ⓓ	56. Ⓐ Ⓑ Ⓒ Ⓓ	81. Ⓐ Ⓑ Ⓒ Ⓓ
7. Ⓐ Ⓑ Ⓒ Ⓓ	32. Ⓐ Ⓑ Ⓒ Ⓓ	57. Ⓐ Ⓑ Ⓒ Ⓓ	82. Ⓐ Ⓑ Ⓒ Ⓓ
8. Ⓐ Ⓑ Ⓒ Ⓓ	33. Ⓐ Ⓑ Ⓒ Ⓓ	58. Ⓐ Ⓑ Ⓒ Ⓓ	83. Ⓐ Ⓑ Ⓒ Ⓓ
9. Ⓐ Ⓑ Ⓒ Ⓓ	34. Ⓐ Ⓑ Ⓒ Ⓓ	59. Ⓐ Ⓑ Ⓒ Ⓓ	84. Ⓐ Ⓑ Ⓒ Ⓓ
10. Ⓐ Ⓑ Ⓒ Ⓓ	35. Ⓐ Ⓑ Ⓒ Ⓓ	60. Ⓐ Ⓑ Ⓒ Ⓓ	85. Ⓐ Ⓑ Ⓒ Ⓓ
11. Ⓐ Ⓑ Ⓒ Ⓓ	36. Ⓐ Ⓑ Ⓒ Ⓓ	61. Ⓐ Ⓑ Ⓒ Ⓓ	86. Ⓐ Ⓑ Ⓒ Ⓓ
12. Ⓐ Ⓑ Ⓒ Ⓓ	37. Ⓐ Ⓑ Ⓒ Ⓓ	62. Ⓐ Ⓑ Ⓒ Ⓓ	87. Ⓐ Ⓑ Ⓒ Ⓓ
13. Ⓐ Ⓑ Ⓒ Ⓓ	38. Ⓐ Ⓑ Ⓒ Ⓓ	63. Ⓐ Ⓑ Ⓒ Ⓓ	88. Ⓐ Ⓑ Ⓒ Ⓓ
14. Ⓐ Ⓑ Ⓒ Ⓓ	39. Ⓐ Ⓑ Ⓒ Ⓓ	64. Ⓐ Ⓑ Ⓒ Ⓓ	89. Ⓐ Ⓑ Ⓒ Ⓓ
15. Ⓐ Ⓑ Ⓒ Ⓓ	40. Ⓐ Ⓑ Ⓒ Ⓓ	65. Ⓐ Ⓑ Ⓒ Ⓓ	90. Ⓐ Ⓑ Ⓒ Ⓓ
16. Ⓐ Ⓑ Ⓒ Ⓓ	41. Ⓐ Ⓑ Ⓒ Ⓓ	66. Ⓐ Ⓑ Ⓒ Ⓓ	91. Ⓐ Ⓑ Ⓒ Ⓓ
17. Ⓐ Ⓑ Ⓒ Ⓓ	42. Ⓐ Ⓑ Ⓒ Ⓓ	67. Ⓐ Ⓑ Ⓒ Ⓓ	92. Ⓐ Ⓑ Ⓒ Ⓓ
18. Ⓐ Ⓑ Ⓒ Ⓓ	43. Ⓐ Ⓑ Ⓒ Ⓓ	68. Ⓐ Ⓑ Ⓒ Ⓓ	93. Ⓐ Ⓑ Ⓒ Ⓓ
19. Ⓐ Ⓑ Ⓒ Ⓓ	44. Ⓐ Ⓑ Ⓒ Ⓓ	69. Ⓐ Ⓑ Ⓒ Ⓓ	94. Ⓐ Ⓑ Ⓒ Ⓓ
20. Ⓐ Ⓑ Ⓒ Ⓓ	45. Ⓐ Ⓑ Ⓒ Ⓓ	70. Ⓐ Ⓑ Ⓒ Ⓓ	95. Ⓐ Ⓑ Ⓒ Ⓓ
21. Ⓐ Ⓑ Ⓒ Ⓓ	46. Ⓐ Ⓑ Ⓒ Ⓓ	71. Ⓐ Ⓑ Ⓒ Ⓓ	96. Ⓐ Ⓑ Ⓒ Ⓓ
22. Ⓐ Ⓑ Ⓒ Ⓓ	47. Ⓐ Ⓑ Ⓒ Ⓓ	72. Ⓐ Ⓑ Ⓒ Ⓓ	97. Ⓐ Ⓑ Ⓒ Ⓓ
23. Ⓐ Ⓑ Ⓒ Ⓓ	48. Ⓐ Ⓑ Ⓒ Ⓓ	73. Ⓐ Ⓑ Ⓒ Ⓓ	98. Ⓐ Ⓑ Ⓒ Ⓓ
24. Ⓐ Ⓑ Ⓒ Ⓓ	49. Ⓐ Ⓑ Ⓒ Ⓓ	74. Ⓐ Ⓑ Ⓒ Ⓓ	99. Ⓐ Ⓑ Ⓒ Ⓓ
25. Ⓐ Ⓑ Ⓒ Ⓓ	50. Ⓐ Ⓑ Ⓒ Ⓓ	75. Ⓐ Ⓑ Ⓒ Ⓓ	100. Ⓐ Ⓑ Ⓒ Ⓓ

THE TEST

Time: 3 1/2 hours
100 questions

> Answer questions 1–8 based on the following instructions.
>
> **Directions:** Study for 5 minutes the following information about the trial of defendant Tom Green. Try to remember as many details as possible. Do not make written notes of any kind during this 5-minute period. After the completion of the 5-minute period, answer questions 1–8. When answering the questions, do NOT refer back to the information.

MEMORY INFORMATION

5-Minute Time Limit

Court:	New City Criminal Court
Date of Trial:	March 19th
Case:	People versus Green
Case Docket Number:	03591215
Defendant:	Tom Green
Complainant:	Lou Broker
Charge # 1:	Robbery
Charge # 2:	Grand Larceny
Charge # 3:	Possession of a Dangerous Weapon
Date of Crime:	January 12th
Date of Arrest:	January 29th
Arrest Number:	95375911
Date of Arraignment:	February 9th
Arraignment Number:	03557912
Magistrate:	The Honorable James Jensen
District Attorney:	Peter Miles
Defense Attorney:	Bill Harris
Court Clerk:	Charles Champion
Court Officer # 1:	Peggy Smart
Arresting Officer:	Police Officer Harry Shields
Bail Bondsman:	Henry Money

DO NOT PROCEED UNTIL 5 MINUTES HAVE PASSED.

1. Who was the Bail Bondsman?

   (A) Harry Shields
   (B) Peggy Smart
   (C) Henry Money
   (D) Charles Champion

2. What was the name of the case?

   (A) New City versus Green
   (B) People versus Green
   (C) Green versus Broker
   (D) Broker versus Green

3. What was the date of the arrest?

   (A) January 12th
   (B) January 29th
   (C) February 9th
   (D) March 19th

4. Charge # 3 was . . .

   (A) Robbery.
   (B) Grand Larceny.
   (C) Possession of a Dangerous Weapon.
   (D) Murder.

5. Who was the Defense Attorney?

   (A) Harry Shields
   (B) Peggy Smart
   (C) Peter Miles
   (D) Bill Harris

6. Who was the Arresting Officer?

   (A) Harry Shields
   (B) Peggy Smart
   (C) Henry Money
   (D) Charles Champion

7. What was the Arrest Number?

   (A) 03591215
   (B) 95375911
   (C) 03557912
   (D) not given

8. How much bail money was posted?

(A) $1000.00
(B) $5000.00
(C) $10,000.00
(D) not given

Answer questions 9–15 based on the following instructions.

Directions: Study for 5 minutes the following information about four wanted persons. Try to remember as many details as possible. Do not make written notes of any kind during this 5-minute period. After the completion of the 5-minute period, answer questions 9–15. When answering the questions, do NOT refer back to the information.

MEMORY INFORMATION

5-Minute Time Limit

Court Officer Don Ginty is assigned to the Metropolis Criminal Court. During roll call training, he is given the following information about four wanted persons who have been attempting to intimidate witnesses in an ongoing homicide trial.

Wanted Person # 1: Larry Ash, male, white, 45 years old, 185 pounds, 6'4", black hair, and blue eyes. He walks with a limp as a result of an automobile accident when he was 12 years old. Larry Ash is wanted for arson. On May 31st of this year, he set fire to the unoccupied automobile of his former girlfriend, Pat Swan. He is an avid fan of country music and frequents country music clubs. He has no previous convictions.

Wanted Person # 2: Don Smart, male, white, 25 years old, 180 pounds, 5'7", brown hair, and brown eyes. He has a 5-inch scar over his right eye as a result of a bar fight when he was 19 years old. Smart is wanted for armed robbery. He is known to carry a handgun and is considered extremely dangerous. He has a lengthy arrest record with many previous convictions. He is a college graduate with a degree in accounting. He is a lifelong sports fan and often attends professional sports events, especially basketball games.

Wanted Person # 3: Pat Wall, male, white, 32 years old, 225 pounds, 5'9", brown hair, and brown eyes. He has a speech impediment. He is wanted for the murder of the husband of his ex-wife. He is an expert knife fighter with a reputation for being armed and dangerous. He has spent time in prison as a result of a previous assault conviction. He is an expert chef who specializes in cooking Italian food.

Wanted Person # 4: Art Champion, male, white, 24 years old, 175 pounds, 5'9", brown hair, and brown eyes. He is wanted for the sexual abuse of an 11-year-old girl. He is known to be an extremely violent person who is often armed with some sort of deadly weapon and should be considered dangerous. He has four previous convictions for various sex offenses. He is known to loiter in the vicinity of elementary schools and often poses as a law enforcement officer when approaching his young victims.

DO NOT PROCEED UNTIL 5 MINUTES HAVE PASSED.

Answer questions 9–15 solely on the basis of the previous information. Do not refer back to the information when answering these questions. You have 15 minutes to complete these seven questions.

9. Which of the wanted persons has a college degree?
   (A) Larry Ash
   (B) Don Smart
   (C) Pat Wall
   (D) Art Champion

10. The wanted person who walks with a limp is . . .

   (A) Larry Ash.
   (B) Don Smart.
   (C) Pat Wall.
   (D) Art Champion.

11. Which of the following wanted persons is an expert knife fighter?

   (A) Larry Ash
   (B) Don Smart
   (C) Pat Wall
   (D) Art Champion

12. The tallest of the wanted persons is . . .

   (A) Larry Ash.
   (B) Don Smart.
   (C) Pat Wall.
   (D) Art Champion.

13. Which of the wanted persons is known to loiter in the vicinity of elementary schools?

   (A) Larry Ash
   (B) Don Smart
   (C) Pat Wall
   (D) Art Champion

14. Larry Ash is wanted for . . .

   (A) armed robbery.
   (B) murder.
   (C) sexual abuse.
   (D) arson.

15. Pat Wall . . .

(A) is a college graduate.
(B) is a country music fan.
(C) is an expert chef.
(D) impersonates law enforcement officers.

Directions: Questions 16–21 are to be answered solely on the basis of the following representation of objects found during an inspection of the holding pens (jail cells) of defendants who are involved in lengthy trials.

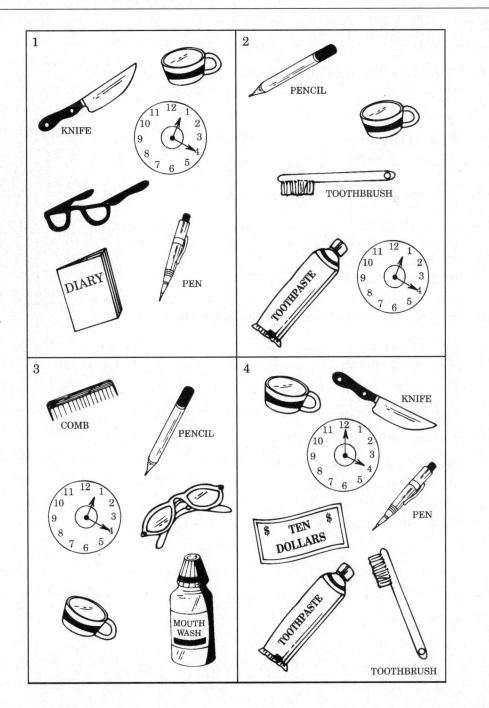

16. A court system rule prohibits defendants from keeping cutting implements in their holding pens. This rule is being violated by . . .

(A) one defendant.
(B) two defendants.
(C) three defendants.
(D) four defendants.

17. The defendant who probably keeps a written record of daily events occupies . . .

(A) holding pen # 1.
(B) holding pen # 2.
(C) holding pen # 3.
(D) holding pen # 4.

18. The clock in which holding pen is probably not working correctly?

(A) holding pen # 1
(B) holding pen # 2
(C) holding pen # 3
(D) holding pen # 4

19. The holding pen with the most objects is . . .

(A) holding pen # 1.
(B) holding pen # 2.
(C) holding pen # 3.
(D) holding pen # 4.

20. The holding pen with the least number of objects is . . .

(A) holding pen # 1.
(B) holding pen # 2.
(C) holding pen # 3.
(D) holding pen # 4.

21. There is a writing implement in . . .

(A) only one holding pen.
(B) only two holding pens.
(C) only three holding pens.
(D) all four holding pens.

METROPOLIS CRIMINAL COURT
MONDAY TO FRIDAY COURT OFFICER WORK SCHEDULE
FOR THE MONTH OF MAY

Court Officer	Assignment	Meal Time
Frank Day*	Main Entrance	Noon
Joe Brown	Main Entrance	Noon
Mark Fish	North Entrance	1:00 P.M.
Sandra Money	Main Entrance	Noon
Fred White	Police Entrance	12:30 P.M.
Don Smith**	Judge's Entrance	Noon
Charles Beach	Arraignment Court	1:00 P.M.
George May**	Trial Court	1:00 P.M.
Jack Fine*	Trial Court	Noon
Mike Branch	Appeals Court	1:00 P.M.
Sam Sweet	Holding Pen Area	Noon
Leon Waters	On Reserve	1:00 P.M.
Tom Banks	On Reserve	Noon

* Officer with CPR training

**Spanish-speaking officer

ASSIGNMENT INFORMATION

1. Officers on reserve are to be used as needed only at the direction of Court Clerk Green.

2. A new work schedule will be prepared each month. In no case shall the same officer be assigned to Reserve Duty for two consecutive months.

3. Officers must take meals in the courthouse cafeteria.

4. Meals must be finished in one hour.

5. Main entrance must be kept open and staffed the entire court day.

22. Which of the following is the most accurate statement concerning the weekday work schedule for the month of June?

   (A) Officer Branch must have a different assignment.
   (B) Officer Brown must have a different assignment.
   (C) Officer White must have a different assignment.
   (D) Officer Waters must have a different assignment.

23. Which of the following officers probably have a conflict in their work schedule?

   (A) Day and Brown
   (B) Smith and White
   (C) Beach and May
   (D) Sweet and Waters

24. A message must be delivered to Judge Smith as soon as he arrives at the courthouse. The assignment to deliver the message would best be given to Officer . . .

   (A) Smith.
   (B) Beach.
   (C) May.
   (D) Fine.

25. Assume that you are a court officer and that it is 1:30 P.M. You need to talk to Officer Branch. To find him, you should look . . .

   (A) in the Appeals Court.
   (B) in the Reserve Room.
   (C) at the front door.
   (D) in the courthouse cafeteria.

26. Assume that you are a court officer and you have been directed by a judge to have Officer Banks assigned to Trial Court. You should . . .

   (A) give the assignment directly to Officer Banks.
   (B) clear the assignment with Court Clerk Green.
   (C) tell the judge that Officer Banks is not available.
   (D) assign Officer Fine to the Trial Court.

27. Assume that you are a court officer and an incident has occurred involving a visitor who speaks only Spanish? Which of the following officers should you attempt to bring to the scene?

   (A) May
   (B) Fine
   (C) Sweet
   (D) Waters

28. Which of the following assignment locations is probably the busiest?

    (A) Trial Court
    (B) Main Entrance
    (C) Police Entrance
    (D) Appeals Court

29. A person in the Arraignment Court is in need of CPR. Which of the following officers should be brought to assist that person?

    (A) Day
    (B) Sweet
    (C) Waters
    (D) Banks

Directions: Answer questions 30–34 based solely on the following information.

The purpose of random drug testing of court officers is to establish a credible deterrent to illegal drug usage. Officers chosen to be tested must be notified at least 24 hours prior to the scheduled test. Officers scheduled for testing must appear at the Court Division's Health Section in civilian clothes at the designated date and time. The only excusals from drug testing shall be given to officers who are on sick report, on a regularly scheduled day off, on military leave, on annual vacation, or on bereavement leave. Officers missing a scheduled test for any reason will be rescheduled for testing as soon as possible irrespective of any random sampling selection. Officers must submit to drug screening. Refusal to submit to testing will result in mandatory suspension and may be grounds for permanent dismissal.

30. The main purpose of random drug testing for court officers is to . . .

    (A) establish a credible deterrent to illegal drug usage.
    (B) provide drug-free public service to the public.
    (C) prevent civil liability.
    (D) maintain a fair and equitable delivery of justice.

31. Which of the following statements concerning the drug policy is most appropriate?

    (A) The random selection must be conducted no more than 24 hours prior to the actual drug testing.
    (B) Officers must be notified 24 hours after the test of the results.
    (C) The test must be given within 24 hours of the officer being notified.
    (D) Officers must be notified at least 24 hours prior to scheduled testing.

32. Shamus Ginty is a court officer. He is ordered to appear for drug testing as a result of being selected randomly. According to the procedure, Ginty should appear . . .

(A) in either uniform or civilian clothes, whichever he chooses.
(B) in uniform.
(C) in civilian clothes.
(D) in either uniform or civilian clothes, whichever his immediate supervisor directs.

33. Court Officer Lewis misses an appointment to be randomly tested for drugs. Unfortunately the officer could not keep the appointment because she was on a regularly scheduled day off. The officer should . . .

(A) be rescheduled within 24 hours.
(B) be rescheduled as soon as possible.
(C) be rescheduled but only if the officer is again randomly selected.
(D) not be rescheduled because the officer had a valid excuse for missing the appointment.

34. If an officer refuses to submit to drug screening, the officer will be subject to . . .

(A) suspension only.
(B) immediate mandatory dismissal.
(C) mandatory suspension and possible dismissal.
(D) possible suspension.

Directions: Answer questions 35–40 based solely on the following information.

Most law enforcement agencies throughout the country use the military method of telling time. The major advantage of the military method of determining time is that it uses a 24-hour clock, which means that it is not necessary to distinguish between A.M. and P.M. Under the civilian method of telling time, which uses a 12-hour clock, the same numbers appears in the time twice a day and are distinguished by adding either A.M. or P.M. For example, under the civilian method, it is 11 o'clock twice during each day, in the morning when it is 11 A.M. and at night when it is 11 P.M. Because the military method uses a 24-hour clock, the same numbers never appear as the time more than once a day. For example, at 11:00 A.M. in the civilian method, it is 1100 hours in the military method, and at 11:00 P.M., it is 2300 hours. Noon in the military method is represented by 1200 hours, and midnight is represented by 2400 hours. The time between midnight and 12:59 P.M. is fairly easy to remember in the military system because it is similar to the civilian method. For example, when it is 3:00 A.M. civilian time it is 0300 hours military time; when it is 4:30 A.M., it is 0430 hours; and when it is 12:59 P.M., it is 1259 hours. It is the time after 12:59 P.M. that becomes a little difficult to determine under the military system. The rule to follow is to add 12 hours to the civilian time to determine the military time during the period between 12:59 P.M. and midnight. For example, when it is 2:25 P.M. in civilian time, it is 1425 hours in military time (2:25 hours plus 12 hours because it is P.M.), and when it is 12 midnight, it is 2400 hours in military time.

35. The major advantage of using military time is that . . .

 (A) it is less confusing.
 (B) it is more accurate.
 (C) the same numbers never appear in the time more than once a day.
 (D) it is not necessary to distinguish between A.M. and P.M.

36. Which of the following is the most accurate statement about military time?

 (A) Civilian time is less accurate than military time.
 (B) All law enforcement agencies use military time.
 (C) Military time was devised by the U.S. Army.
 (D) Military time uses a 24-hour clock.

37. The military time equivalent of 3:28 P.M. is . . .

 (A) 0328 hours.
 (B) 1528 hours.
 (C) 1828 hours.
 (D) 2028 hours.

38. At 35 minutes after noon, it is . . .

 (A) 12:35 A.M. and 0035 hours.
 (B) 12:35 P.M. and 0035 hours.
 (C) 12:35 A.M. and 1235 hours.
 (D) 12:35 P.M. and 1235 hours.

39. The correct military time when it is 4:45 P.M. civilian time is . . .

 (A) 0445 hours.
 (B) 0045 hours.
 (C) 1445 hours.
 (D) 1645 hours.

40. What does the A.M. stand for in civilian time?

 (A) after midnight
 (B) ante meridian
 (C) apres minite
 (D) not given in passage

On August 3rd, at 50 minutes after midnight, an explosion took place in front of the Metropolis Family Court Building. One hour and 10 minutes prior to the explosion, a bearded man was observed loitering in front of the court building. Fifty-five minutes after the explosion, a telephone call was received at police headquarters stating that the explosion was the responsibility of the Anti-marriage Coalition. At 1:45 P.M. on the same day, a rock was thrown through the window of the main entrance door to Family Court injuring two judges. Fifty minutes prior to this rock-throwing incident, the same beaded man was observed in front of the courthouse. At 8:35 P.M., the bearded man was arrested by Police Officer Alicia Schroeder when he once again returned to the area around the Family Court.

41. At what time was the bearded man first observed in the vicinity of the Family Court building?

    (A) 0050 hours
    (B) 2340 hours
    (C) 0210 hours
    (D) 0010 hours

42. At what time was the telephone call made to police headquarters claiming responsibility for the explosion?

    (A) 0135 hours
    (B) 0055 hours
    (C) 0435 hours
    (D) 0145 hours

43. At what time was the bearded man arrested?

    (A) 2035 hours
    (B) 0835 hours
    (C) 1435 hours
    (D) 1345 hours

The two powers that peace and police officers have that set them apart from ordinary citizens are the power of arrest and the authority to use legal force. Because the authority to use legal force leaves much potential for abuse, the necessity to have very strict guidelines regulating the use of firearms by police and peace officers is very pressing. The following guidelines are typical of those that exist in most law enforcement agencies. They are not meant to restrict a peace or police officer in the performance of his/her lawful duty, but they are intended to reduce shooting incidents and, consequently, to protect life and property. In every case, the policy is that only the minimum amount of force be used consistent with the accomplishment of the mission.

In addition to Penal Law restrictions on the use of deadly physical force, peace and police officers will adhere to the following guidelines concerning the use of firearms.

A. Use all means before using a firearm when effecting an arrest or when preventing or terminating a felony, or when defending yourself or others.

B. Do not fire warning shots.

C. Do not discharge a firearm to summon assistance, except when your safety or the safety of others is endangered.

D. Do not discharge your firearm from or at a moving vehicle unless deadly physical force is being used against you or others by means other than a vehicle.

E. Do not discharge your firearm at dogs or other animals unless there is no other way to bring the animal under control.

F. Do not discharge your firearm if innocent persons may be endangered.

44. These guidelines are meant to . . .

   (A) restrict an officer's performance.
   (B) protect life and property.
   (C) eliminate the need to discharge firearms.
   (D) prevent all abuses of authority from occurring.

45. In addition to these guidelines, other restrictions on the use of firearms can be found in . . .

   (A) the Criminal Procedure Law.
   (B) the City Charter.
   (C) the Penal Law.
   (D) the Administrative Code.

46. Police officers are always prohibited from . . .

   (A) firing their firearms to summon assistance.
   (B) firing warning shots.
   (C) firing shots from a moving vehicle.
   (D) firing shots at animals.

47. Why is it so important to have strict guidelines regulating the use of firearms by peace and police officers?

(A) The potential for abuse is significant.
(B) The protection of life is a paramount concern.
(C) Innocent persons must be protected from injury.
(D) The prospect of civil liability is great.

48. What policy covers every use of force occurrence?

(A) Never shoot at a fleeing felon.
(B) Never fire a shot into the air.
(C) Never shoot from a moving vehicle.
(D) Never use more than the minimum amount of force required.

49. The guidelines presented here are . . .

(A) those found in all law enforcement agencies.
(B) not typical of those that actually exist in law enforcement agencies.
(C) those that exist in progressive law enforcement agencies.
(D) commonly found in many law enforcement agencies.

50. The use of nonlethal devices is . . .

(A) highly recommended.
(B) very experimental.
(C) quite risky.
(D) not covered in the guidelines.

Directions: Answer questions 51–56 solely on the basis of the following legal definitions. Do not base your answers on any other knowledge of the law you may have. You may refer to the definitions when answering the questions.

Definition: A search warrant is a court order directing an officer to conduct a search of a designated premises or designated vehicle or designated person, for the purpose of seizing designated property and to deliver the property to the court that issued the warrant.

Property subject to seizure: In addition to property designated to be seized by a search warrant, an officer executing a search warrant may also seize:

A. Stolen property, or

B. Property that is unlawfully possessed such as contraband, or

C. Property used in the commission of a crime, or

D. Evidence that a crime has been committed.

When executable:

   A. A search warrant must be executed not more than 10 days after the date of issuance and it must thereafter be returned to the court of issuance without unnecessary delay.

   B. A search warrant may be executed on any day of the week. It may be executed only between the hours of 6:00 A.M. and 9:00 P.M. unless the warrant expressly authorizes execution thereof at any time of the day or night.

Execution of a search warrant: In executing a search warrant, an officer must make a reasonable effort to give notice of his authority and purpose to an occupant thereof before entry and show him the warrant or a copy of the warrant upon request.

However, if there are reasonable grounds to believe that the property sought may be destroyed or disposed of or someone's safety will be endangered, the officer executing the warrant may be given privilege not to announce his purpose and authority before executing the warrant.

If denied access to the premises, the officer may use that force which is necessary to enter and conduct the search.

Disposition of property: Property seized under the authority of a search warrant, along with an inventory of such property, must be returned to the court that issued the search warrant. In addition, a receipt must be given by the officer seizing the property to the person from whom the property was seized. If the property was seized from a premises and no owner can be established, a receipt must be left in a conspicuous place in the premises by the officer seizing the property.

51. A certain officer lawfully executes a search warrant and obtains the property named in the search warrant. Under such circumstances, it would be most correct for the officer to return the property . . .

    (A) to the officer's headquarters.
    (B) to the officer's supervisor.
    (C) to the court that issued the search warrant.
    (D) to the nearest court.

52. When a search warrant is executed, in addition to property designated to be seized by the search warrant, all the following may also be seized except . . .

    (A) any property that anyone named in the search warrant may be carrying.
    (B) stolen property.
    (C) evidence that a crime has been committed.
    (D) contraband.

53. A search warrant to search a specific premises has just been issued on April 1st. Of the following dates, which indicates the latest date that this search warrant may legally be executed?

(A) April 6th
(B) April 10th
(C) April 15th
(D) April 30th

54. Court Officer Parks is recently graduated from the Court Officers Training Academy. She approaches Court Officer Meadows and asks her when a search warrant can be executed. Court Officer Meadows would be most correct if she gave which of the following answers?

(A) "On any day of the week, but it must always be executed between the hours of 6 A.M. and 9 P.M."
(B) "Only on weekdays but at any time of the day or night."
(C) "It could be at any time of the day or night if expressly authorized as such."
(D) "On any day of the week, but it must be executed between 9 P.M. and 6 A.M."

55. Officer Collars wishes to obtain a No Knock search warrant. That is, she wishes to be given privilege not to announce her purpose and authority before executing a certain search warrant. Officer Collars would be most likely to obtain such a search warrant if there are reasonable grounds to believe that . . .

(A) the property sought may be destroyed.
(B) a person named in the search warrant may be alarmed by the officer making such an announcement.
(C) the persons inside the premises have been arrested many times before.
(D) the property sought is expensive stolen property.

56. After a certain officer executes a search warrant and seizes property named in the search warrant, the officer would be most correct if he . . .

(A) always left a note in the form of a receipt in a conspicuous place in the premises.
(B) gave an inventory sheet of the property seized to the person in charge of the premises.
(C) in all instances did not leave the premises until he personally gave a receipt for the property seized to the lawful owner of the property.
(D) gave a receipt to the person from whom the property was seized.

A. Petit larceny is committed when a person steals the property of another and the
value of the property is $1000 or less. Petit larceny is a misdemeanor.

B. Grand larceny is committed when a person steals the property of another and

    a. the value of the property is more than $1000, or

    b. the property stolen is a public record, or

    c. the property stolen is a credit card, or

    d. the property is stolen from the person of the owner regardless of the value of the
property, or

    e. the property stolen is a secret scientific formula, or

    f. the property stolen is a firearm such as a handgun, or a rifle.

57. Jay steals $999 from Bob's pocket while they are riding on a crowded bus. The most
serious crime Jay has committed is . . .

    (A) a misdemeanor because of the dollar amount stolen.
    (B) a felony because of the dollar amount stolen.
    (C) petit larceny because of the fact that the property was taken without the use
of force.
    (D) grand larceny because of the fact that the property was taken from a person's
pocket.

58. Which of the following constitutes the offense of petit larceny?

    (A) the theft of a credit card
    (B) the theft of a deed from the county clerk's office
    (C) the theft of a ring worth $750
    (D) the theft of a secret formula used in scientific experiments

59. Maria is in court as the complainant in a past assault case. During a recess, Maria
leaves her purse in the courtroom unattended. In her absence from the courtroom, a
male, whom Maria does not know, reaches into her unattended purse and removes
a credit card intending to steal it. Court Officer Kegler observes what has taken
place and places the male under arrest. In such an instance, the most serious charge
against the male would be . . .

    (A) petit larceny, mainly because the property was not on Maria's person.
    (B) grand larceny, mainly because a purse is an article that is usually carried on
someone's person.
    (C) petit larceny, mainly because the property was actually taken was not more than
$1000.
    (D) grand larceny, mainly because the article taken was a credit card.

60. Pat enters the locker room of some court officers assigned to the court without permission. He removes an unloaded handgun legitimately valued at less than $400 from one of the lockers and is about to leave when he is detected and arrested by Court Officer Hues. In such an instance, the most serious charge against Pat would be . . .

(A) petit larceny, mainly because although the object is a handgun, its value is less than $1000.

(B) grand larceny, mainly because the object is a handgun.

(C) petit larceny, mainly because, although the object is a gun, it was unloaded at the time of the theft.

(D) grand larceny, mainly because the value of the handgun might be more than $1000 if sold illegally on the street.

Directions: Answer questions 61–65 solely on the basis of the following legal definitions. Do not base your answers on any other knowledge of the law you may have. You may refer to the definitions when answering the questions.

A. An order of protection is a written court order that regulates the behavior of a specific person when dealing with another person.

B. Criminal contempt in the second degree is a misdemeanor and occurs when a person:

  a. acts in a disorderly manner while in a court and such behavior interrupts the business of the court, or

  b. unlawfully refuses to be sworn by a court to give testimony or after being properly sworn refuses to answer lawful questions

    (Note: this subdivision does not apply to grand jury matters), or

  c. fails to obey a verbal order of a judge presiding over a court, or

  d. within a 200-feet radius of a courthouse, shouts, holds, or displays signs calling for specific action by the court or jury involved in an ongoing hearing.

C. Criminal contempt in the first degree is a felony and occurs when a person:

  a. refuses to be sworn in by, or answer the lawful question(s) of, a grand jury, or

  b. violates an order of protection by subjecting another to fear by means of

    i. injury with a weapon, or

    ii. repeated phone calls, or

    iii. any physical contact, or

    iv. damaging property in the amount of more than $250.

61. Tom is standing outside a courthouse holding a placard that advocates the acquittal of his son Pat, who is being tried for murder. Tom could be charged with criminal contempt if the distance he is standing from the courthouse is . . .

(A) within a radius of 250 feet.
(B) more than a radius of 200 feet.
(C) within a radius of 200 feet.
(D) more than a radius of 250 feet.

62. Evaluate the following statements.

1. Criminal contempt is always a felony.

2. Criminal contempt could be committed by a person who is actually in his or her own home.

Which of the following choices is most accurate concerning these statements?

(A) Only statement 1 is correct.
(B) Only statement 2 is correct.
(C) Both statements 1 and 2 are correct.
(D) Neither statement 1 nor 2 is correct.

63. Tab is a witness to a crime. After being sworn in by a grand jury, he refuses to answer any questions about his observations. In such an instance, Tab could be charged with . . .

(A) a felony.
(B) a misdemeanor.
(C) a felony or a misdemeanor.
(D) no crime because a person can never be forced to give testimony if such person wishes not to give testimony.

64. Which of the following violations of an order of protection would be least likely to result in a charge of criminal contempt in the first degree?

(A) subjecting another to fear by means of injury with a weapon
(B) subjecting another to fear by means of repeated phone calls
(C) subjecting another to fear by means of any physical contact
(D) subjecting another to fear by means of damaging property in the amount of more than $200

65. Evaluate the following statements.

1. An order of protection is a verbal court order that regulates the behavior of a specific person when dealing with another person.

2. Refusing to be sworn in by any court is a felony.

Which of the following choices is most accurate concerning these statements?

(A) Only statement 1 is correct.
(B) Only statement 2 is correct.
(C) Both statements 1 and 2 are correct.
(D) Neither statement 1 nor 2 is correct.

Directions: Answer questions 66–70 based solely on the following information.

Court officers shall comply with the following regulations mandated by the court:

A. Force shall be defined as deliberate physical contact made by a court officer with a prisoner during a confrontation to control the behavior of the prisoner or enforce a lawful order.

B. Force may be used against a prisoner to

a. defend oneself or another court employee, prisoner or visitor to the court from a physical attack, or

b. prevent the commission of an offense, escapes, or prisoner disturbances, or

c. overcome resistance to an arrest, or

d. prevent serious damage to property, or

e. prevent a prisoner from self harm, or

f. generally enforce rules and orders of the court but only as a last resort.

In general, force may not be used to punish a prisoner. Thus the following are prohibited:

a. Striking a prisoner to discipline the prisoner for not obeying an order.

b. Striking a prisoner when pushing the prisoner would have achieved the desired result.

c. Continuing to use force after the prisoner ceases to offer resistance or to engage in prohibited conduct.

d. Hitting a prisoner with an unauthorized object such as flashlights, keys, or handcuffs.

e. Striking a prisoner who is already restrained by mechanical restraints. Except that a restrained prisoner can be struck if such prisoner continues to pose a threat to an employee, a visitor, or other prisoner. Such an incident should be immediately reported to the shift supervisor who shall make a written report to the court desk officer.

f. Using a choke hold or a blackjack. Note that a regulation baton club may be used but only as a last resort.

66. During a session of night court, Court Officer Rems enters the detention pens to prevent Tom White, a prisoner, from destroying the lighting fixtures inside the detention pens. Officer Rems strikes White several times with a flashlight to prevent White from further seriously damaging the fixtures. In this instance, the officer acted . . .

(A) properly, mainly because the officer probably prevented more serious damage to the fixtures.
(B) improperly, mainly because flashlights should not be used to strike prisoners.
(C) properly, mainly because the situation might spread to other locations where prisoners are being held.
(D) improperly, mainly because force may never be used to merely prevent damage to property.

67. Which of the following actions would be least appropriate in connection with the use of force by court officers?

(A) using force against a prisoner to defend oneself
(B) using force against a prisoner in the form of a choke hold
(C) using force against a prisoner who is attempting to escape
(D) using force against a prisoner who is attempting to strike her attorney who is visiting her

68. Jay is a prisoner who is being subdued by a court officer after Jay attempted to strike another prisoner. After a brief struggle, the officer is able to restrain Jay with mechanical restraints. In this situation, the officer . . .

(A) is prohibited from ever striking the prisoner after the prisoner is mechanically restrained.
(B) could strike the prisoner even though the prisoner is restrained.
(C) is prohibited from striking the prisoner unless authorized by the shift supervisor.
(D) could strike the prisoner but only if directed by the court desk officer.

69. Court officers are generally to use the least amount of force as possible. Nonetheless, however, as a last resort, which of the following items would be most appropriate for a court officer to use against a prisoner who is attempting to injure another prisoner?

(A) a blackjack
(B) a set of keys
(C) a set of handcuffs
(D) a regulation baton club

70. According to court regulations, which of the following least accurately describes a characteristic of force that may be used by a court officer against a prisoner?

(A) The force must be physical.
(B) The force must be deliberate.
(C) The force may be used to control the behavior of a prisoner.
(D) The force may be used to enforce any order.

A court officer is prohibited from engaging in any of the following conduct:

A. Using discourteous or disrespectful remarks regarding another person's ethnicity, race, religion, gender, or sexual orientation.

B. Consuming intoxicants while in uniform, whether on or off duty.

C. Bringing or permitting an intoxicant to be brought into a court building or facility, or vehicle assigned to the court, except in the performance of duty.

D. Steering business, professional, or commercial persons to a prospective client requiring such services except when transacting personal affairs.

E. Riding in any vehicle, other than an official vehicle to which assigned, while in uniform, except when authorized or in an emergency. (Does not apply to Court Officer Captains and above.)

F. Using the official court officer logo unless authorized by the Commanding Officer of the Court Officer Personnel Bureau.

G. Making a false official statement.

H. Engaging in card games or other games of chance in a court facility.

I. Engaging in illegal gambling anywhere.

J. Soliciting money for a political club or committee.

71. After an overtime tour of duty, Court Officer Mary Downs comes directly home. Her husband greets her at the door and offers her a glass of wine to relax her while she is still wearing her uniform. Mary accepts and sits down to discuss her day. In this situation, Mary's actions were . . .

(A) proper, mainly because she is now off duty.
(B) improper, mainly because she is still in uniform.
(C) proper, mainly because, even though she is a court officer, she can do as she pleases in her own home.
(D) improper, mainly because a court officer may never consume any intoxicants.

72. Court Officer John Baker and his boss Court Officer Captain Mary Best are driving to work one day in Officer Baker's personal car. They are both in uniform. According to regulations, . . .

(A) both Baker and Best are in violation.
(B) neither Baker nor Best is in violation.
(C) only Baker is in violation.
(D) only Best is in violation.

73. A group of court officers from a certain city court are seeking to form a softball team to play against other city agencies while off duty. Although they are off duty and do not represent their agency, the court officers' plan is to wear a uniform that displays their official court officer logo. In such an instance, it would be most appropriate if . . .

   (A) the permission of the Commanding Officer of the Court Officer Personnel Bureau was sought.
   (B) the court officers sought the permission of the commanding officer of the court to which they are assigned.
   (C) the court officers went ahead with their plan because no permission would be required for any such off-duty activity.
   (D) the permission of a captain or above was sought.

74. Court Officer Barks joins a political club within the confines of the city where the officer is employed. While a member of the club, the officer decides to contribute money to the club. Such actions of the officer are . . .

   (A) appropriate because there is no prohibition against joining and contributing to a political club.
   (B) inappropriate because even though there is no prohibition against joining a political club, contributing money to a political club is prohibited.
   (C) appropriate because court officers are even allowed to solicit funds for a political club.
   (D) inappropriate because it is prohibited to join a political club within the city.

75. Evaluate the following statements:
   1. A court officer is prohibited from engaging in illegal gambling while out of state on vacation.
   2. A court officer is permitted to play cards in a court facility's lunch room with another officer as long as they are both on a meal break and not playing for money.

   Which of the following choices is most accurate concerning these statements?

   (A) Only statement 1 is correct.
   (B) Only statement 2 is correct.
   (C) Both statements 1 and 2 are correct.
   (D) Neither statement 1 nor 2 is correct.

A court officer shall:

a. Obey lawful orders and instructions of a supervising officer.

b. Be punctual when reporting for duty.

c. Maintain a current state driver's license and notify the commanding officer of the unit to which assigned, with pertinent details, when the license is suspended, revoked, or not renewed.

d. Keep assigned locker neat, clean, and secured with combination lock (without an identifying serial number displayed on it) that conforms to specifications established by the Commanding Officer of the Equipment Section. The identifying serial number should not be displayed anywhere on the locker nor should a record of such number be kept by the court.

e. Affix a Locker Sticker to assigned locker with rank, name, shield, and squad number captions filled in.

f. Be fit for duty at all times, except when on sick report.

g. Refrain from consuming intoxicants to the extent that the officer becomes unfit for duty.

h. Give name and shield number to anyone requesting them.

i. Be courteous and respectful.

j. Avoid conflict with agency policy when lecturing, giving speeches, or submitting articles for publication. Questions concerning fees offered will be resolved by Commanding Officer, Press Relations Division, who shall be consulted before a court officer accepts any fee.

k. Not smoke in public view outside a court building while in uniform.

l. Not patronize an unlicensed premises such as an unlicensed bar except in the performance of duty.

76. Evaluate the following statements concerning court regulations.

    1. A court officer must obey all orders and instructions of a supervising officer.

    2. A court officer must be punctual when reporting for duty.

    Which of the following choices is most accurate concerning these statements?

    (A) Only statement 1 is correct.
    (B) Only statement 2 is correct.
    (C) Both statements 1 and 2 are correct.
    (D) Neither statement 1 nor 2 is correct.

77. At the Metropolitan Superior Court, Joe Lewis is a court officer. One day Lewis receives a notification that his state driver's license has been revoked. In such a situation, Lewis is required to notify . . .

(A) his commanding officer.

(B) the commanding officer of the Motor Transport Division.

(C) the commanding officer of the Press Relations Section.

(D) no one in his agency because it is his own personal business.

78. One afternoon Probationary Court Officer Singer arrives at the Hamilton Special Sessions Court for assignment. The captain on duty assigns a locker to Officer Singer who then proceeds to the locker to secure it with a lock. Officer Singer then secures the locker by using a combination lock that conforms to specifications established by the Commanding Officer of the Equipment Section. According to official regulations the lock should . . .

(A) not have a serial number displayed on it.

(B) have a serial number displayed on it.

(C) not have a serial number displayed on it, but the serial number should be entered on the Locker Sticker.

(D) not have a serial number displayed on it, but the serial number should be kept on file with the Commanding Officer of the Equipment Section.

79. John Jay College of Criminal Justice has asked Court Officer Bard to address a seminar on jury selection. The College has offered Officer Bard a modest fee for his services. In this situation, Officer Bard should . . .

(A) refuse to make the speech.

(B) accept the fee and not notify anyone because the fee is modest.

(C) notify the Commanding Officer Press Relations Division before accepting any fee.

(D) notify the Commanding Officer Personnel Bureau before accepting any fee.

80. Evaluate the following statements:

1. A court officer in uniform is never permitted to smoke in uniform outside a court building.

2. A court officer shall never patronize an unlicensed premises such as an unlicensed bar.

Which of the following is most accurate concerning these two statements?

(A) Only statement 1 is correct.

(B) Only statement 2 is correct.

(C) Both statements 1 and 2 are correct.

(D) Neither statement 1 nor 2 is correct.

The purpose of random drug testing of court officers is to establish a credible deterrent among employees to illegal drug usage. As such, the following steps shall be taken when such testing is required:

a. Court officers shall be notified at least twenty-four (24) hours prior to scheduled testing.

b. Court officers selected shall appear at the Health Section in civilian clothes at the designated date and time.

c. Court officers must report to the Health Section when notified except if said court officer is on:

  i. Sick report

  ii. Regularly scheduled day off

  iii. Military leave

  iv. Annual vacation

  v. Bereavement leave

  Court officers missing a scheduled test for any reason will be rescheduled for testing as soon as possible irrespective of any random sampling selection.

d. Court officers must submit to drug screening. Refusal to submit to test will result in mandatory suspension and may be grounds for dismissal from the agency.

81. The main purpose of random drug testing for court officers is . . .

    (A) to establish a credible deterrent to illegal drug usage among defendants before the court.
    (B) deter drug use among the employees.
    (C) gain information on who is selling drugs.
    (D) encourage defendants before the court to model themselves after court officers and remain drug free.

82. According to the procedure governing random drug testing, which of the following statements is most appropriate?

    (A) The random selection must be conducted no more than 24 hours prior to the actual drug testing.
    (B) Court officers must be notified 24 hours after the test of the results.
    (C) The test must be given within 24 hours of the court officer being notified.
    (D) Court officers must be notified at least 24 hours prior to scheduled testing.

83. Tab is a court officer. He is ordered to appear for drug testing as a result of being selected randomly. According to the procedure, Tab should appear . . .

(A) in either uniform or civilian clothes, whichever he chooses.
(B) in uniform.
(C) in civilian clothes.
(D) in either uniform or civilian clothes, whichever his immediate supervisor directs.

84. Court Officer Barns misses an appointment to be randomly tested for drugs. Unfortunately the officer could not keep the appointment because the officer was on a regularly scheduled day off. Barns should . . .

(A) be rescheduled within 24 hours.
(B) be rescheduled as soon as possible.
(C) be rescheduled but only if the officer is again randomly selected.
(D) not be rescheduled because the officer had a valid excuse for missing the appointment.

85. If a court officer refuses to submit to drug screening, the court officer will be subject to . . .

(A) suspension only.
(B) immediate mandatory dismissal.
(C) mandatory suspension and possible dismissal.
(D) possible suspension.

Directions: Answer questions 86–90 based solely on the following procedure.

When a court officer is to be tested as a result of the agency's random drug testing program, the following procedure shall apply:

A. Prior to testing, the individual officer being tested shall prepare a form listing all foods, alcohol, mixes, and medicine ingested in the past seventy-two (72) hours.

B. At the testing location, the officer being tested shall present his/her shield and identification card to ensure that the proper individual has reported for testing.

C. Privacy and dignity will be protected. Urine samples will be given in maximum feasible privacy. Only one (1) person of the same sex will be present with the officer being tested when urine is collected.

D. No more than two (2) samples will be taken, each in a separate vial.

E. Prior to testing, a code number assigned to the officer and the date of the testing will be affixed to each vial. The code number will be logged separately with the officer's name.

F. Immediately after giving the urine sample, the officer being tested will then initial the vial sticker. The vials will be sealed in the officer's presence after the sample has been given. Appropriate procedures to create and follow a strict accounting of custody will be followed at all times.

G. Negative test results will not be maintained but will be destroyed.

H. Positive test samples will be maintained by the laboratory involved and will remain confidential unless and until disciplinary action by the agency is taken.

I. An officer whose test is positive may, within sixty (60) days of notification of such result, submit a written request to the Agency Attorney's Office for further independent retesting of the original sample.

J. Testing will be done only for illegal drugs and controlled substances. No other substances will be screened.

86. Prior to testing, Court Officer Teller, who is being randomly tested for drugs, should prepare a form listing all foods, alcohol, mixes, and medicine ingested . . .

(A) in the past 7 days.
(B) in the past 5 days.
(C) in the past 72 hours.
(D) in the past 24 hours.

87. When urine samples are given in connection with random drug testing, the maximum number of people present while the urine is being collected is . . .

(A) one, just the person being tested.
(B) two, and both persons must be of the same sex.
(C) three, with at least one of the persons the same sex as the employee.
(D) four, with two persons of each sex present.

88. Regarding the actual giving of urine, which of the following statements is most appropriate according to the procedure concerning random testing for drugs?

(A) A minimum of two samples will be taken.
(B) A maximum of two samples will be taken.
(C) Exactly two samples must be taken.
(D) If multiple samples are taken, they shall not be put in separate vials.

89. Court Officer Pat Volts is undergoing random drug testing and is, therefore, giving a urine sample. Pat has just completed giving the urine sample. What should Pat do next?

(A) Seal the vials.
(B) Initial the vial sticker.
(C) Write his name on the vial sticker.
(D) Write the date on the vial sticker.

90. May is a court officer who has tested positive during a random drug test. She strongly denies the use of drugs. If May wishes to protest she should do which of the following?

(A) Immediately make a phone call to the Agency Attorney's Office protesting the results of the test.
(B) Submit a written request to the laboratory that conducted the test asking for further independent retesting of the original sample.
(C) Immediately make a phone call to the laboratory that conducted the test protesting the results of the test and asking that a new sample be tested by them.
(D) Submit a written request to the Agency Attorney's Office for further independent retesting of the original sample.

Directions: For questions 91–100, each question contains a sample consisting of a defendant's name and criminal identification number. You are to select as your answer the choice that contains the exact same name and criminal identification number as the sample.

---

91. Harry Nalbandion   5205186bx93

    (A) Harry Nalbandian   5205186bx93
    (B) Harry Nalbandion   5205186xb93
    (C) Harry Nalbendion   5205186bx93
    (D) Harry Nalbandion   5205186bx93

92. Clement DiMaio   143406915ttn43

    (A) Clement DiMaio   143406915ttn43
    (B) Clement DiMiao   143406915ttn43
    (C) Clement DiMaio   143406915tnt43
    (D) Clemint DiMaio   143406915ttn43

93. Harvey Rabinovitz   B-27*493270ert78

    (A) Harvey Rabinovitz   B-27-493270ert78
    (B) Harvey Rabinovitz   B-27*493270ert78
    (C) Harvey Rabinovits   B-27*493270ert78
    (D) Harvey Rabinovitz   B-27*49327Oert78

94. Willyses Gordon   T#4897766567#97

    (A) Willyses Gordon   T#4897766765#97
    (B) Willyess Gordon   T#4897766567#97
    (C) Willyses Gordon   T#4897766567#97
    (D) Willyses Gordon   T#4897766567&97

95. Cookie Laventowski   908OO458 & 5bt

    (A) Cookye Laventowski   908OO458 & 5bt
    (B) Cookie Laventowsky   908OO458 & 5bt
    (C) Cookie Laventowski   908OO458 & 5bt
    (D) Cookie Laventowski   908OO458 + 5bt

96. Lucifer Labryinth   650Gr10451cyrp44577t.

    (A) Lucifer Labyrinth   650Gr10451cyrp44577t.
    (B) Lucifer Labryinth   650Gr10451cyrp44577t.
    (C) Lucefir Labryinth   650Gr10451cyrp44577t.
    (D) Lucifer Labryinth   650gR10451cyrp44577t

97. Feliciana Moutanasse   Tkrm5566677490gy

    (A) Feliciana Moutanasse   Tkrpm566677490gy
    (B) Feliciano Moutanasse   Tkrm5566677490gy
    (C) Feliciana Moutanasse   Tkrm5566777490gy
    (D) Feliciana Moutanasse   Tkrm5566677490gy

98. Freddy Matterettezky   Cmp#5768-908-99ty

    (A) Freddy Matterettezky   Cmp#5768-908-99ty
    (B) Freddy Matterettesky   Cmp#5768-908-99ty
    (C) Fredie Matterettezky   Cmp#5768-908-99ty
    (D) Freddy Matterettezky   Cmp#5768-909-98ty

99. Marie Dillenger   clt456-098=37

    (A) Marie Dillengir   clt456-098=37
    (B) Marie Dillenger   clt456-098-37
    (C) Marie Dillenger   clt456-098=37
    (D) Maria Dillenger   clt456-098=37

100. Peter Echierverria   SanQ456908rckis34

    (A) Peter Echierverrea   SanQ456908rckis34
    (B) Peter Echierverria   SanQ4569O8rckis34
    (C) Peter Echierverria   SanQ456908rckes34
    (D) Peter Echierverria   SanQ456908rckis34

ANSWER KEY
Practice Exam Four

1.	C	26.	B	51.	C	76.	B
2.	B	27.	A	52.	A	77.	A
3.	B	28.	B	53.	B	78.	A
4.	C	29.	A	54.	C	79.	C
5.	D	30.	A	55.	A	80.	D
6.	A	31.	D	56.	D	81.	B
7.	B	32.	C	57.	D	82.	D
8.	D	33.	B	58.	C	83.	C
9.	B	34.	C	59.	D	84.	B
10.	A	35.	D	60.	B	85.	C
11.	C	36.	D	61.	C	86.	C
12.	A	37.	B	62.	B	87.	B
13.	D	38.	D	63.	A	88.	B
14.	D	39.	D	64.	D	89.	B
15.	C	40.	D	65.	D	90.	D
16.	B	41.	B	66.	B	91.	D
17.	A	42.	D	67.	B	92.	A
18.	D	43.	A	68.	B	93.	B
19.	D	44.	B	69.	D	94.	C
20.	B	45.	C	70.	D	95.	C
21.	D	46.	B	71.	B	96.	B
22.	D	47.	A	72.	C	97.	D
23.	A	48.	D	73.	A	98.	A
24.	A	49.	D	74.	A	99.	C
25.	D	50.	D	75.	A	100.	D

DIAGNOSTIC CHART

Section	Question Numbers	Area	Your Number Correct	Scale
1	1–15	Memory (15 questions)		15 Right—Excellent 13-14 Right—Good 11-12 Right—Fair Under 11 Right—Poor
2	16–50	Reading Comprehension (35 questions)		33-35 Right—Excellent 30-32 Right—Good 27-29 Right—Fair Under 27 Right—Poor
3	51–65	Legal Definitions (15 questions)		15 Right—Excellent 13-14 Right—Good 11-12 Right—Fair Under 11 Right—Poor
4	66–90	Applying Court Officer Procedures (25 questions)		25 Right—Excellent 22-24 Right—Good 18-21 Right—Fair Under 18 Right—Poor
5	91–100	Clerical Ability (10 questions)		10 Right—Excellent 8-9 Right—Good 7 Right—Fair Under 7 Right—Poor

How to correct weaknesses:

1. If you are weak in Section 1, concentrate on Chapter 2.
2. If you are weak in Section 2, concentrate on Chapter 1.
3. If you are weak in Section 3, concentrate on Chapter 4.
4. If you are weak in Section 4, concentrate on Chapter 3.
5. If you are weak in Section 5, concentrate on Chapter 5.

Note: Consider yourself weak in a section if you receive a score other than excellent in that section.

ANSWERS EXPLAINED

1. **(C)** The person who put up the bail was Henry Money. Hopefully, you noticed the ready-made association that the examiner provided you with. Henry Money put up the money for the bail.

2. **(B)** People versus Green is the name of the case.

3. **(B)** Putting the dates in the order they occur is quite helpful. The crime was committed on January 12th, the arrest was made on January 29th, the arraignment occurred on February 9th, and the date on the trial was March 19th.

4. **(C)** Whenever you see a numbered series of items you must find a quick way to remember the sequence of the series. In this case, Charge Number 3 was Possession of a Dangerous Weapon.

5. **(D)** The Defense Attorney was Bill Harris. Defense attorneys always present bills to their clients.

6. **(A)** The arresting officer wore a shield, and his name was Harry Shields.

7. **(B)** If you noticed that the arrest number ended in 911, you would have had an easy time with this question.

8. **(D)** Whenever one of the choices suggests that the information asked for was not given, you must always consider the possibility of that choice being the answer.

9. **(B)** Don Smart has a college degree. The association, we hope, was obvious to you. Note that questions using this format rely heavily on the differences among the wanted persons.

10. **(A)** An alphabetical association, Larry Ash walks with a limp would have guaranteed your answering this question correctly.

11. **(C)** Pat Wall is an expert knife fighter with a reputation for being armed and dangerous.

12. **(A)** Once again, the question involved differences among the four wanted persons. Note that the differences are usually pronounced ones. Larry Ash is the only wanted person over 6 feet tall.

13. **(D)** Art is a subject one takes in school, and Art Champion loiters around schools.

14. **(D)** Arson causes ashes, and Larry Ash is wanted for arson.

15. **(C)** Pat Wall is an expert chef who specializes in cooking Italian food.

16. **(B)** The knives in holding pens #1 and #4 are the only objects in all four holding pens that could be classified as cutting implements.

17. **(A)** Holding pen #1 contains a diary, which is defined as being a daily journal of activities.

18. **(D)** The clocks in holding pens #1, #2, and #3 all indicate that it is about the same time. The clock in holding pen #4 indicates a different time. Note that the word *probably* in the stem of the question allows you to make certain assumptions to arrive at the correct answer. Remember, however, that such assumptions must be based on facts. In

this question, it is a fact that the clocks in three holding pens all indicate the same time. Furthermore, the instructions tell you that the objects were found during an inspection. It is therefore safe to assume that the items were all found at about the same time.

19. **(D)** Holding pen # 4 has seven objects depicted.

20. **(B)** Holding pen # 2 has five objects depicted.

21. **(D)** There is a pen in holding pen #1; a pencil in holding pen #2; a pencil in holding pen #3; and a pen in holding pen #4.

22. **(D)** Officer Waters is on reserve duty, and, according to the assignment information, he cannot be given reserve duty again next month.

23. **(A)** Officers Day and Brown are both working the main entrance, and they both have meal time at noon. Additionally, the assignment information indicates that the main entrance must stay open. Finally, the third officer assigned to the main entrance, Officer Money, also has a meal time scheduled for noon.

24. **(A)** Officer Smith is assigned to the judge's entrance.

25. **(D)** Officer Branch is on meal time from 1:00 to 2:00 P.M., and according to the assignment information, officers must take their meals in the courthouse cafeteria.

26. **(B)** Officer Banks is on reserve duty, and according to the assignment information, officers on reserve are to be used only at the direction of Court Clerk Green. Don't let the fact that the direction comes from a judge distract you. Answer based solely on the information given to you.

27. **(A)** The double asterisk next to Officer May's name indicates that he is a Spanish-speaking officer.

28. **(B)** The main entrance is the only assignment location that has three officers assigned to it.

29. **(A)** The single asterisk next to Officer Day's name indicates that he is trained in CPR.

30. **(A)** All the choices sound like good reasons to have drug testing, but Choice A is the only one mentioned in the passage.

31. **(D)** Officers chosen to be tested must be notified at least 24 hours prior to the scheduled test.

32. **(C)** It very clearly states in the passage that officers must appear in civilian clothes.

33. **(B)** Officers missing a scheduled test for any reason will be rescheduled as soon as possible irrespective of any random sampling selection.

34. **(C)** Refusal to submit to a drug test will result in mandatory suspension and may be grounds for permanent dismissal.

35. **(D)** Because it uses a 24-hour clock, it is not necessary to distinguish between A.M. and P.M.

36. **(D)** As stated in the passage, a 24-hour clock is used in the military and is the major advantage of military time.

37. **(B)** When it is after 12:59 P.M., add 12 hours to the civilian time to get military time. So, when it is 1:00 P.M. civilian time, it is 1300 hours in military time.

38. **(D)** 12:35 P.M. in civilian time is equivalent to 1235 hours in military time.

39. **(D)** It is as simple as this: 4 plus 12 equals 16.

40. **(D)** Be careful. Don't introduce personal knowledge into the answering of reading comprehension questions. The information asked for in the question is not given in the passage.

41. **(B)** This question requires that you use information in two places in the paragraph to get the right answer. The explosion took place at 0050 hours (50 minutes after midnight). The bearded man was first seen 1 hour and 10 minutes prior to that, which is 2340 hours.

42. **(D)** The explosion took place at 0050 hours, and 55 minutes later the telephone call was made. Fifty-five minutes after 0050 hours is 0145 hours.

43. **(A)** The bearded man was arrested at 8:35 P.M., which is 2035 hours.

44. **(B)** This will be accomplished by reducing shooting incidents.

45. **(C)** Although each of these four laws undoubtedly imposes restrictions on the use of firearms, the only one mentioned in the passage is the Penal Law.

46. **(B)** Warning shots are prohibited with no exceptions.

47. **(A)** Because the authority to use legal force leaves much potential for abuse, the necessity to have very strict guidelines regulating the use of firearms by police and peace officers is very pressing.

48. **(D)** In every case, the policy is that only the minimum amount of force be used consistent with the accomplishment of the mission.

49. **(D)** The passage indicates that the guidelines are typical of those that exist in most law enforcement agencies.

50. **(D)** Once again, we caution against picking answers that sound good but are not covered in the information upon which you should base your answers.

51. **(C)** Property seized under the authority of a search warrant, along with an inventory of such property, must be returned to the court that issued the search warrant.

52. **(A)** A search warrant does not allow the officer executing the warrant to seize anything someone named in the warrant may be carrying (e.g., a photo of one's child).

53. **(B)** The search warrant must be executed within 10 days of the date of issuance. Of the suggested dates, April 10th is the latest date on which the warrant could be legally executed.

54. **(C)** A search warrant may be executed on any day of the week but only between the hours of 6:00 A.M. and 9:00 P.M., unless the warrant expressly authorizes execution thereof at any time of the day or night.

55. **(A)** If there are reasonable grounds to believe that the property sought may be destroyed or disposed of or someone's safety will be endangered, the officer executing

the warrant may be given privilege not to announce his or her purpose and authority before executing the warrant.

56. **(D)** Choice A is incorrect because a receipt must be left in a conspicuous place in the premises by the officer seizing the property if the property was seized from a premises and no owner was able to be established. Choice B is incorrect because an inventory sheet should be returned to the court. Choice C is incorrect because it is when no one is present that a receipt for property taken from a premises must be left in a conspicuous place. Choice D is correct because a receipt must be given by the officer seizing the property to the person from whom the property was seized.

57. **(D)** In this instance, the offense is grand larceny because the property, regardless of its value, was stolen from the person of the owner.

58. **(C)** Choices A, B, and D indicate instances of grand larceny. Only Choice C represents an instance of petit larceny where the property stolen is $1000 or less.

59. **(D)** Theft of a credit card is an instance where a charge of grand larceny would be appropriate.

60. **(B)** Choice B is correct because according to the information provided, the theft of a firearm such as a handgun or a rifle constitutes grand larceny. There is nothing to support the assumption stated in Choice D, namely that the sale of such a gun would bring more than $1000. When answering legal definition questions, unless otherwise instructed, answers should be based on the information provided and not assumptions.

61. **(C)** Any time numbers are part of the given legal definitions, pay particular attention to them. Examiners often ask questions involving numerical distances, weights, and ages mentioned in the legal definitions.

62. **(B)** Criminal contempt can be either a felony or misdemeanor. Someone in his or her own home could commit criminal contempt by violating an order of protection by subjecting another person to fear by means of repeated phone calls.

63. **(A)** Criminal contempt in the first degree is a felony and occurs when a person refuses to be sworn in by, or answer the lawful question(s) of, a grand jury.

64. **(D)** Criminal contempt in the first degree is a felony and occurs when a person violates an order of protection by subjecting another to fear by means of damaging property in the amount of more than *$250*.

65. **(D)** An order of protection is a written court order and not verbal. Remember to read carefully and to concentrate. Also refusing to be sworn in, in connection with a grand jury, not just any court, is a felony. As we warned earlier in the book, be careful whenever you see absolute words such as *any, always*, and *all*.

66. **(B)** Choice D is incorrect because force could be used to prevent serious damage to property, but according to the procedure, a flashlight should not be used to strike a prisoner.

67. **(B)** Choke holds are prohibited by the regulations.

68. **(B)** Striking a prisoner who is already restrained by mechanical restraints is usually prohibited. But if such a prisoner continued to pose a threat, an officer could justifiably

strike such a prisoner. The incident should be immediately reported to the shift supervisor who shall make a written report to the court desk officer.

69. **(D)** Choices A, B, and C suggest items whose use is prohibited.

70. **(D)** Choices A , B, and C represent characteristics, but Choice D does not. The force may be used to enforce a *lawful* order, not any order.

71. **(B)** The officer is in uniform, and intoxicants cannot be consumed in uniform regardless of being on or off duty.

72. **(C)** Court officer captains are excluded from the prohibition against riding in uniform in a private vehicle.

73. **(A)** To use the official court officer logo, the permission of the Commanding Officer of the Court Officer Personnel Bureau would be required.

74. **(A)** The regulation prohibits soliciting funds for a political club. Choice D is incorrect because no such prohibition was included in the regulations.

75. **(A)** Statement 1, is correct, but statement 2 is incorrect because engaging in card games or other games of chance in a court facility is prohibited.

76. **(B)** Statement 1 is incorrect because a court officer must obey all *lawful* orders and instructions of a supervisor. Statement 2 is correct.

77. **(A)** The commanding officer of the unit to which the court officer is assigned (i.e., his commanding officer) must be notified.

78. **(A)** The identifying serial number should not be displayed anywhere on the locker nor should a record of such number be kept by the court.

79. **(C)** Any fee for a speech should be first cleared by the Commanding Officer Press Relations Division.

80. **(D)** A court officer shall not smoke *in public view* outside a court building while in uniform. Also a court officer could patronize an unlicensed bar in the performance of duty.

81. **(B)** The aim of this procedure is to deter drug use by employees, not defendants.

82. **(D)** The court officer concerned must be notified at least 24 hours prior to scheduled testing.

83. **(C)** The procedure mandates that the court officer being tested be in civilian clothes.

84. **(B)** If an employee has a valid reason for missing an appointment, the employee is to be rescheduled as soon as possible.

85. **(C)** Refusing a drug test calls for mandatory suspension and may be grounds for dismissal from the agency.

86. **(C)** As stated in the procedure, Choice C is correct.

87. **(B)** Only two persons will be present, and they shall be of the same sex.

88. **(B)** According to the procedure, no more than two samples will be taken, each in a separate vial.

89. **(B)** Immediately after giving the urine sample, the officer being tested will initial the vial sticker.

90. **(D)** Such a request must be made within 60 days of the notification of such results.

91. **(D)** Choice A is incorrect Nalbandian. Choice B is incorrect 5205186xb93. Choice C is incorrect Nalbendion. Choice D is the answer.

92. **(A)** Choice B is incorrect DiMiao. Choice C is incorrect 143406915tnt43. Choice D is incorrect Clemint. Choice A is the answer.

93. **(B)** Choice A is incorrect B-27-493270ert78. Choice C is incorrect Rabinovits. Choice D is incorrect B-27*49327Oert78. Choice B is the answer.

94. **(C)** Choice A is incorrect T#4897766765#97. Choice B is incorrect Willyess. Choice D is incorrect T#4897766567&97. Choice C is the answer.

95. **(C)** Choice A is incorrect Cookye. Choice B is incorrect Laventowsky. Choice D is incorrect 9080OO458±5bt. Choice C is the answer.

96. **(B)** Choice A is incorrect Labyrinth. Choice C is incorrect Lucefir. Choice D is incorrect 650gR10451cyrp44577t. Choice B is the answer.

97. **(D)** Choice A is incorrect Tkrpm566677490gy. Choice B is incorrect Feliciano. Choice C is incorrect Tkrm5566777490gy. Choice D is the answer.

98. **(A)** Choice B is incorrect Matterettesky. Choice C is incorrect Fredie. Choice D is incorrect Cmp#5768-909-98ty. Choice A is the answer.

99. **(C)** Choice A is incorrect Dillengir. Choice B is incorrect clt456-098-37. Choice D is incorrect Maria. Choice C is the answer.

100. **(D)** Choice A is incorrect Echierverrea. Choice B is incorrect SanQ4569O8rckis34. Choice C is incorrect SanQ456908rckes34. Choice D is the answer.

A Final

WORD

The Final Week

What should be done during the week right before the exam? To begin with, if you have prepared for the exam, you should do well. If your efforts have been honest and you have practiced answering the various types of questions, especially those that seem to give you difficulty, your score on the exam should reflect how hard you have worked. Each time you sat down and prepared with this text, you were in reality helping yourself pass the actual exam. When the actual test is imminent and only a week away, you should realize that even though you will take your actual exam in a few days, you have already begun passing the exam by studying hard, learning test-taking strategies, and answering practice questions. Exam day should be thought of as appearing at the exam site to collect what is owed you for the hard work you have already done. The real work is over. When you take the exam you are actually collecting a reward for what you have already done.

Nonetheless, the legitimate question still exists, What should be done in the days right before the exam and even on the day of the exam? Here are our recommendations.

SEVEN DAYS BEFORE THE EXAMINATION

About a week before the exam, you should wind down your study efforts and focus on certain specific areas. By reviewing the Diagnostic Examination you took in the beginning of this text, you should be able to identify those question types that are hardest for you and seem to give you the most difficulty. These question types along with the chapters dedicated to them and the practice questions in these areas are what you should be devoting your preparation time to in the days immediately preceding the exam.

In addition, sometime during the week you should take a trip to the examination site. If you plan to use public transportation, then actually go to the site using public transportation. Find out what stop to get off at, how best to go from the bus or train stop to the site, and what the transportation schedule will be on the day of the examination. Very often the examination will be given on weekends when a reduced transportation schedule is in effect. On examination day, do not be left waiting for a train or bus that never comes. All the preparation in the world is of no use if you don't get to the examination site and take the examination.

If you decide to use a private auto, drive there during the week that precedes the examination. Make sure you know what parking will be available on the day of the examination. Make sure that your car is in good mechanical order. Many students have someone drive them to the site. If car trouble should then develop, the car can be left with the driver, and the candidate can proceed on to the site alone. The bottom line is that you should know where the exam site is, how to get there, and, if driving, where to park your car safely and legally. A candidate once reported to us that after hurriedly parking his car and entering the examination site, he began the examination. A little while later, he looked up and through a window saw his brand new car being towed away. Apparently because he was unfamiliar with the area and somewhat in a hurry, he had neglected to notice that he parked his car in a No Parking area. He now had to continue taking the examination with the stress of knowing that when he finished, he then had to undergo the unpleasant and expensive experience of getting his car back. Taking an examination while you are unnecessarily preoccupied about your car certainly is not a good idea. You should give yourself every advantage and be able to concentrate exclusively on your examination.

SIX AND FIVE DAYS BEFORE THE EXAMINATION

Reread the chapters that deal with what you have found to be difficult. Do not waste your time with areas that come easily to you. For example, if reading comprehension is difficult for you but memory questions seem easy for you, then you should be concentrating on the chapter and any questions that deal with reading comprehension. Continuing to study the chapter on memory and continuing to answer practice questions on memory, which you find easy, would not be the most effective use of your time in the days remaining before the examination.

FOUR, THREE, AND TWO DAYS BEFORE THE EXAMINATION

Review the practice examinations that appear in the text. However, you should make everything as close as possible to actual examination conditions. For example, you should sit in a chair at a desk or table, just like you will be called upon to do when you take your examination. Time yourself and make sure you can finish the practice examinations in the time allotted. Use the same kind of pencil or pen that you will be required to use on the day of the examination. Usually you will be required to bring and use a number two pencil. If on each of these three days, you review the practice examinations under simulated examination conditions, when you finally do take your examination in few days, you will be used to sitting in one place for a fairly long period of time without tiring.

ONE DAY BEFORE THE EXAMINATION

Study the chapter in the text dealing with test taking and how to maximize your test score, especially the part that gives you strategies for handling multiple-choice questions. It is not a good idea to try to cram. Your study efforts are over. On the day before the examination, you should begin to relax and mentally prepare to take the examination the next day.

The night before the exam, you should eat your usual dinner and lay out what you will need the next day including any admission cards, pencils, and other equipment you may want to take to the examination. Regarding test-taking equipment, you should have ready anything that the testing agency requires you to bring such as pencils, an identification card, and so on. In addition, we recommend bringing a sweater. If the room is too cool, you can wear it. If it becomes too warm you can remove it and sit on it. A sweater can soften a desk seat, which after several hours can become quite hard and uncomfortable.

Anything else? We recommend a reliable watch to help you keep track of your time, extra pencils with erasers, and if required a pen to sign your name. If you wear glasses, bring a spare pair and something to clean them with. Some candidates have found it helpful to bring a few packets of alcohol wipes to refresh themselves while remaining in their seats thus saving time by not having to leave their seats. If allowed and it does not present dietary problems, you might want to bring along an appropriate snack of your choice as a quick source of energy during the examination.

Regarding bringing and using a watch, we recommend that you bring two watches, both accurately set. However, when the examination actually begins, take one of the watches and place it safely and conspicuously on your desk. Then set this watch to noon when the monitor signals you to begin the examination. In this way you can quickly look at the watch and determine at anytime during the examination how much time you have used. For example when this watch indicates 12:48, this means 48 minutes have elapsed since the beginning of the examination. When the watch indicates 2:27, that would mean 2 hours and 27 minutes have passed. This obviously eliminates your wasting time to determine how much time has elapsed since the beginning of the examination. Because examinations do not always begin exactly on the hour (e.g., 9:00 A.M.) and instead more realistically begin at several minutes past the hour (e.g., 9:07 A.M.), if a watch indicates 10:52 A.M., then a candidate would have to consciously subtract 9:07 A.M. from 10:52 A.M. to determine that 45 minutes have elapsed. This takes time and could be done erroneously which might lead a candidate to believe that he or she has more time than is available

Continuing, get what is for you a good night's sleep. Some candidates have asked if they should take sedatives to help them get to sleep. We do not recommend this practice unless there is some medical reason, and such sedatives have been recommended by a physician. Otherwise, it might be harmful to you the next day, examination day.

The idea is to treat yourself as you would any other day. Remember that you have already taken the steps necessary to help you pass the examination. Exam day is just the day when you demonstrate what you have learned during your many weeks of preparation.

EXAMINATION DAY

Wake up with enough time to dress and get ready without having to hurry. It is not a bad idea to have a friend call you to make sure that you are up. Have your normal breakfast and check over whatever test-taking equipment you have decided to take with you to the examination.

Upon arriving at the examination site, follow the instructions you receive from the monitors. When directed, proceed to your assigned room and seat. Now is the time to look over your seat. If there are any problems with your seat, report them immediately to the test monitor. Follow all instructions exactly. Relax and get ready to demonstrate what you have learned as a result of your many hours of study and preparation. If you follow what has been outlined for you in this text, you should be successful. Believe in your preparation effort and ability.

Good Luck!

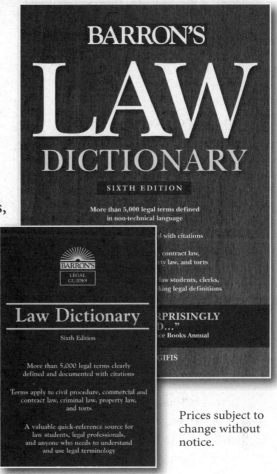

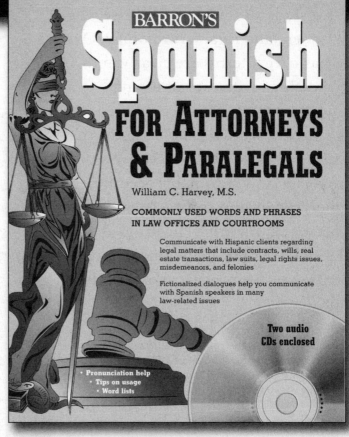